LEARNING JAZZ

American Made Music Series

ADVISORY BOARD

David Evans, General Editor
Barry Jean Ancelet
Edward A. Berlin
Joyce J. Bolden
Rob Bowman
Curtis Ellison
William Ferris
John Edward Hasse
Kip Lornell
Bill Malone
Eddie S. Meadows
Manuel H. Peña
Wayne D. Shirley
Robert Walser

LEARNING JAZZ

Jazz Education, History, and Public Pedagogy

KEN PROUTY

University Press of Mississippi / Jackson

The University Press of Mississippi is the scholarly publishing agency of the Mississippi Institutions of Higher Learning: Alcorn State University, Delta State University, Jackson State University, Mississippi State University, Mississippi University for Women, Mississippi Valley State University, University of Mississippi, and University of Southern Mississippi.

www.upress.state.ms.us

Portions of chapter two have appeared in a different form in *Popular Music and Society* 37, no. 5 (2014): 595–617. https://doi.org/10.1080/03007766.2014.909202.

The University Press of Mississippi is a member of the Association of University Presses.

Copyright © 2023 by University Press of Mississippi
All rights reserved

∞

Library of Congress Cataloging-in-Publication Data

Names: Prouty, Ken, author.
Title: Learning jazz : jazz education, history, and public pedagogy / Ken Prouty.
Other titles: American made music series.
Description: Jackson : University Press of Mississippi, 2023. | Series: American made music series | Includes bibliographical references and index.
Identifiers: LCCN 2023032796 (print) | LCCN 2023032797 (ebook) | ISBN 9781496847904 (hardback) | ISBN 9781496847911 (trade paperback) | ISBN 9781496847928 (epub) | ISBN 9781496847935 (epub) | ISBN 9781496847942 (pdf) | ISBN 9781496847959 (pdf)
Subjects: LCSH: Jazz—History and criticism. | Jazz—Historiography. | Jazz—Instruction and study—United States—History. | Jazz—Social aspects—United States—History. | Jazz—Analysis, appreciation. | Jazz musicians—United States. | Big bands—United States. | Music and race—United States—History.
Classification: LCC ML3506 P76 2023 (print) | LCC ML3506 (ebook) | DDC 836.815/74—dc24/eng/20230719
LC record available at https://lccn.loc.gov/2023032796
LC ebook record available at https://lccn.loc.gov/2023032797

British Library Cataloging-in-Publication Data available

DEDICATION

Beverly Jean Forbus
1937–2022
Thanks for everything, Mom

CONTENTS

Acknowledgments ix
Introduction 3

Chapter 1: To Jazz, or Not to Jazz: Pedagogy and Publishing in
    Early Jazz Method Books 11

Chapter 2: We Don't Know What We Don't Know: Historiography
    and the "Lost Voice" in Jazz 50

Chapter 3: Sight-Reading, Virtuosity, and Identity: Big Bands and
    Race in Jazz Education 81

Chapter 4: Understanding Jazz Education's "Race Problem" 122

Chapter 5: Jazz People and Public Pedagogies 157

Coda: What's in a Domain Name 196

Notes 199
Index 225

ACKNOWLEDGMENTS

The list of those to thank for this project might constitute a book all by itself, but there are some individuals whom I'd like to publicly acknowledge. My colleagues at Michigan State University have been a constant source of support and good cheer. Thanks to my fellow faculty in Musicology: Michael Largey, Kevin Bartig, Sarah Long, Marcie Ray, Joanna Bosse, Chris Scales, and Nick Field. And special thanks to my colleagues in the Jazz Studies program, including Diego Rivera, Michael Dease, Antony Stanco, Randy Napoleon, Xavier Davis, Randy "Uncle G" Gelispie, and most especially Rodney Whitaker. Their level of talent and dedication to nurturing this music leaves me in awe. Thanks as well to Juliet Hess, Ron Newman, Joe Luloff, and David Stowe, who have provided support and encouragement in my career. I would also like to thank our administrative staff, Dean Jim Forger, Associate Deans Michael Kroth and David Rayl, and a special thanks to Shawn Myrda Mahorney and Anne Simon, without whose efforts our college would almost certainly grind to a halt. Many students over the years have endured long-winded explanations of my sometimes hare-brained ideas; my particular thanks to Matthew Kay, Kelli Smith-Biwer, Christine Glassman, and Emily Demski. And an enormous thank you to recently minted PhD and professor Jonathan Gomez, my former student, thesis advisee, and continuing friend. Our time together was some of the most rewarding of my professional career, always challenging and sharpening my thinking. His imprint on this book is exceeded only by my pride in all he has done and will continue to do.

Many peers and colleagues from around the world show up in my work in some form or another: Chuck Hersch, Gabriel Solis, Mark Lomanno, Lewis Porter, David Ake, Kim Teal, Andrew Berish, Christi Jay Wells, Darren Mueller, Tammy Kernodle, John Howland, Mike Heller, Aaron Johnson, David Borgo, Nichole Rustin-Paschal, Alan Stanbridge, Tim Wall, Sherrie Tucker, George McKay, John Gennari, Ingrid Monson, Scott DeVeaux, Steve Pond, Bruce Boyd Raeburn, Krin Gabbard, and so, so many others with whom I have had the great pleasure of interacting over the years. A special thanks to the organizers of the Rhythm Changes research consortium, without whose efforts I would not be in the position I am in today: Tony Whyton, Walter van de Leur, Catherine Tackley, Nick Gebhardt, Loes Rusch, and Christa Bruckner-Haring have all gone above and beyond the call many times over in organizing some of the most engaging and rewarding meetings it has even been my pleasure to attend. Two individuals who have left us were particularly important in shaping my work. John Murphy provided exactly the right kind of critical feedback in the best sense of the term. His presence is sorely missed by so many, as is that of David Baker, whose insights, support, and wisdom were always freely and generously given. And to my teachers and mentors, especially Stan Buchanan, David Joyner, Andrew Weintraub, and the late Nathan Davis, my debt to you is simply beyond description.

Research for this book was conducted with the support of the Humanities and Arts Research Program at Michigan State as well as the Center for Black Music Research, from which I was fortunate to receive a travel grant to visit the archive. Research was also conducted at the Library of Congress, the Hogan Jazz Archive at Tulane University, the Chicago Jazz Archive, and the Institute of Jazz Studies; I sincerely thank staff members at these institutions whose assistance contributed to this project. A special thanks to Ella Campbell for her help with accessing materials at the Hogan Archive.

Finally, my thanks to the editorial staff and board at the University Press of Mississippi, and in particular Craig Gill, for continuing to support my work and for their constant encouragement of leading-edge research in jazz studies. I'd also like to acknowledge the assistance of Katie Turner for her guidance and Debbie Burke for her diligent editing. I am in very good company as a UPM author.

LEARNING JAZZ

INTRODUCTION

In 2016, America bade farewell to the presidency of Barack Obama, whose affinity for jazz was clearly and publicly expressed, replaced by the political ascendancy of Donald Trump, for whom jazz was not, it seemed, even the faintest blip on his cultural radar. Jazz people more or less did not know what to do with or about Trump. Where Obama had been mostly celebrated for his interest in jazz, Trump's presidency was met by uncertainty and, in some cases, hostility. Wynton Marsalis generated a minor controversy when the trumpeter and Jazz at Lincoln Center artistic director explained to a group of students that he would not necessarily refuse to perform at the new president's inauguration, preferring to take a wait-and-see attitude.[1] A few months later, Marsalis had apparently seen enough, blasting the Trump administration's proposal to eliminate the National Endowment for the Arts, an action which would leave the American public "more ignorant."[2] Others were more pointed. In 2018, *JAZZIZ* ran a special issue on "Jazz in the Age of Trump." What is most remarkable, perhaps even more than any specific comments to emerge from the various participants, is the very fact that this event took place, that the election of Trump necessitated it. And perhaps it did. In the introduction to the piece, the convenors discussed the idea behind the panel:

> The idea was to sit together in a room for a couple hours and discuss the challenges of creating and presenting thoughtful art during a precarious moment in the United States. When we met in January, the nine of us strained the capacity of a friend's dining room table in Harlem and represented some of the diversity present in today's jazz community.[3]

Individual participants expressed a wide range of opinions, although, for the most part, the general consensus was more clearly conveyed by trumpeter and composer Terence Blanchard, who stated that "I listened to Duke Ellington and John Coltrane, I toured with Art Blakey. I'm not going to stand on the shoulders of these guys who struggled to better their communities and then water down who I am and what I think."[4] On the other hand, Wadada Leo Smith, while not dismissing what Trump's presidency meant, points to a more systemic, historical perspective, noting that "[t]he times haven't changed because one man got elected. There's been a long struggle for what's right and a long tradition of what's wrong, and I think we have taken our eye off the ball for too long."[5] While the panel hashed out the implications of Trump's election, others took a different perspective, even going so far as to liken Trump to jazz itself. Writing in the *Washington Post*, David van Drehle refers to Trump's "jazz combo of national distraction," in which "[Trump's] fingers fly over the keyboard of his phone like Charlie Parker burning up the alto saxophone. But imagine Bird sitting in with a high school band: He must take every solo."[6] Meanwhile, in *The Atlantic*, David Graham makes a similar connection between Trump's erratic, "improvisational" approach to another jazz icon:

> Trains have long been a staple of Donald Trump's iconography. Trane, less so. But the recent North Korea crisis provides a moment to consider the parallels between John Coltrane, the iconic tenor saxophonist who died 50 years ago this summer, and the 45th president.
>
> Trump and Coltrane both began their careers in fairly traditional ways, and each got more esoteric as he got older, producing what some listeners found brilliant and what others called incoherent and hard to listen to. Both are prodigious improvisers, tending to whip up new ideas and thoughts on the spot. And both seem unsure where to stop improvising.
>
> "I don't know what it is," Coltrane once told Miles Davis, in whose band he was playing. "It seems like when I get going, I just don't know how to stop." Davis, never one to beat around the bush, replied, "Why don't you try taking the horn out of your mouth?"
>
> This week, some of President Trump's advisers wish he'd just taken the horn out of his mouth.[7]

Comparisons such as these might seem a bit extreme, but they demonstrate the way in which, for the most part, jazz people aligned against the Trump presidency with uniformity and urgency. A number of benefit concerts to support the Biden/Harris campaign were held in the lead-up to the 2020 election; of these, none was of a higher profile than "Jazz for America," an event held in October which featured numerous jazz luminaries including John Scofield, Ravi Coltrane, Dee Dee Bridgewater, and Christian McBride, among others. Given the fact Biden and Harris were successful in the election, one might assume that these types of events played a significant role in shaping public opinion; that is, until we are reminded that jazz has stubbornly remained an increasingly modest aspect of American cultural discourse.

A statement like this, especially in the context of a book on jazz, might come off as being overly pessimistic. And perhaps, I'll admit, there is some truth to this. But it is something I see nearly every day: many (if not most) students, including many who are advanced-level players in classical forms, know absolutely nothing about this music, not even the "big names" like Louis Armstrong and Duke Ellington. Yes, they may have heard these names before, but seldom do they have any particular knowledge of what they did. This is the unquestionably discomforting reality faced by jazz practitioners. But musicians, fans, and others who might align themselves with what has often been termed the "jazz community" never seem to lose hope that, with just the right "education," more of the masses of jazz-ignorant music fans can be reached and converted. One can't fault them for their efforts or their outlook.

I'd like to turn for a moment to terminology. In my previous book, I wrote extensively about the concept of the "jazz community."[8] In short, I suggested that this term, which is still used with great frequency, does not really have a specific meaning that aligns with conventional understandings of "community." Following Benedict Anderson, I argued that the jazz community, such as it is constituted, is largely "imagined," and that such a perspective allows us to connect with others not only across physical distances but also in temporal terms. Through recorded media, listeners can participate in a type of community that is generated through the process of recording and that is completed by the act of listening. Following on from this, I have chosen to avoid using this phrase for the most part, save for when it appears in a quotation. Instead, I use the term "jazz people" when referring to large-scale, nonspecific entities, as I find this term to be somewhat more useful in conceptualizing the larger jazz world. While individuals may differ vastly in their engagement with jazz, in the final analysis, they are all "people" who share an interest in the music.

Whether it is explicitly defined this way or not, jazz people today are increasingly occupied (or preoccupied) with advocating for jazz, with *educating* the public. Indeed, statements by musicians and others regularly invoke the need to educate audiences; jazz musicians are increasingly engaging in public service and advocacy designed to introduce jazz to new audiences and maintain a positive public image of the genre. This is not easy, to be sure, as the advent of digital listening and distribution has simultaneously opened up new worlds of music and culture and also has had the effect of shrinking the actual listening experience. A case in point: a few years ago, I was leading a discussion of the 1959 docudrama *The Cry of Jazz*. The story of this film, the goal of which was to establish jazz as Black music, is centered on a jazz listening club meeting. In our discussion of the film, one student raised his hand and asked, "Professor, do people still do this, have jazz listening parties?" The answer I gave, as I recall, was along the lines of "not as long as the main way we listen to music is to stuff earbuds in our heads." Jazz listening among the nonspecialist public used to be more widely social, as did many other aspects of the music and its culture; the same might be said about many other genres. Social listening has been supplanted by social media, creating an interactive dynamic that is simultaneously more global and more solitary. Again, change has been rapid and profound.

Jazz education, too, has changed. A number of pioneering figures in the field have left us, including David Baker, Donald Byrd, and Nathan Davis, to name just a few. And we lost one of our most endearing and enduring figures in bringing jazz to the public, Marian McPartland, whose weekly *Piano Jazz* program was a fixture on public radio since the 1970s. This is to say nothing of the numerous jazz artists, writers, and other key jazz figures: musicians like Dave Brubeck, Yusef Lateef, Chick Corea, Ornette Coleman, Geri Allen, Curtis Fuller, Roy Hargrove, Wayne Shorter; jazz writers including Stanley Crouch, Nat Hentoff, Gunther Schuller, and Albert Murray; industry figures like George Wein; and many others too numerous to list here. The COVID-19 global pandemic has had a devastating impact on jazz, taking some of its most illustrious figures, such as Ellis Marsalis and Lee Konitz, as well as the countless local and regional figures whose deaths did not make the pages of *DownBeat* or the *New York Times*. This is to say nothing of the nearly incalculable loss of livelihood experienced by countless musicians, venues, and others who suffered devastating disruptions to their careers. These losses have left jazz in a very different place than it was even a few years ago. As time goes on, the temporal distance between jazz education and the actual historical worlds of the music that serve as a basis for study potentially grows even wider. This is the inevitable trajectory of time, but the oft-expressed anxiety over jazz morphing into a static, "museumified" music risks becoming even more entrenched.

And yet, in some ways, the past few years have opened new doors and presented new opportunities. Collaborative online performance, which has long been overlooked due in part to concerns about synchronization and limits on communication speeds, became, in some cases, the only way for musicians to collaborate. Performers from school ensembles to professional artists adapted to the online world. Many ensembles made recordings that were recorded separately and then mixed together; sometimes, the results were haphazard, but in other cases, the performances are exceptionally strong. One example can be seen in the recordings made by the Quarantine Big Band Helsinki that produced a series of YouTube videos featuring composite performances. Comprised—as the name would imply—of a group of Finnish musicians, the band recorded several challenging charts, including Vince Mendoza's arrangement of the Brecker Brothers' "Some Skunk Funk."[9] The band members are unquestionably very good players, and the syncing of the parts produces a performance that, if heard from a live band, would be classified as being very "tight." Institutions such as Jazz at Lincoln Center presented virtual performances, carried live across platforms like YouTube and Spotify; not only did this allow regular patrons to continue their engagement with jazz, but the increased use of virtual performance through streaming has potentially opened new paths to connect with audiences that are not limited by how close they live to a venue. Jazz education programs moved teaching and performing online, using platforms such as Zoom to keep students and teachers connected, and although it was by no means an ideal scenario, it provided a means to keep going in the face of what was truly an existential threat.

The pandemic was initially approached as a fight for survival and not just in terms of public health. Already on the ropes in terms of waning public popularity, COVID threatened to erase the entire economic basis of jazz, its central performative and community space: the club. And indeed, many venues were impacted, in too many cases resulting in closure.[10] But jazz people were already well versed in the ins and outs of keeping the music alive in the face of stiff challenges from the early musicians who struggled for acceptance to jazz educators who often faced hostile academic environments to fans of the music who desperately want to preserve what they see as a vital, important form of cultural expression. In confronting the pandemic, jazz people fell back on what they knew best: they improvised.

The creation of new jazz people, be it through a college jazz history class, a Twitter exchange, a motion picture, or a casual conversation, has thus become an even greater imperative; in all of these contexts, there is one constant: at the risk of stating the obvious, jazz is something that is learned. Learning jazz has largely been addressed in scholarship with respect to the pedagogy of learning how to play the music and in learning about its main practitioners. And indeed, these are important perspectives. But all such contexts must be understood in relation to forces outside the recording studio, the classroom, the stage, and the club. Learning about jazz takes place in many different forms, settings, contexts, and communities. In the following chapters, I examine a number of distinctive case studies ranging from historical publications and critical perspectives to recent events concerning jazz advocacy and the music's place in media to the often poorly understood topic of race and its role in how jazz is learned and taught within institutions of learning. Any interaction relating to the music will, by its very nature, involve learning in some way, be it an exercise in improvisational theory, a jazz appreciation class, or a jazz fan explaining to a friend why they should give the music a chance. All of these studies involve the work and nature of particular kinds of institutions that play a role in learning about jazz. Some of these are formal, such as schools or civic arts organizations that have particular, often well-defined missions. Some are less formal, such as jazz criticism and publishing, which have their own kinds of practices, rules, and perspectives. And some involve the building of knowledge about jazz in less overtly defined ways, emerging from diverse communities within which jazz occupies an important place. Initiatives to foster a greater appreciation for the music among the general public are not the sole purview of educational and civic entities; jazz fans themselves serve as advocates for the music. Particular ideas about the nature of jazz—what it is, what it means, whom it belongs to—are shaped, taken apart, and shaped again, be it through a masterclass, a book, a conversation, a movie, or a tweet. Public jazz pedagogy has, it seems, become an institution in its own right.

In the first chapter, I engage in a close reading of jazz trombone method books in the first decade or so of jazz's emergence in the public sphere, engaging an audience of musical learners whose understanding of jazz was still very limited. The proliferation of instructional books in jazz speaks to its increasingly vital presence in both professional music performance and with respect to the development of a general understanding of the music as a whole. The 1919 publications by Henry Fillmore, Mayhew Lake, and Fortunato Sordillo all endeavored to present not only practical musical guidance but to work toward a definition for and understanding of what jazz is. Later books in the mid to late 1920s continue these ideas, establishing an understanding of the music through particular musical and textual devices, often capitalizing on the increasing popularity of recordings. This is followed in chapter two by a discussion of "lost voices" in jazz historiography. Specifically, I present two particular case studies that speak to the question of why some individuals' voices carry through the years while others seem to fall into relative obscurity. In the first case study, my focus is the jazz writer Paul Eduard Miller, a widely known and published critic in the mid to late 1930s who, by the 1950s, had been eclipsed by peer figures such as Marshall Stearns. In looking at Miller, I examine both his published columns for *DownBeat* as well as a pair of unpublished book manuscripts housed at the Center for Black Music Research in Chicago. The next case study turns toward performers, and in particular, a related question of why some artists are "picked" for fame while others are relegated to relative historiographic insignificance. In doing so, I position "canonic" figures as *outliers*, drawing on the work of Malcolm Gladwell; specifically, I also examine the nature of the "ordinary" jazz musician whose appearances in the canon are generally a function of brushes with greatness.

Chapter three focuses on the culture of the big band in jazz education and how this emerged historically. In the first of two main case studies, I look at the relationship between Stan Kenton and jazz education in the 1950s and 1960s. Specifically, I examine the relationship between Kenton and Leon Breeden, the director of the jazz program at North Texas State (now the University of North Texas). Kenton and Breeden, I argue, shared many ideas and perspectives about what jazz ought to be and how it should be situated in education. Then, the chapter turns to a study of Kenton's protégé, trumpeter Maynard Ferguson. I situate Ferguson as a significant influence on jazz education in the 1970s based on a combination of covers of popular hits and an intensely virtuosic, physical style of performance that resonated deeply with an audience consisting overwhelmingly of young White men. Both Kenton and Ferguson, I contend, sent ripples through the jazz education system that are still being felt today. The next chapter serves as something of a counterpoint, focusing on the ways in which Blackness has asserted itself in jazz education. The first part of the chapter looks at the stories of two bands from predominantly Black schools that, in 1972, succeeded in what were largely White spaces. The first of these, a band from Chicago's Malcolm X College, would make waves with their performance at the Notre Dame Collegiate Jazz Festival, winning both awards and accolades. This band, hailing from a community college renamed for the late Black Nationalist leader, stood at an intersection between jazz education and the imperatives of social justice. The other band discussed in this part of the chapter is the Kashmere Stage Band. A high school group from Houston, the Kashmere band would stun the jazz education world by winning the 1972 All-American High School Stage Band Festival in Mobile, Alabama. Their win was an important occasion in the world of high school stage bands, long the province of White schools and ensembles. The chapter concludes with an assessment of Jazz at Lincoln Center's "Essentially Ellington" competition for high school bands. I position this program as a critical corrective initiative that attempts to redress the historical underrepresentation of students of color in jazz education programs. But even with the centering of Duke Ellington as a link to the institution's larger aesthetic goals, the political economies of American music education are deeply entrenched, and a number of inequities persist.

In the final chapter, I turn to the topic of "public pedagogy," the ways in which jazz people attempt to bring jazz to audiences that are unfamiliar with it and, at the same time, attempt to shape the public understanding of the genre. After a discussion of jazz "defensiveness," I examine the ways in which the "jazz metaphor" has been employed as a vehicle for public pedagogy, predicated on a view of jazz as a democratic, collaborative art form. These programs will often involve a pedagogical component centered on particular understandings of the music that are accessible to "lay" audiences. In the final case study in this chapter, I examine the films of Damien Chazelle, particularly *Whiplash* and *La La Land*. As both films placed jazz at the center of their narratives and were very successful commercially and critically, they generated significant discussion in the jazz media, much of which was decidedly negative. The release and success of these films seemed to necessitate responses that sought to "correct the record," to defend jazz against what was seen as, at best, a distortion of jazz, and at worst, an outright attack. The reality is, I argue, more complicated, calling for a more nuanced interpretation.

I would also like to make a brief comment about positionality. The studies that follow in this book are written from the perspective of a White, American, college-jazz-educated musician and musicologist. Having been a student and teacher in several different jazz education programs over the course of more than three decades, I consider myself something of an insider to this field, but in other contexts, some of which are discussed in this manuscript, I am looking in from the outside, at communities and histories that are not always my own. In saying this, in no way do I want to suggest that ideas that are not addressed here are not vitally important, and indeed, groundbreaking scholarship has been and continues to be done on such topics, much of which is a result of the work of nonmale and non-White scholars. This is very important work, and it is imperative that it be supported by those of us in this field. In general, I do not address topics emerging from outside the United States. In saying this, I likewise do not wish to dismiss or otherwise overlook this important scholarship. Indeed, many non-American jazz scholars, including some who are cited in this book, have made invaluable contributions to my development and are doing important work in understanding the ways in which jazz plays out as a global system. My voice and my perspectives are but a modest part of a multitude of communities of scholars, musicians, fans, and others around the world. I hope this work will open other paths and other avenues for inquiry from vantage points that are far removed from my own.

Chapter 1

TO JAZZ, OR NOT TO JAZZ

Pedagogy and Publishing in Early Jazz Method Books[1]

INTRODUCTION: A GLISS IS JUST A GLISS . . . OR IS IT?

On February 12, 1924, an audience at Aeolian Hall in New York bore witness to a landmark event in American musical lore: Paul Whiteman's infamous "Experiment in Modern Music," which would introduce *Rhapsody in Blue* to the world and make a bona fide star of its composer, George Gershwin. And there is perhaps no more memorable moment in this piece than its opening passage, featuring a drawn-out rising glissando over the course of about five seconds and one and one-half octaves played by clarinetist Ross Gorman.[2] It was Gorman, in fact, who originally came up with the idea to play the glissando during rehearsals for the piece; Gershwin liked the effect, and he (through Whiteman's orchestrator Ferde Grofé) added it to the score.[3] The rest, as they say, is history: the opening phrase of *Rhapsody in Blue* is among the most iconic single figures in the American orchestral canon. What Gorman likely knew when he played it and what Gershwin must have immediately understood when he heard it was that the glissando was a musical gesture that was rich with cultural significance. There is some discussion about the cultural genesis of this passage. A number of commenters have pointed to the resonance of the passage with klezmer music; music critic Norman Lebrecht notes that Gershwin, who was certainly quite familiar with the style, told Gorman to make the passage "wail."[4] But given the nature of the rest of the piece and of Whiteman's overall project with the "Experiment" program (to say nothing of the commission of *Rhapsody in Blue* itself),[5] there is little question, I think, about the context in which this phrase was interpreted by the audience, regardless of its specific origin. During the previous two decades, the device was frequently employed in musical forms that were associated with genres and idioms that were, to put it simply, understood as "Black."

It might seem odd to devote so much attention to what seems, on the surface, to be a rather simple musical device. But the simplicity of the glissando belies its unique identity in early twentieth-century popular music, especially jazz. In particular, I turn my attention in this chapter to the appearance of several method books related to the learning and playing of jazz on the trombone, in which the glissando plays a central role. I have chosen to focus on the trombone for two main reasons. First, I am a trombonist myself, having been "jazz educated" on the instrument since junior high and having made part of my career as a freelance performer. I am, for lack of a better way to put it, drawn to the instrument. Second, and perhaps more importantly, a focus on the trombone, where the design of the instrument lends itself easily to the playing of glissandi, allows us to zero in on a particular aspect of jazz's nascent pedagogical discourse. Glissandi were often regarded as an essential, or even *the* essential, musical marker of the jazz style. Historical associations of the glissando with particular musical ideas and cultural characteristics, often conflated with a backstory based in blackface minstrel shows and novelty band pieces, complicate these matters even further. This can be seen in the appearance of a number of early jazz method books for the trombone in which the glissando is explicitly characterized as jazz's defining feature. An assessment of these texts reveals an intersection of music, pedagogy, publishing, race, and other factors that come into play in the history of early jazz.

THE ROAD TO SUCCESSFUL JAZZING: THE JAZZ TROMBONE METHODS OF HENRY FILLMORE AND HIS CONTEMPORARIES[6]

It is within this context that I wish to discuss the work of Henry Fillmore, who, by any measure, is an individual who would be seen as marginal in contemporary discussions of jazz. A prolific composer of popular band music, Fillmore was a central figure in the generation of composers that emerged from the shadow of John Philip Sousa and whose work centered on the creation of music for military band, mainly in the form of marches ("The Klaxon" is probably Fillmore's best-known work in this regard). His greatest notoriety, however, came with the creation of a series of compositions written to capitalize on the idiosyncrasies of the trombone. This series of works, which Fillmore would later market as a set, drew heavily on the novelty character of the instrument as well as crude racial stereotypes. The members

To Jazz, or Not to Jazz: Pedagogy, Publishing in Early Jazz Method Books   13

Figure 1: Advertisement for Fillmore's "Trombone Family" Collection, c. early 1920s.

of this "trombone family," as Fillmore called it, first appeared in 1908 with the composition "Miss Trombone (A Slippery Rag)." The "slippery" nature of the piece is undoubtedly due to its extensive use of the device, which is evident from the very beginning of the piece, kicked off with a boisterous glissando.

Fillmore would continue to publish his "trombone smears,"[7] as they were called, over the course of the next decade, resulting in works such as "Teddy Trombone" (1911), "Lassus Trombone" (1915, probably the most famous of the series), "Pahson Trombone" (1916), "Sally Trombone" (1917), and "Slim Trombone" (1918), among others. Fillmore continued publishing such novelty trombone works during the 1920s, though the "family theme" seems to have been abandoned. The marketing of these pieces draws heavily on the same kinds of racialized imagery and language that departs very little from the traditions of blackface minstrelsy and the "coon songs" of the turn of the century, as we can see in advertisements for Fillmore's compositions (Figure 1).[8]

The trombone novelty piece itself has a long association with these kinds of ideas. This dates back to at least 1899 with the publication of what might be regarded as the first trombone-centric novelty rag, "A Coon Band Contest," written by Arthur Pryor, a member of the John Philip Sousa band and perhaps the first significant virtuoso performer on the slide trombone. By the late 1890s, Pryor served increasingly as a relief conductor and composer/

Musical Example 1: "Coon Band Contest" trombone glissandi.

arranger; his compositions, especially those based on popular forms, were often programmed and recorded by Sousa. One of these was "A Coon Band Contest," recorded by Sousa's band in 1900 for Victor, with Pryor himself conducting. The piece was subtitled "The Song That Won the Ham for That Coon Band," a not-so-subtle conflation of the glissando with common representations of Black comic affect. In the trio section (the piece generally follows a standard ragtime form), we see a pronounced glissando (Musical Example 1) scored with specific pitches. As Trever Herbert notes, the trombone glissando was not a common feature in the classical trombone repertoire at this time. Herbert cites Arnold Schoenberg's performance note in the trombone parts for *Pelleas und Melisande* (1903), indicating that the technique was so unusual that it required explanation.[9]

French composer Charles-Marie Widor seemed equally unfamiliar with the technique, reacting with astonishment at hearing an ensemble—almost certainly Sousa's band, who stopped in Paris on a 1900 tour—using the device. "Astounding," he wrote in his widely read orchestration text, noting that the glissando was "very easy to execute."[10] Judging from the example Widor includes in the book, it is nearly certain that the piece he heard was "A Coon Band Contest" (Musical Example 2).

Contemporary method books for slide trombone often took a grim perspective on the use of the glissando. Carl Weber's 1897 *Premier Method* was a widely used and very influential turn-of-the-century method book, in many ways the standard for developing slide trombonists. The glissando seems to be wholly absent from Weber's method. While Weber does include a discussion of techniques for executing a portamento, the last sentence in

Musical Example 2: Excerpt from Charles-Marie Widor's *The Technique of the Modern Orchestra: A Manual of Practical Instrumentation* (1906).

this passage is revealing: "The Portamento is an expression of a sound being slurred into another. Increase the sound when from low to high, decrease it when from high to low notes. The portamento must only be applied in parts especially adapted for this phrasing, but it should not be overdone, *otherwise it sounds ridiculous*."[11] No mention is made of the glissando here, or indeed anywhere else, in Weber's book. But it might not be too much of a stretch to imagine that this last bit might be an implicit admonition against it. At about the same time, R. N. Davis's *Imperial Method for Slide Trombone* appeared. Davis's discussion of articulation, and of slurs in particular, is notable. In describing the playing technique for the slur, he states, "When two or more notes are connected by a curved line placed over or under them, the first note only is produced by the tongue, the others being made by the same breath without repeating the stroke of the tongue."[12] What Davis describes here could easily be heard as a glissando, yet it is doubtful that this was his intent. The accompanying exercises seem fairly straightforward. Davis goes on the write the following:

> To make a good slur on the trombone is indeed difficult, more so than on any other instrument in fact [*sic*] many otherwise good performers upon this instrument fail very signally [*sic*] in this particular, for when they try to slur they either move the slide in such a clumsy manner and at the same time manage the breath in such a way as to produce all the intermediate sounds between the two tones or else they use their tongue so the notes are not connected at all.[13]

In order to avoid such effects, the trombonist should do the following:

> If the second note [of the slur] is found in another position, the slide must glide gently to it at just the proper time and the directions in regard to the action of the lips and control of the breath apply the same as before, the greatest care being taken to avoid any *disagreeable sound* while the slide is moving from one position to the other.[14]

It is clear that what Davis is describing here (at least in his first example) is a glissando, and it is equally clear that, in his view, it is something that should be scrupulously avoided. Davis's explanation seems somewhat labored; this, I suggest, speaks to the relatively unknown nature of the glissando; there simply was not a language to talk about it. It was, as Davis writes, a "disagreeable sound." But precisely what was disagreeable about it is never made clear.

One of the first method books to explicitly refer to the glissando was written by Thomas H. King (perhaps better known today as the founder of King trombones) and first published in 1908. But like earlier methods, the glissando was not an effect that was to be encouraged among developing students. In the midst of a larger section discussing slurring techniques, King states that "[t]he so called Trombone Glissando is not to be taken seriously. However, if you must gliss do so on page 94."[15] Turning to page 94, one finds a number of exercises devoted to the glissando; most of these are basic exercises that consist of short glisses between positions. One wonders what King would have thought of the fact that his instruments would become favorites among jazz trombonists.

Even as late as the mid-1920s, the use of the glissando was still a contentious issue in discussions of trombone playing. In an exchange centered on a 1925 essay in the *Musical Times* by J. A. Westrup, in which the author decries what he feels is inferior writing for trombone by various composers (especially Cesar Franck), one J. H. Reginald Dixon writes, in a letter to the editor of the same periodical (in which he argues that Westrup's criticisms of Franck are misplaced as the composer likely was writing for valve trombone), that "[t]he valve trombone has at least one merit, i.e., the freedom from slithering up to the note in the horrible way beloved by the purveyors of jazz noises."[16] In a later issue, another letter writer named Harold Watts shares Dixon's concerns, suggesting that the young student would do well to put aside the "free, agile 'stunt' treatment of this dignified instrument, as exemplified in much modern instrumentation (including the hybrid known as the 'jazz' band), and follow the practice of the 'wise men of old.'"[17]

Was Fillmore's penchant for using the glissando an attempt to corner the market on such a mysterious, dastardly musical effect? Or was it intended to cater to an audience that craved such novelty? The answer is not entirely clear, and at any rate, both considerations likely have merit (and are certainly not mutually exclusive by any means). What is clear, however, is that the use of this instrumental technique in early jazz recordings made between 1916 and 1918 seemed to have a profound impact on the manner in which Fillmore positioned himself within the popular music market of the day. Though the term "jazz" (with various spellings) had been in common use for some time,[18] there is no evidence to suggest that Fillmore used the term in describing his "smear" compositions; there is no reference to jazz in any of his scores, and it seems that for Fillmore, the trombone smear was, simply put, one in a number of popular band styles of the day.

All this changed in 1919, when Fillmore published what is almost certainly the first method book for jazz trombone playing and possibly for jazz as a whole. Titled *Henry Fillmore's Jazz Trombonist: A Unique Treatise Showing How to Play Practical Jazzes and How and Where to Insert Them into Plain Trombone Parts*, this book is a fascinating document, appearing at a moment when jazz was first becoming popular. In producing the book, Fillmore takes advantage of the general sense of mystery and unfamiliarity with which many in the contemporary audience regarded the music, turning jazz's murky origins and practices to his own advantage. In the preface to the book, he quotes liberally (and without complete attribution) from a 1918 article in *Current Opinion*, which itself quotes liberally (and also without complete attribution) from Walter Kingsley's essay in the *New York Sun* from August 1917 (a work that is today considered a landmark of early jazz criticism), emphasizing jazz's relationship to such ideas as "voodoo drums." That Fillmore's first invocation of jazz is imbued with a sense of primitivism should not be surprising given his previous trafficking in heavily racialized minstrel stereotypes in the marketing of his novelty trombone pieces.

In pedagogical terms, Fillmore treats jazz as not simply a genre of music but rather as a specific musical approach that, in his view, stemmed from a sense of comedy that is apparent even from the book's cover illustration. A trombonist is seen practicing in an apartment; his cheeks puff to the side as his slide, extended to the end of its reach, nearly hits his cat, which frantically scurries out of the way. On the street outside, neighbors point with alarm to his window; on the sidewalk, a stern-faced, baton-wielding policeman investigates, and a dog lets out a howl (figure 2). Jazz, as presented in this illustration, is imbued both with a sense of comedy and with a sense of outsider identity, reflected in the consternation with which others (even a dog) greet the music.

Figure 2: Henry Fillmore's *Jazz Trombonist*, cover, 1919.

The humor of jazz also is a function of the mode of musical production. As Fillmore notes in the introduction to the book, "The Jazz effect in music is supplied by the humorous qualities of instruments. In the brass family the slide trombone, because of its slurring possibilities, may be called the *premier jazz producer*."[19] The "Jazz effect" in question is, of course, the glissando, that staple of his own compositions for the previous decade. Thus, Fillmore's foray into jazz does not require anything really new but only a simple relabeling of what he has already been doing. Further, it is the trombone, specifically, that has the ability to achieve this effect. And indeed, Fillmore was not the only one to make such a case. As noted in a 1920 essay in *Literary Digest* (quoting an earlier piece in the *New York Tribune*), "The demand for trombone-players, for what are called 'jazz' bands, has not only made it difficult to keep them in symphony orchestras, but it is destroying their artistic efficiency. The principal characteristic of 'jazz' music is the vulgar sliding from tone to tone."[20] Fillmore, by virtue of his previous work in novelty trombone music, seems a likely candidate to meet just such a demand.

Let us return to Fillmore's book specifically. Fillmore includes numerous exercises intended to familiarize the trombonist with playing what he refers to as "jazzes." Fillmore's theory of "jazzing" is predicated on several important elements. First, he draws a distinction between "home" and "out" positions. "Home" positions are the pitches that are, in essence, the "normal" positions on the slide (i.e., middle C in third position). "Out" positions are those that we might think of as "alternate" positions (i.e., middle C in sixth position). The intent of this is to train the trombonist to begin thinking about the relationships between pitches, especially starting and ending pitches, in the glissando, and in a more general sense, to learn to "get around" the instrument and to explore different ways of thinking about it. After a few pages of such alternate position studies, Fillmore moves on to the discussion of "practicable jazzes." Beginning with half-step figures (moving from one position to the next), Fillmore attempts to build the trombonist's ability to gliss between pitches. Gradually, Fillmore increases the intervals and thus the distance between positions, leading to wider and wider glissandi. Following this is a section on "Compound Jazzes," in which the student is introduced to figures that include both ascending and descending motion, and a brief section on "practicable pedal jazzes," involving glissandi based on pedal tones.

Once the student has become comfortable moving about the instrument in this way, Fillmore extends his method to include the lengths of the figures. He identifies three main lengths, "short jazzes," "medium jazzes," and "long jazzes," all of which refer, as the labels imply, to the length (in terms of position change) of the glissando motion. Short jazzes are simple half-step figures (a movement of one slide position), while medium jazzes move two or three positions; glisses that involve motions of four or more positions are long jazzes (Musical Example 3).

At this point, with diligent practice, the student should have mastered the technical aspects Fillmore has outlined. He now embarks on the more creative aspects of his method: where and how to employ these effects. Over

Jazz Lengths

The length of a jazz may be short, medium or long. A short jazz is one that takes in the movement of one (or fraction of one) position. *Example*: From A to B flat is a short jazz.

A medium jazz takes in from two to four positions. *Example*: From G to B flat is a medium jazz.

A long jazz takes in from five to seven positions. *Example*: From F to B flat is a long jazz.

Short jazzes because of the limited slide movement are the easiest, so we will take this style first.

Scale Exercises in the most used Keys with short Jazzes preceding each note

Musical Example 3: "Jazz" lengths from *Henry Fillmore's Jazz Trombonist* (1919).

the course of a number of exercises, Fillmore draws comparisons between "plain" and "jazzed" phrases, demonstrating how to convert one to the other. The section on short jazzes tends to treat them mainly as ornaments, scoops that precede each main pitch. In the discussion of applying medium and long jazzes, the glissandi are, of course, longer, and would seem to have, in some (but not all) cases, more of a connective function. Fillmore's advice on applying the compound jazz is to use it to provide the effect on sustained notes, supplying the stereotypically comic effect associated with his "smears." Fillmore also includes a section devoted to "A Few Old Timers Jazzed Up," in which older songs are presented as vehicles for "jazzing." Among these songs are "Annie Laurie," a favorite of trombonists, and "The Old Oaken Bucket." Fillmore concludes his book by coming full circle, as he includes his own "family" of trombone smears, thus using his own compositions as a model for the jazz process.

At times, Fillmore refers to "jazzing" as a larger-scale musical process, reflecting the act of using a "jazz" in performance. Fillmore thus sees jazz trombone playing, and indeed, jazz itself, as a matter of simply inserting particular effects into the melody, effects that, not coincidentally, he pioneered in his "family" of trombone smears. In essence, Fillmore is converting his previous experience as a composer into an early form of improvisational pedagogy (though the term improvisation is itself never used). In an entry for his *Illustrated History for the Modern Trombone, Tuba, and Euphonium Player*, trombonist Douglas Yeo writes that such use of the term "jazz . . . should not be confused with the musical style of the same name."[21] Looking back from the vantage point of a century later, this assessment makes sense. But at the time, it's likely that the sense of confusion and instability about the nature of jazz was precisely what enabled Fillmore to make such claims.

There are a number of important things we can take from Fillmore's method book. First, jazz was still an idea whose identity was in flux. It was not precisely a genre of music nor precisely a way of playing. It is easy to dismiss Fillmore's use of the term "jazz" today as Douglas Yeo does, but in 1919, there was no similarly established understanding of jazz that it could be measured against. Second, Fillmore's book seems to reflect an attempt by a composer attuned to the changes in the popular market to capitalize on such changes. Prior to 1919, Fillmore makes no mention of "jazz" as a characteristic of his works. A more expansive interpretation of this might suggest that Fillmore's actions were nothing less than an attempt to assert his role as not only an expert in "jazzing," but as one who was in a very real way responsible for the emergence of the form. In this line of thinking, jazz was nothing new; he had been doing it for years.

Somewhat surprisingly, Fillmore's book was not the only work devoted to the topic of jazz trombone playing to be published in 1919. Mayhew Lake, writing under the name M. L. Lake, authored the curiously titled *The Wizard Trombone Jazzer*, subtitled "A Short, Concise Treatise on Practical Glissandos (or 'Smears') showing how and when they should be employed." Lake was a contemporary of Fillmore, and the two men occupied very similar spaces in the popular music industry of the day, though Fillmore was certainly the better known of the two. During the same period in which Fillmore was giving birth to his "trombone family," Lake was producing pieces like "Slidus Trombonus," first published in 1916. It seems likely that Lake was trying to capture the same spirit of humor and novelty through the use of the glissando that had put Fillmore on the pop music map. Little is known about any specific relationship between Fillmore and Lake. In the Paul Bierley biography of Fillmore, there is no mention of Lake; by the same token, Lake does not mention Fillmore in his own autobiography.[22] Given the similarity between the two men's careers and musical output, however, it is difficult to believe that, at the very least, they were not aware of each other and that there was not, at some level, a degree of professional rivalry.

Published by Carl Fischer, for whom Lake was an executive, and priced at seventy-five cents, *The Wizard Trombone Jazzer* was obviously going after the same market as Fillmore's book and was in direct competition with Fillmore for this new generation of trombonists. As with their novelty compositions for trombone during the preceding several years, this raises a critical question: to what extent might one book have been a copy of the other? A search of archival records from the US Copyright Office indicates that Fillmore's book was registered on February 27, 1919, with receipt of copies dated to March 6 (approximately one week later). Lake's book, by contrast, was not registered with the Copyright Office until later in the year, with an application dated September 18, 1919, with copies not received until December 12. Clearly, then, Fillmore's book appeared first, and it appeared that he had beaten Lake to the punch.

In comparing Lake's book with Fillmore's, there are, of course, a number of similarities. Both books engage with the same basic topic, namely, the application of the glissando to "regular" trombone solos. As with Fillmore, Lake's views on jazz were infused with assumptions about race. And as in Fillmore's book, Lake immediately weighs in on the debate about jazz's origins and meaning in the preface to *The Wizard Trombone Jazzer*:

> The word jazz is by no means new, but has been used for many years by travelling showman, particularly on the circus lot, where it was quite a common occurrence to hear one negro hail another of his race with "Hello Jazz!" The word, used in this manner had no meaning "musically" but rather portrayed the slow, shiftless, indolent negro. The best exponents of these same characteristics were the colored bands travelling with the shows.[23]

The essential aspects of Lake's method are conspicuously similar to those seen in Fillmore's earlier work. "Jazzes" are, as with Fillmore, identified as discrete musical techniques to be learned and applied in performance (Musical Example 4).

Musical Example 4: "Jazzes" from Lake, *The Wizard Trombone Jazzer* (1919).

Explaining "jazzes," Lake writes that "[a] proper jazz should start and end on component tones of the chord which is being played against it. For this reason, the trombonist who possesses a good 'ear' for chords has the advantage in jazzing the proper intervals."[24] He goes on to give several examples of "jazzes" that illustrate this principle along with advice for their specific application. Later in the book (following a chart of all "legitimate jazzes" on the instrument), Lake includes a section called "Improvising Jazz," which engages in a more focused discussion of the stylistic considerations of jazz trombone performance. Lake cautions the student against over-employing the "jazz," noting that its overuse could lead the player to sound "monotonous and very tiresome."[25] Lake helpfully provides a notated example of such a performance, showing glissandi applied to every note in a rendition of "Rocked in the Cradle of the Deep." The final section of Lake's book, like Fillmore's, is devoted to trombone solos, notated with the appropriate "jazzes" to add the desired effect. As was the case with Fillmore, Lake was not shy about promoting his own work; of the twelve pieces included, four were his own works.

Yet another method book that appeared on the heels of Fillmore's was written by Fortunato Sordillo. Sordillo is not a figure whose life and career are generally well known today, even among trombonists. Born near Naples in 1885, he arrived in Boston in 1898 and would become an American citizen in 1960.[26] After stints as a trombonist and euphonium player with Arthur Pryor (with whom he studied) and John Philip Sousa, Sordillo established himself as an active presence on the musical scene in Boston, where he performed with the Boston Symphony from 1918 to 1920.[27] Sordillo was emphatically not a jazz trombonist. He was, rather, a pedagogue and something of an educational entrepreneur, and indeed, teaching seems to have taken up a good deal of his time. In the May 1921 edition of *Jacobs' Band Monthly*,[28] for example, he placed an ad for the "Sordillo Correspondence School of Music," heralding the "Sordillo-Gardner Course in Music" which had been established in 1917 ("Gardner" was percussionist and fellow Boston Symphony alum Carl E. Gardner).[29] This course included, according to the ad, options for all brass and percussion instruments as well as options for studying music theory, composition and arranging, and conducting.[30] By the mid-1920s, Sordillo had become a teacher in the Boston Public Schools, serving as instrumental music supervisor in 1924 and assistant director of music in 1926.[31] By the 1930s, he was active as a composer and arranger of music for school ensembles, his works frequently reviewed and highlighted in the *Music Educators' Journal* and similar publications. Sordillo was also active with community musical organizations such as the Boston Consolidated Gas Company Band, established under his leadership in 1934.[32] If this were not enough, Sordillo also tried his hand at inventing. Most notable among the patents he had registered through the US Patent and Trademark Office is a mute that could, Sordillo claimed, better facilitate the creation of the "jazz effect."[33]

Given Sordillo's tendency to find opportunities in many different areas of music and education, it makes sense that his "jazz" method book might represent yet another example of musical opportunism. Titled *The Art of Jazzing for the Trombone: A treatise, not only upon the jazzing possibilities of the instrument, but also upon the complete possibilities of the seven positions for the slide in artistic trombone playing*, the book was priced at a very competitive seventy-five cents (as opposed to Fillmore's relatively exorbitant $1.35), Sordillo's book is, like Fillmore's, concerned with the practice of the glissando, an effect that the author characterizes as being at the core of jazz trombone performance practice. Sordillo writes that:

> ... these very exercises form the ideal foundation for jazz trombone playing. As is well known, glissandos between various notes of a part form the "stock in trade" of the jazz trombonist. In order to be prepared to insert glissandos at any time, the trombonist must know the possibilities of the various positions on the slide .... the player will add to his technical equipment and thus be better prepared to play all kinds of music; and he will also be acquiring the knack of playing the jazz, which is highly desirable at this time.[34]

A few observations are in order here. First, as alluded to previously, Sordillo approaches the idea of "the jazz" in a way that is very similar to that of Fillmore (Musical Example 5). Jazz is defined less as a genre of music and more as a particular ornamental effect, i.e., a glissando. And, like Fillmore, there is at least a hint of improvisation; jazzes are things to be "inserted" in the course of playing, with the trombonist having a good deal of discretion as to how this effect is achieved.

But the similarities do not end at the broad conceptual level. Many aspects of Sordillo's book are very similar to Fillmore's, and one wonders if the former had seen the latter's work; given the similarity in the usage of terms like "compound jazz," it seems likely that he did. If this were the case, it would not be out of the ordinary for writers and publishers of trombone methods generally, as I noted previously. A number of method books in the early twentieth century drew heavily on previous works, even to the level of direct copying of textual and musical material. C. Weber's discussion of appoggiaturas, for example, uses language that is identical to that of Otto

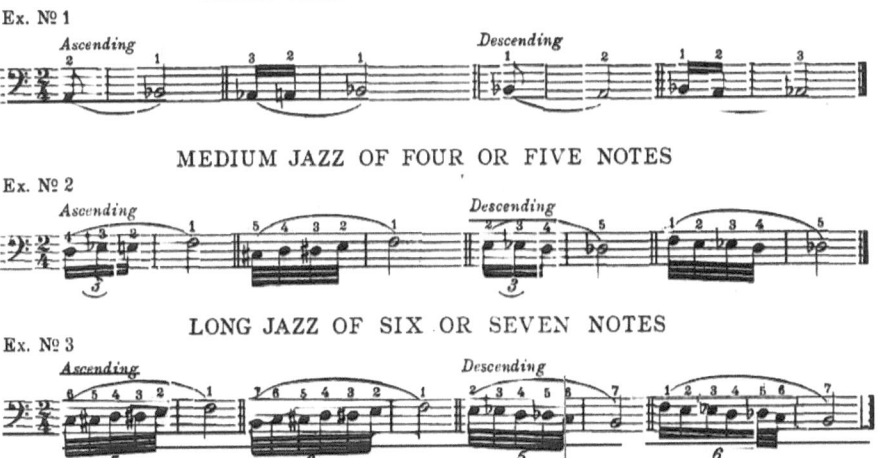

Musical Example 5: "Jazzes" from Sordillo, *Art of Jazzing for the Trombone* (1919).

Langey's earlier method book, and early methods are rife with such "borrowings." Pedagogical materials, it seems, were fair game for imitation and copying, and this tendency is evident in Sordillo's book, which owes a great deal to Fillmore's previous work.

Unlike Fillmore, Sordillo does not spend a great deal of time ruminating on the origins of jazz. He does not incorporate perspectives on the music (as Fillmore did in borrowing indirectly from Walter Kingsley) that speak to its racial character. On the other hand, Sordillo does devote substantial discussion to a more philosophical approach to understanding popular trends in music. In an introductory essay, he writes:

> A late fad in popular music is the "Jazz." You have heard trombones and saxophones play weird sounds and runs that synchronize and harmonize with the rest of the music .... The "Jazz" is here, and trombone players should put themselves immediately to the task of mastering its difficulties, so that they may be familiar with all the possibilities of each position of the instrument.[35]

If Fillmore's book can be read as an attempt by the author to capitalize on a recent musical trend that he believes (and not without some justification) that he pioneered, Sordillo's book might be read as being more pragmatic. Although serious trombonists might lament the current state of affairs in contemporary popular culture, this situation is, Sordillo argues, not going to change; musicians had to "get with it," so to speak, or risk being left behind. This sort of half-grudging acceptance of jazz was not uncommon in this era. No less than Sousa himself, whose bands were pivotal in the popularity of both ragtime and "the jazz" through the works of Arthur Pryor, noted in a 1924 *Etude* magazine feature on "The Jazz Problem" that "Jazz, like the poor, are ever with us."[36]

Smears, Jazzes, and Novelty Music

It is likely that all of these texts sought to do the same thing, to capitalize on a new musical craze that had enormous appeal both to popular audiences and to trombonists who wished to court those audiences. While it is tempting to view these developments as simply an attempt to capture market share in a new popular idiom, I suggest that we must also understand them as part of an active and engaging public discourse on the very nature of jazz itself. Jazz is, and this likely comes as little surprise to those who have conducted any degree of historical work in the genre, a form whose commentators are often preoccupied with self-definition. From the very outset of the style, the idea of what jazz is (or is not) has provoked vociferous debate. Even before the 1917 Original Dixieland Jass Band recordings, earlier works appeared that played on these ideas. One notable example can be found in a recording that was made in late 1916 by the comedy duo Arthur Collins and Byron Harlan. Called "That Funny Jas Band from Dixieland," this recording sought to educate its audience on the nature of the new music. Most notable for the present discussion is the middle section of the recording, in which the musicians demonstrate different musical characteristics that typify the genre. It is notable that the first effect demonstrated is a trombone glissando; "Henry" explains the sound, while "Sal," his counterpart, laughs ecstatically and comments in racially encoded dialect. As Tim Gracyk notes in his book *Popular American Recording Pioneers: 1895–1925*, there is no small measure of irony in the fact that jazz was already being parodied even before it had become a widely known popular form.[37]

If jazz was an object of fun and parody in 1916, by 1919, it was certainly big business, and it would need to be treated as such. This is not to say that the humor of the novelty trombone style was lost on Fillmore and others. Indeed, Fillmore's direct reference to jazz's "humorous qualities" speaks to this exact point. Fillmore is not arguing that jazz is something different from the earlier novelty pieces. In fact, he embraces this identity. More importantly, he places himself squarely in the middle of the conversation. Jazz and novelty, as articulated through the trombone smear, are really one and the same.

Indeed, this is an idea that I wish to pursue further.[38] Jazz historians and historiographers have often made a clear distinction between "jazz" and "novelty." Groups like the ODJB, whose place in the canon has always been somewhat suspect, are often saddled with the designation of "novelty." As Charles Hiroshi Garrett writes in an essay in the volume *Jazz/Not Jazz*, the ODJB's "Livery Stable Blues"

> ... integrated musical incongruities into a parody of rural life, complete with imitation barnyard sounds. At that moment in jazz history, the contrast between the slapstick comedy of this primitivist novelty and, say, a classical symphony or a parlor song, was inordinately clear to amused record buyers, and the ODJB emphasized their knack for clowning around in their promotional materials.[39]

I take issue with nothing that Garrett writes here. The ODJB, at some level, clearly *was a novelty group*. Their own promotional materials, in fact, point to this very idea, as they advertised themselves as "the first sensational amusement novelty of 1917."[40] And as Garrett notes, such novelty was likely readily apparent to most observers.

But I am less interested in juxtaposing the ODJB and early novelty jazz as a whole against a classical symphony and more interested in examining its relationship to the jazz tradition itself, within which such groups are often dismissed. More to the point, early novelty jazz is often used as a foil for later, more "artistic" efforts. In such discourses, groups like the ODJB are "mere" novelty and are thus not "really" jazz, or at the very least, represent jazz of a lower standard. And to be clear, whatever one thinks about the ODJB's music or its identity when considered in the context of sometimes-inflammatory comments made by the group's members, one cannot dispute that these were seasoned, experienced players. We can see such rhetorical gestures invoked in discussions of early jazz trombone playing itself. One notable example of this comes from the late Lawrence Gushee. Writing about Edward "Kid" Ory's 1922 recording of "Ory's Creole Trombone" on a ragtime recording set in the 1970s, Gushee describes the recording with an enormous qualifier, noting Ory's "avoidance of novelty instrumental effects (notwithstanding the trombone glissandos)."[41] Yet in listening to the recording, the novelty character of "Ory's Creole Trombone" is, to be blunt, fairly obvious, right down to the self-referential title, which is not too far of a departure from the titles of pieces in Fillmore's "trombone family" (Musical Example 6). In considering this recording, I find Gushee's hedge on explicitly referring to "Ory's Creole Trombone's" novelty character to be a good representation of

Musical Example 6: Kid Ory, a phrase from "Ory's Creole Trombone" with slide positions (1922). Transcribed by the author.

the reluctance that many jazz historians have seemed to express in dealing fully with the music's relationship to novelty forms. Gushee was an astute scholar, to be sure, and his contributions to our understanding of early jazz are nothing short of groundbreaking; this makes his remark here all the more puzzling. Why such reluctance to link Ory more directly with novelty music? I believe that this speaks to the way in which Ory, in particular, has often been used as a dividing line between earlier jazz styles and the more mature New Orleans-derived style of the late 1920s, best epitomized in his work on Louis Armstrong's recordings between 1926 and 1928. Put simply, jazz trombone prior to Ory is often seen as novelty; starting with him, it simply becomes a part of "early jazz."

I propose that this type of historiographic exercise distorts our view of the jazz genre as it was developing in these formative years. Jazz was, at the time, just one part of a matrix of popular styles that included ragtime, popular song, early blues, band music, and novelty songs, among others. Figures such as Fillmore, Lake, and Sordillo, it seems, saw no distinction between "popular music," "novelty," and "jazz," save for where these ideas served as a way for them to market their products more effectively. For Fillmore, a working musician who was trying as best he could to capitalize on the newest popular style, such a shift was as easy as applying a new label to what he had been doing for over a decade. Historical debates that loom large in today's jazz discourse might seem trivial to someone in this position.

The juxtaposition of novelty with what are deemed to be more authentic examples of early jazz only works if we accept the premise that there is an inherently lesser quality in popular novelty music. And to be clear, I am in no way suggesting that the novelty genre, taken as a whole, was not deeply problematic on many levels, not the least of which was its all-too-common invocation of the crudest of racial stereotypes. But even here, such strategies may miss the bigger point, that detaching jazz from popular novelty music may not be possible. At least in terms of recording, the period of jazz's history from 1917 to 1922 was dominated (at least publicly) by White artists, whose work and demeanor are frequently aligned with novelty styles. And they are so aligned because often they *were* novelty acts and were often explicitly conceptualized that way. To simply dismiss such artists as not being "real" jazz robs us of the opportunity to examine the dynamics of the music industry more critically at this important moment in American popular culture. In the context of the industry, jazz in 1919 was simply the latest new craze, the fad that had kids dancing and their parents in an uproar. It was not "America's Classical Music" but simply one of a number of threads that comprised the tapestry of American music.

Henry Fillmore, by laying claim to the term "jazz" in such an overt and public way, seems to have understood this better than most. For him, jazz was not a special idea—it was simply a marketing category and one that he felt he could capitalize on given his previous work. His *Jazz Trombonist* provides us with a fascinating snapshot of this process, a particular moment when jazz was not a tradition with a long and storied history but was a narrative that was yet to be written. As audiences became more serious about the music and as the style eventually changed, Fillmore's claims of being an authority on jazz faded, and he returned to his previous identity as a bandleader, teacher, composer, and publisher. But Fillmore's claim to defining jazz was likely no more or less problematic than numerous others. And, like all attempts at defining the music, time is the ultimate arbiter.

I do not wish to suggest that we need to regard Fillmore, Lake, or Sordillo as central figures in the early jazz scene. To the contrary, their works seem to have been, shall we say, a blip on the radar. What is more important in this discussion is that these books emerged at a moment when jazz had no perceived center, at least not as we recognize it today. The character and identity of jazz were concepts that were not yet settled, and these kinds of claims to authority reveal an attempt by individuals involved with the publishing of popular music to identify with the newest trends. Jazz, as both a musical system and a discourse, was seemingly up for grabs. All too often as a function of identity, some were better positioned to grab it than others.

DIRTY TRICKS AND HOT LICKS: METHODS AND THE CONCEPT OF JAZZ IN THE 1920S[42]

In the years following the release of "Livery Stable Blues," the question of "what is jazz?" seemed to preoccupy many in the press and beyond. Even the very name of the style was in question. Efforts to find an alternative name for jazz were many and are a well-documented part of jazz's historical narratives. Alan Merriam and Fradley Garner's 1968 study makes note of a contest sponsored in 1924 by one Meyer Davis to find a new term for jazz. One hundred dollars was promised for the winning entry in the *Musical Courier*, but according to Merriam and Garner, the results of the contest have been lost to history.[43] Other terms which appeared in print included "syncopep," which is supposed to have "represent[ed] an honest effort to provide something new within the limitations of its exponents."[44] Terminology, like the music of the time itself, remained in a state of flux.

This lexical instability can also be observed in other kinds of publications. At nearly the same moment that "syncopep" had its brief moment in the sun, the creation and proliferation of books devoted to jazz "breaks" were developing into something of a cottage industry, with the appearance of scores of books, pamphlets, and other printed materials intended to provide developing players with "tricks of the trade." To date, the only significant scholarly attention that has been paid to these works seems to be an essay by Lawrence Gushee on the discourses of improvisation in jazz's "middle period."[45] Specifically, Gushee examines the way in which the practice of improvisation was characterized in jazz writing through the 1930s; instructional texts, Gushee notes, were an important step in this process. Of particular importance were books that were attributed to well-known "real world" jazz players. This is illustrated by a pair of books published in 1925 and 1926 by trombonist Miff Mole, which shed light on the ways that publishers tried to capitalize on the fame and influence of particular players. Referencing the 1925 text in which Mole emphasizes his own approach and style, Gushee writes: "Trombonist Mole, in his 1925 self-published collection, claimed that he was responding to numerous letters asking for a book 'that will teach my original style and method of playing a trombone . . . . My style is not copied from other musicians' ideas . . . . Every break and chorus is my own improvisation.'"[46] Authors and publishers of such books lured nascent jazz players with promises of an authentic connection to the professional music world, but to what extent was the musical material contained within them—the actual notated breaks—connected to "real-world" practice? Gushee writes that the breaks in Mole's books were "transcribed from records," but there is no specific information provided that links the musical content and particular jazz recordings. Still, Gushee's theory might seem to be supported in the foreword to Miff Mole's 1926 book, which states that "the material in this volume has been successfully used by the author in playing many well-known phonograph dance records and with Ross Gorman's Orchestra at the Earl Carroll's Vanities and Club Monte Carlo, New York."[47]

Considering that these were commercial objects whose purpose may have been, at least in part, to generate more publicity for the artist-authors, it might seem that omitting specific information about the source of this material would be a lost opportunity for cross-marketing to encourage would-be players to seek out specific recordings (and, one would think, buy them). It is certainly within the realm of possibility that Gushee is correct, that these breaks are drawn from the language of jazz improvisation as it was practiced instead of being original material that was written "in the style of" a certain artist.[48] Yet Mole's own discography seems to weigh against this interpretation. To date, I have been unable to locate any record of Mole's appearing on a recording of "Beale Street Blues," which is included as one of the "hot choruses" in his 1925 book.[49] And while there is a record of a 1924 version of "Some of These Days" with an ensemble called The Ambassadors that may have included Mole, it appears that song was only used as an introductory section on the recording[50] and is thus unlikely to be the source of the solo chorus under that title in Mole's book. This is not to say that these materials were not derived from actual performance, but it does not seem to be supported by anything in the discographic record. Regardless of whether they were derived from recordings or were generated as original material (or some combination of the two), these texts provided aspiring players with a way to both learn the language of jazz and have a sense of connection with working jazz musicians.

The musical materials that comprised Mole's books will be addressed in more detail later in this section. But for the moment, I'd like to return to the topic of wording. Nowhere in Mole's 1925 book can one find the word "jazz." The only description that is given is the description of "Original Breaks" and "Hot Choruses." Would potential buyers associate his book with "jazz" or might they instead think that this was a fine example of "syncopep"? Perhaps there was another term with which we aren't familiar. This is precisely the idea that Gushee was getting at in his essay, situating method books within a broader body of work in which an understanding of the concept of "jazz improvisation" was being shaped. Method books and pedagogical materials, he notes, played an important role in this process in a way that is, I would suggest, similar to the way that Henry Fillmore's book advanced its own definition of jazz. It was not simply a matter of understanding how to play jazz but of *the very understanding of what the music was.*

In the discussion that follows, I turn to the publication of several method books for jazz trombone in the 1920s, precisely at the moment that the main paradigm for jazz's performance practice was about to undergo a profound shift. What characterizes these texts is a move away from the idea of the glissando as the defining characteristic of jazz and toward the development of what I term an "idiomatic improvisational language." In using this phrase,

I am referring to the overlap between a) melodic concepts related to pitch selection, phrasing, harmonic/melodic relationships, and other aspects of the improvisational language of jazz that is in development, and b) idiomatic aspects of the instrument itself, referring to particular characteristics, challenges, technical demands, and other considerations of trombone playing. It is in the overlap of these two areas, of musical language and instrumental technique, where much learning in jazz performance takes place.

Despite a new focus on the development of language in these later works, we can see a similar relationship to our earlier examples: Fillmore, Lake, and Sordillo were all concerned with a particular musical gesture that is idiomatic to the instrument (the glissando) and how it could be applied in performance. By the mid to late 1920s, authors of pedagogical works were engaging with similar problems at the intersection of instrumental performance and improvisational practice, and they did so within the context of a literature that was attributed to working jazz musicians of the time, linking the worlds of pedagogy and performance. Here, learning was not an isolated act but one that was done with a metaphorical musician looking over your shoulder, guiding your progress and development. A crucial aspect of these works is how to classify the various musical approaches. Would they be understood as "jazz" or as something else?

Method, Marketing, and the Case of Milfred "Miff" Mole

In the history of jazz trombone playing, Miff Mole occupies an unusual place. He was, by nearly every account, among the most technically formidable players on the 1920s jazz scene, easily the equal of such stalwarts as Kid Ory, George Brunies, and Charlie Green. By the middle of the decade, he had risen from an unheralded local player to a first-call, in-demand musician, steadily climbing the ladder of the Jazz Age musical marketplace. After a few years of associations with musicians such as Ray Miller and Ross Gorman, Mole made his first of a series of recordings as a leader in January 1927 with a group that featured his frequent musical partner Red Nichols, with whom Mole had made numerous recordings during the previous few years. For Mole, this date must have been especially significant, the culmination of a long period of paying dues, of contributing to other artists' work. Mole thrived within the traditional New Orleans-based ensemble format in which the most important role for horn players was still the contrapuntal interplay of the frontline. At this, Mole was indisputably a master, effortlessly matching the cornet and clarinet note for note, playing fluid lines that evinced a formidable technique but that also dripped with blues sensibilities. Occasionally,

Mole would punch through the ensemble with a break or even a short solo chorus, and on this first 1927 date, he gave himself plenty of space to play on each of the three sides recorded that day.

Why history taps some individuals for greatness while others fade into memory is the subject of the following chapter. But one consideration is that at exactly the same moment that Mole was beginning to emerge as a player on his own, there were signs that this music was beginning to point to a new approach, a new sound, that would occur over the course of the next few years. With a style based on a disjunct, highly technical approach that worked well in the context of a traditional frontline counterpoint, Mole did not seem to adapt to the kinds of melodic-based improvisational approaches that were being popularized by other players.

It would be useful here to get a fuller sense of what Mole was doing in the years leading up to this point. Tom Lord's *Jazz Discography* lists Mole's first recording session as being with the Original New Orleans Jazz Band in 1919, but there is some dispute as to whether this was, in fact, Mole or Frank Lhotak, a peer of Mole's who was also active on the New York scene by the early 1920s. At any rate, the trombone is mainly relegated to tailgate countermelodies that were in the style of Eddie Edwards of the Original Dixieland Jass Band. It would be another three years before Mole's name would appear again on a recording, embarking on a course that would make him one of the busiest trombonists on the New York jazz scene. The year 1922 was, in terms of recording, a particularly fruitful year for Mole as he entered the studio on nearly three dozen occasions between January and November. Although he worked as an on-call player for various groups, his most steady recording work came with the Original Memphis Five; many of the groups with which Mole recorded were, in fact, drawn from the same core roster.[51]

Mole was, relatively speaking, a "local" to the New York scene. Born in 1898, Mole grew up on Long Island, not far from the city. By the age of fifteen, he had taken up the trombone (after playing piano and violin), and in his late teens, began to work with a number of New York-based ensembles, including groups led by Gus Sharp and Jimmy Durante. Little has been written about Mole's early years in the New York world, with most discussion of his work centering on his efforts as a bandleader in the latter part of the decade and his work with cornetist Red Nichols. But for a brief period in the early 1920s, he was a major presence on the New York scene, and his prodigious recorded output enables a closer examination of his style. In a series of recordings made with Leona Williams, a New Orleans-born singer who had relocated to New York, it is clear that Mole has absorbed the essential elements of the New Orleans style, exhibiting a bluesy sound that frequently featured both sweeping glissandi and intricate passagework. These early recordings supporting Williams—with a group of musicians whose members also recorded as the Original Memphis Five, Jazzbo's Carolina Serenaders, and The Cotton Pickers—allowed few opportunities for Mole to take on a foreground role. What we don't know is this: to what extent were these kinds of counterlines improvised, and to what extent might they have been predetermined? In Mole's case, the answer seems to lie somewhere in between. This can be heard in two recorded versions of "I Wish I Could Shimmy Like My Sister Kate," first by The Cotton Pickers in September 1922 and then by the Original Memphis Five in the following month. Mole's playing across both versions uses several of the same figures at similar points in the form. Of particular note is a two-bar break at the midpoint of the second chorus in each version, in which Mole plays an identical figure. Overall, his playing on these early recordings is consistently clean, fluid, and expressive.

It is probably more useful to compare the materials in Mole's books with his playing as captured in his recordings from the summer and fall of 1924. As with others in the New Orleans-derived style, the question of improvisation, particularly as it relates to countermelodies, is always of foremost importance in such assessments. In a June 1924 recording of "Where Is That Old Girl of Mine" with Ray Miller's Brunswick Orchestra, one gets a good sense of the group's Whiteman-based approach. Characterized by precise, crisp ensemble work, Miller's group is going for a similar aesthetic as Whiteman. At the same time, the Miller group has a somewhat livelier feel and a more pronounced sense of swing. And while such tightly controlled arrangements often afforded little opportunity for a player like Mole to shine through, there were notable exceptions. One example of his playing can be heard in a recording of "Prince of Wails" from another November 1924 session with The Cotton Pickers.[52] Mole's presence is felt throughout the recording, consisting of counterline work that is technically challenging (particularly impressive are a number of abrupt register shifts). But he does get the chance to take a brief solo just before the end of the recording; like his ensemble work, Mole's solo playing showcases his exceptionally smooth, fluid style that often masks its more technical aspects. Mole's playing at this moment in time is a clear match for that of any other trombonist in jazz.

Hearing these early records, it is not difficult to imagine why Mole might have attracted a good deal of attention on the New York jazz scene of the time. It's also not difficult to imagine why such a musician might have an ambition to become something more than a background player. He was, simply put, coming into his own, fast becoming a model for developing trombonists. Scott Yanow suggests that this period likely represented the high-water mark of Mole's career and his influence in the development of jazz trombone playing:

> During 1926–27, Miff Mole emerged as one of the first trombonists to truly liberate his horn from its percussive function, treating it as a solo instrument that could be played nearly with the facility of a trumpet. While Mole's unusual style (with its wide interval jumps and eccentric choice of notes) was well utilized with Red Nichols' groups, it was soon overshadowed by the legato playing of Jimmy Harrison and particularly Jack Teagarden, whose arrival in New York in 1928 was a major event.[53]

Mole, it would seem, understood this all very well. By the end of 1924, he was positioned at precisely the right place, at exactly the right time, to take the next steps in establishing himself as a major player. The jazz world had undergone a tectonic shift over the course of the year. In February, Paul Whiteman's premiere of Gershwin's *Rhapsody in Blue* at Aeolian Hall redefined the parameters of jazz, both musical and societal; meanwhile, at the Roseland Ballroom, up-and-coming bandleader Fletcher Henderson had his own hand to play, heralded by the brash sounds of a young trumpeter from New Orleans by way of Chicago, Louis Armstrong, and featuring the tight, swinging arrangements of Don Redman.[54] As 1924 turned into 1925, he likely saw an important opportunity to advance his position in the market. The publishing of a pedagogical pamphlet, seen in this light, is yet one more way to make inroads into this new world and to establish a reputation as an authoritative voice. And so, in 1925, Mole published what would be the first of two pedagogical works, the second coming the following year. Let us examine these works in greater detail.

The first of the two books, *"Original Breaks" and "Hot Choruses" for Trombone and Alto Saxophone*, is a modest book (at only eight pages in length) that seems to have been self-published and distributed; the only publication information included is for "Ability Printing Co.," located on 48th Street in New York.[55] The booklet serves as part method book, part publicity package, with Mole's picture prominently displayed on the front cover; on the back cover, another photo is used, this time featuring Ray Miller's Brunswick Orchestra with Mole featured prominently in the foreground. The conventional wisdom of pedagogy publishing in this period is that it was driven by publishers who were looking for any way possible to capitalize on the newest trends, as companies like Alfred and Melrose would demonstrate. But in Mole's case, where it is the musician that is trying to enter the market directly,

Musical Example 7: Miff Mole, break in F Major from *Original Breaks and Hot Choruses* (1925).

we must consider a different dynamic, that of the working jazz musician who sees educational materials as an opportunity for commercial and career advancement. The book provides a series of two-bar breaks in various keys as well as a few single-chorus solos based on popular songs. There is nothing that we might classify as "instruction" in the book; the examples stand on their own, to be practiced and applied as the user sees fit. As for the exercises themselves, they generally tend to exhibit the core aspects of Mole's playing; intricate passagework, abrupt changes in register, and a bluesy sensibility that is represented here in the carefully placed glissandi that can be easily heard in his playing. There is little question that a skilled trombonist could, upon mastering these exercises, play in a style that, at the very least, resembles Mole's playing. This, I would think, is precisely the point (Musical Example 7).

His subsequent book, meanwhile, published in 1926 by Alfred and Co., is different in some significant ways. Titled *100 Jazz Breaks*, the book is notable both for its use of the term "jazz" and its more explicit connection with "real world" practice, which the written introduction to the book suggests is a close one. Yet aural evidence for this kind of direct connection is scant; breaks and choruses, as recorded by Mole throughout this period, do not seem to correlate directly to the material included in the books. But there is another way of looking at this question: to what extent did the material in these books reflect Mole's overall approach, his style of playing in a broad sense? There is one other factor that complicates the connection between these books and Mole's actual playing. This is particularly evident in the 1926 book, where a few passages hint that someone other than Mole might have been responsible for the actual writing of the book(s). While there is no specific evidence that Mole did not, in fact, write the book, or at least the exercises contained within it, there are a few irregularities to be found in its pages. In one passage from the book's foreword (which is credited to "The Author"), the following text appears: "The author suggests that to get the best results these breaks be gradually committed to memory. Careful attention must also be given to accents, *fingering*, and phrasing."[56] The reference to "fingerings" is a curious term in a book intended to be played by slide trombonists and that was purported to be written by one of the foremost jazz trombonists of the day. This leads me to speculate that perhaps this text was not, in fact, written

Musical Example 8: Miff Mole, four breaks in C Major from *100 Hot Breaks for Trombone* (1926).

by Mole but could have been penned by a copywriter for Alfred. If this were the case (and again, I admit that this is speculation), might this also be true of the breaks themselves? Could they also have been written by someone else? There is little likelihood that this will ever be definitely determined, but, at the very least, it is an interesting idea to ponder.

As for the actual breaks, the included exercises consist entirely of two-bar breaks in commonly played keys from A♭ to D♯. Each break is a self-contained figure ready to be "plugged in" to a performance situation. The structure of these figures is generally similar to that in the previous book; the main difference is simply that there are more of them. Glissandi are not notated specifically but instead are indicated with the "gliss" marking, which would seem to indicate that the idea was commonly understood by this point (Musical Example 8).

And as with the previous book, there is very little in the way of actual instruction or advice for the trombonist in *100 Jazz Breaks*. The only thing approaching this is a passage in the foreword that gives some very general guidance:

> The player will find that by memorizing the breaks he will easily be able to fit them into the playing of popular dance melodies. However, where and when to use them must be left entirely to the discretion of the individual. There are no definite rules of improvising breaks, but this should become a reality after practice and study of the construction of the breaks in this book.[57]

By emphasizing the creation of an arsenal of breaks and solos, Mole and his collaborators seem to have two main goals. First, they are meant to give the player a "bag of tricks" that can be easily deployed as needed. Second, these breaks can serve as models for players to construct their own figures, to play in a "Mole-like" manner. But there is another unstated goal that might be as important as the first two, namely the amplification of Mole's reputation. Mole's books seem to have appeared right at the peak of his influence, just as the performance practice of jazz trombone playing was about to move in a dramatically different direction.

Crozier, Miller, and Dorsey

Mole's 1926 book would not be the only one published by Alfred during this period. Also appearing was a series of "loose leaf" folios credited to George Crozier, an arranger and trombonist whose greatest notoriety likely came as a member of McMurray's California Thumpers in the early 1920s as well as Eddie Elkins's Orchestra, both based in Los Angeles. Crozier does not appear to have recorded with either group; his only recording credits seem to be a few sides with Don Parker's Western Melody Boys recorded from March to October 1923. Both Parker's ensemble and Crozier's playing are, to be frank, somewhat unremarkable. For his part, Crozier's approach to improvisation tends toward the stiff side, certainly proficient in terms of technique but without much of Mole's fluidity and sense of ease.

Crozier seems to have had more success as an arranger, creating charts for Tommy Dorsey, Fletcher Henderson, and Jean Goldkette, among others. Despite his billing as the "hottest arranger of them all," little else is known about Crozier, with the exception of this series. In keeping with the spirit of similar publications, Crozier takes the idea of "inserting" his jazz breaks into existing parts to its logical—and literal—conclusion, as can be observed from this passage in the introduction to his 1926 trombone book:

> The object of this book of *50 Jazz Breaks* is not merely to furnish the player with breaks in the various keys to be memorized wherever possible, but rather to simplify their application by making them LOOSE LEAF *so that they may be cut and pasted in the dance arrangement.* This eliminates the necessity of memorizing, thereby permitting the player to be sure of accurately playing the breaks which are all carefully phrased and accented.... While of course the best way to eventually acquire the art of improvising is to memorize the breaks and study their construction, the author believes that by using them in the

manner suggested above (pasting them in the dance arrangement) the player will gradually be able to learn how to improvise, and at the same time be able to MAKE HIS PLAYING STAND OUT, while acquiring this technique.[58]

I draw attention to Crozier's suggestion, which I have highlighted with italics in the above quote, to insert these breaks directly into a score. There is a consistency among Crozier's books in that all of them suggest that these musical figures can be "inserted" into actual playing situations. In this sense, the books are geared toward the professional trombonist who wishes to enhance their "toolkit" for playing jazz in the most literal sense possible. Crozier's trombone book—as is the case with the rest of those in the series—is simple in construction, consisting entirely of a series of two-bar breaks in common keys in both dominant and tonic harmonic contexts (Musical Example 9).

Crozier also makes direct connections to performance with respect to the origins of his material, writing in the author's note that they were "used in

Musical Example 9: George Crozier breaks in E♭ Major from *Jazz Breaks in Loose Leaf Form* (1926). Breaks 1–3 are intended to be used on dominant chords, while 4–5 are used on the tonic. Note the perforation lines between the breaks.

making phonograph arrangements" for a number of top orchestras, including Jean Goldkette, Fletcher Henderson, and Ross Gorman.[59] Yet the individual breaks are not identified as having been used in particular recordings, making such an assessment difficult.

Crozier would remain, it seems, a relatively unheralded figure in jazz. But the following year, additional pedagogical publications would appear that offered a more fundamental and tangible sense of connection to the professional jazz world. Two books are of particular interest, pitting rival trombonists against one another: Glenn Miller and Tommy Dorsey. Miller and Dorsey would be most closely associated with the later big band boom of the 1930s, but in 1927, both men were in the midst of careers as well-regarded freelance trombonists, demonstrating a high degree of flexibility and skill. In this sense, Miller and Dorsey occupied similar spaces on the scene and had similar styles of performance, and one would imagine that, at some level, they saw each other as professional rivals. That two publishers would release method books with Miller and Dorsey as the respective authors would seem to underscore this idea. Miller's book was published by Melrose, the Chicago-based music publishing house that is probably best known today for its collaborations with Jelly Roll Morton.[60] Melrose saw itself as a major player in the emerging jazz scene, forming relationships with numerous jazz players of the time. Dorsey's book, meanwhile, would be published by Robbins-Engel, a New York-based publisher that had close connections to Tin Pan Alley, Broadway, and the still-active silent film industry. Let us examine these works individually.

The first thing I would note is the direct and explicit use of the term "jazz" in Miller's book; there is no ambiguity or hedging in the use of this term. In the foreword to the book (which is identified as a "Publisher's Note"), the publishers sing Miller's praises and establish his bona fides as an authority on jazz trombone playing:

> Glen [sic] Miller, feature trombonist of Ben Pollack's Recording Orchestra, and author of this book, is recognized everywhere as a finished artist. His style is modern, individual, and effective. The manner in which he interprets rhythm and builds up his break attacks is a class of work that only comes from the artist who is master [sic] of his instrument.[61]

In typical fashion, the publishers go on to offer some modest advice for the aspiring trombonist:

Perfection in any endeavor is only gained by study, concentration, and determination to win . . . . The breaks in this book are the ultra-modern style of jazz breaks. They are genuine inspirations. MEMORIZE THEM. They can be used in playing any and all dance melodies. To obtain the best results it is imperative that all phrasings be carefully observed and all positions played as marked.[62]

Miller's exercises are presented through a repeated pattern of four breaks in all twelve keys. For each key center, three different harmonic/melodic contexts are used: major, dominant (on the same root), and the relative minor. The breaks are not transposed; instead, new breaks are created for each particular harmonic context. In many cases, the breaks that Miller includes are relatively idiomatic to the trombone. For instance, in the very first example, a two-bar break features a half step from C to B going from the first to the second measure, which is marked with a "gliss" designation (Musical Example 10).

Musical Example 10: Glenn Miller, four breaks in C Major from Glenn Miller's *125 Jazz Breaks for Trombone* (1927).

Overall, Miller seems to be sensitive to creating breaks that "lay well" on the instrument that do not require large, rapid movements between positions, unlike those of Mole, which require a high degree of flexibility to properly execute.

Like Mole's publications, Miller's book reads as an attempt to capitalize on his rising profile in the recording industry. His most notable recordings in this period were made with bands led by Ben Pollack and Benny Goodman, with occasional dates with Red Nichols and Sam Lanin; Miller was, like Mole, an in-demand freelancer on the late 1920s New York jazz scene in the truest sense of the word. Pollack's band, which was modeled largely on that of Paul Whiteman, tended to afford little opportunity for playing breaks. In fact, it seems as though much of Miller's work on record in these early days of his career was aligned with the so-called "sweet bands," which leaned more heavily on popular melody and less on improvisation. Nevertheless, there are several recordings featuring Miller's jazz playing that are worth examining. One of the best and clearest examples of Miller's playing in this period can be heard in a December 1926 session with Pollack, which resulted in two sides, "When I First Met Mary" and "Deed I Do." Both feature solos by Miller, and they provide starkly different perspectives on his developing style. In the first of these, Miller's playing is squarely in the "sweet" style, featuring a deep, vibrato-infused sound over the course of an eight-bar phrase. But in "'Deed I Do," Miller uncorks a sprightly, virtuosic, and likely improvised solo (Musical Example 11). Though relatively brief (again, relegated to a single eight-bar phrase), Miller's playing exhibits many of the same ideas that will appear the following year in his breaks book. His solo is, to employ a commonly used characterization, "all over the horn"; in comparison to Miff Mole, he demonstrates a more relaxed fluidity and sense of ease with the instrument, both in terms of slide technique and with respect to range and register. His playing is also notable for its pronounced use of short gliss-like figures in stepwise movements (i.e., glissandi between two tones in a neighboring relationship). A similar effect can be observed in a number of the breaks that would be included in Miller's book. In the very first break, Miller uses a minor second gliss that falls on the downbeat of the second bar of the break, creating a slight emphasis on B. But by any measure, the gliss plays a more modest role in Miller's improvisational language, both in recorded work and in his publication. We might position Miller as a player whose approach is pointing more to the future of jazz than that of Mole, who remained more squarely in the New Orleans-Chicago aesthetic.

Musical Example 11: Glenn Miller's solo on "'Deed I Do," Ben Pollack Orchestra (1926). Transcribed by the author.

Musical Example 12: Tommy Dorsey, four breaks from *100 Hot Breaks for the Trombone* (1927).

The cover of Miller's book centers on a portrait of the trombonist, which frames and presents him as a serious, even studious figure. Tommy Dorsey's book[63] takes a different approach. The cover features a photo of Dorsey in the center with caricatured drawings of trombonists on either side (both White and in formal attire), while flames shoot up from the bottom of the page, visually signifying the title *100 Hot Breaks for the Trombone*. Dorsey's book, like Miller's, presents a series of breaks in different keys, although, unlike Miller, Dorsey provides breaks only in the "common" keys that a contemporary trombonist might realistically encounter. The nature of the individual breaks is not significantly different from his rival's. Like Miller, Dorsey places an emphasis on specific articulations, as can be seen in the frequent use of accents and slurred passages (Musical Example 12).

Meaningful distinctions between the books of Miller and Dorsey are difficult to easily identify, and given the relative similarity of their playing styles of the time, this should not be too surprising. Determining which of these came first is a bit of a challenge. While Dorsey's book is dated in the official US Copyright registry on April 2, 1927, Miller's book does not seem to appear in the registry for that year, nor for the years immediately preceding or following. In light of this, it is difficult to reconstruct precisely how the publication of these two works played out in 1927. But in the larger sense, they were part of the same milieu of works intended to bring the "real" jazz language into the studios, practice rooms, and homes of aspiring musicians.

Trix Trombonix and the Lexicon of Improvisation

If books like those credited to Miller and Dorsey reflected a link between pedagogy and real-world performance, others approached the jazz language more from the outside. One such example, also published in 1927, proves very instructive in this regard. Published by Carl Fischer, *Trix Trombonix* was credited to Lester Brockton, a somewhat marginally known name on Tin Pan Alley, who had penned a few modestly successful songs. However, there is more to this story; as it turns out, Lester Brockton was, in fact, a pseudonym for Mayhew Lake, the very same renowned band composer who penned novelty trombone works such as "Slidus Trombonus" as well as *The Wizard Trombone Jazzer*. Lake produced a number of pedagogical works in the 1920s and was a fairly well-known and influential figure in educational music publishing. In 1920, he penned a treatise titled *The American Band Arranger: A Complete and Reliable Self-instructor for Mastering the Essential Principles of Practical and Artistic Arranging for Military Band* (also published by Carl Fischer). By the time this book was published, any lingering attachment to the valve trombone seemed to have vanished; he notes that the slide trombone is the "only effective and legitimate instrument to consider."[64] Yet Lake writes very little about the instrument, confining his discussion mainly to elements of notation, voicing, and orchestration. There is no discussion of glissandi or other jazz or novelty effects, despite his own use of such figures in his compositions.

As was noted previously, Lake was most closely associated with the Carl Fischer publishing house, where he remained for over three decades as an editor of the publisher's band and orchestral music departments.[65] It is likely that his position with Carl Fischer, one of America's leading publishing houses for concert music, would have afforded him an opportunity to indulge his interests in popular genres as well. Lake published works under a number of false names including Paul DuLac, Charles Edwards, William Lester, Robert Hall, and Alfrey Byers, in addition to Lester Brockton.[66]

As for *Trix Trombonix*, Lake identifies the book as a primer on "how to play jazz choruses—'hot' choruses . . . 'dirt' choruses,"[67] and "how to improvise with proper 'smears' against a given melody."[68] This is, perhaps, the most notable aspect of the book. In his preface, as was the case in *The Wizard Trombone Jazzer* several years before, we again find Lake pontificating on the nature of jazz itself. In the foreword to the book, Lake writes that "[j]azz is modern 'ragtime,' its effects based on various accents of rhythm and everchanging harmonies." Lake draws a distinction between playing jazz in a "clean" or "dirt" manner, noting specifically that "[i]n 'clean' jazz the figurations employed against the melody (variations, counter-melodies [sic], etc.) do not 'blur' with the melody but bear a close relationship to the chords which are sounding at the time. In 'dirt' the opposite is true—dissonant tones are purposely interpolated, giving a sort of 'savage' effect to the music."[69] As in *The Wizard Trombone Jazzer*, Lake engages in a bit of racialized theorizing about the music, though this might be considered a modest improvement over his attribution of glissandi to "shiftless negro" tendencies in his previous work. That said, the glissando does play a key role here, as Lake notes that "[n]aturally in trombone jazzes, the glissandos are employed often."[70]

The remainder of *Trix Trombonix* is given over to specific patterns that are variously classified as "jazz," "hot," or "dirt," and it is here, I think, that we should turn our attention to the development of terminology. As discussed previously, "dirt" phrases involve some sort of harmonic clash or dissonance. This is evident in the very first exercise in the book. Three figures—one "jazz," one "hot," and one "dirt"—are presented, all in the key of F major. The "jazz" figure is entirely within the key, while the "dirt" chorus contains numerous examples of dissonance; the first note, for example, is an E♭ over the F major triadic harmony. The "hot" chorus, meanwhile, might be said to fall somewhere between "jazz" and "dirt." It is generally consonant, at least in comparison with the "dirt" chorus, but it also uses a number of instrumental effects. The most notable of these is the glissando, which is specifically notated as such, and without the use of chromatic pitches between the beginning and end of the gliss (Musical Example 13).

Musical Example 13: Lester Brockton (Mayhew Lake), "Jazz," "Hot," and "Dirt" figures, *Trix Trombonix* (1927).

As with Lake's *The Wizard Trombone Jazzer*, *Trix Trombonix* functions as part sourcebook for specific phrases and part method book. Later in the book, Lake includes a discussion of how to improvise that gives specific guidance for the player in negotiating a harmonic framework. Lake writes that

> [a]ll embellishments, counter-melodies and variations are based upon (and subject to) these two factors—the melody and the harmony. The simplest manner of improvising a counter melody is to embellish the component tones of the existing chord (the chord which is sounding at that period . . . . The next step is to employ "passing tones," tones not included in the existing chords but CONNECTING them). In this case it is best for the chord tones to sound ON THE BEAT—[and connecting tones] sounding on the UNACCENTED parts of the measure. Another effective method is to improvise a melody entirely foreign to the melody proper, playable with the same accompaniment, but which WILL NOT "BLUR" when played against the melody proper. This is more difficult.[71]

Lake's explanation is remarkably thorough and relatively sophisticated within the context of the pedagogical literature of jazz at the time and is not terribly far removed from the application of chord-scale theory that would be popularized through the work of figures like George Russell, David Baker, and Jamey Aebersold in later decades. The specific examples he offers in the remainder of the book, in which he admonishes the student to "study . . . carefully,"[72] illustrate his approach. For instance, in one example, Lake provides a series of figures set to a piano accompaniment that represents what would later be called a "ii-V-I" in C, although in Lake's example, specific notation is used rather than abstract chord symbols. Line A of the example is entirely within the harmonic structure—there are no tones that are not present in the given chords. Line B, meanwhile, is a variation on the previous passage but with passing tones between chord tones. The final line (C) is labeled as a "free melody"; it is "free" only in the sense that it does not consist merely of chord tones and passing tones but uses other pitches in the key.

PUBLISHING AND PERFORMANCE

Where, specifically, did the musical material in these books come from? One piece of evidence, which is by no means definitive but relevant nonetheless, comes from Louis Armstrong's *125 Jazz Breaks for Hot Trumpet*, which was published by Melrose in 1927. In the foreword to the volume, the publisher makes the following claim:

> The breaks in this book depart in principle of production from any breaks on the market. They are genuine inspirations obtained, not by the old method of the artist writing down his breaks one note at a time, but from actual recordings. Special phonograph recording apparatus was employed to make them. They are red hot inspirations extracted from red hot jazz recordings.[73]

Melrose's claim, taken at face value, would suggest that the books attributed to Mole, Miller, Dorsey, and their peers were created and notated by the artists themselves and not transcribed from recordings. Armstrong's book, by contrast, is described as being taken from actual sound recordings made by the artist—"red hot inspirations extracted from red hot jazz recordings." James Lincoln Collier recounts the process by which Armstrong was said to have created his "breaks" for Melrose:

> In order to do this, they brought Louis into a studio and had him improvise solos and breaks, which were recorded on cylinders, a nineteenth-century recording system still in use at the time. The improvisations were transcribed by Elmer Schoebel and issued in books as *125 Jazz Breaks for Cornet*, priced at a dollar, and *50 Hot Choruses for Cornet*, priced at two dollars.[74]

Schoebel, a Chicago pianist who also worked for Melrose at the time, tells a similar story in a 1968 interview of his involvement in the creation of Armstrong's books, which provides some crucial details about the process:

> During the Chicago days I was sharing an office with Walter Melrose of the "Melrose Music Co." One day, in 1927, Melrose said he was going to publish a set of Louis Armstrong breaks, but there was a technical problem of getting the Armstrong "hot" breaks down on paper. Finally, Melrose and I hit on the idea of having Armstrong record his breaks. We bought a $15 Edison cylinder phonograph and 50 wax cylinders, gave them to Louis and told him to play. The cylinders were duly filled up by Armstrong and the "breaks" were copied into written form. I transcribed the "breaks" which were published.[75]

A couple of observations are in order with respect to Schoebel's recollections. First, the number of cylinders (fifty) does not correspond to the number of "breaks" in Armstrong's *125 Jazz Breaks*. It does, however, correspond to the number of choruses in Armstrong's *50 Hot Choruses for Cornet*, also published in 1927 by Melrose, and it seems likely that this is the book Schoebel is referring to.[76] Second, this account would provide some support for the claims made by Melrose as noted above; although the specific origin of the material in other contemporary books is not definitively established, it would follow that they were *not* recorded and transcribed in a manner similar to what Schoebel describes, if Melrose's claims are to be believed.

Why does this matter, the idea that other methods, such as those we've examined in this discussion, were likely "composed" by the respective authors (as attributed) and not derived directly from recordings? Does it somehow make them less "authentic" when compared to those whose origins come from actual sound recordings? Armstrong was, by nearly every account, an experienced reader and writer of music by this point in his career; why could he not have transcribed these recordings himself (or, for that matter, simply "composed" them)? What was the nature of the "technical problem of getting the Armstrong 'hot' breaks down on paper"? Why could they not simply be transcribed from Armstrong's existing recordings? The historical record unfortunately has not yet provided answers to these questions.

Nevertheless, Melrose seemed to believe that a direct connection between the breaks and choruses on the one hand and the recordings from which they were transcribed on the other would be an important selling point. There are, as far as I am able to determine, no surviving business records from this era that would give an indication of how these books sold, making a comparison of the popularity of Armstrong's books relative to others impractical. But one might speculate that Armstrong's book likely sold well. At precisely this moment (1927), Armstrong was in the middle of what was likely the most musically significant period of his career, leading the influential "Hot Five" and "Hot Seven" recording sessions, which would position him at the vanguard of a revolutionary shift in jazz performance, the result of which would set jazz on a course in which virtuoso solo improvisation would arguably become the genre's defining feature. While the impact of these recordings has been covered thoroughly by numerous observers over the years, this pair of method books might also shed a bit of light on these changes. It is telling, I think, that both the "breaks" and "choruses" books would appear at this moment. Might this itself indicate a shift in Armstrong's approach to playing, and more generally, to the idea that the traditional break was being overshadowed by the solo as the main point of interest in improvisation?

There is nothing definitive to support this claim, but it is nonetheless an intriguing possibility.

The learning of jazz requires some kind of system through which those who wish to teach the music can impart knowledge to those who wish to learn. Words matter, as simple rote instruction is actually quite uncommon. In the context we have discussed here, the creation of such a system is sometimes a work in progress. And I might suggest that this is a good way to understand how the pedagogy of playing jazz would emerge during this early period. The establishment of a language for communication about the music is itself something that is being created alongside the music. Why did "jazz" emerge as a better term than, say, "hot" or "dirt"? Why do some terms survive while others fade from memory? Method books are but one venue where the language through which we communicate about this music has been built. By 1927, one would think that a potential user of Miff Mole's *Original Breaks and Hot Choruses* or Tommy Dorsey's *100 Hot Breaks for the Trombone* would associate these with "jazz." But can we be certain of this? Such an assumption is made from the perspective of our twenty-first-century vantage point. Lake's *Trix Trombonix* might do the best job of capturing the lexical instability of the style. Throughout this process and in the pages of these texts, "jazz" has meant different things, from a specific musical figure to a particular type of melody to an entire genre. Numerous other books of the time will exhibit similar qualities, and taken together, they form a body of works that have been unfortunately overlooked in jazz scholarship.

Chapter 2

WE DON'T KNOW WHAT WE DON'T KNOW

Historiography and the "Lost Voice" in Jazz

INTRODUCTION: VOICES LOST AND FOUND

It's a semi-annual ritual, that moment when, peering into your mailbox in the departmental office, you see the distinctive shape of a set of papers, folded over, stapled at the edge. It's student evaluation time, and nothing makes the heart of early-career faculty beat faster than the anticipation of reading what their students had to say about their classes, and not without good reason, as such evaluations often play a critical role in decisions concerning tenure, promotion, retention, merit pay, and so forth. For a musicologist, a common point of concern (and critique) is very often related directly to course coverage. The frequency of the "why didn't we talk about so and so" critique that so often stands out on evaluations points to this problem. Decisions about what to include—and by necessity, what to exclude—are often the catalyst for fierce disagreements, and with respect to evaluative processes, can have real, lasting professional consequences. Such moments are but one manifestation of the larger conversations surrounding historiography, canonicity, and representation that pervade musicological discourse, and indeed, historical studies in general. Which stories are told and whose voices are heard are not simply esoteric concepts that preoccupy academics and critics; they are, in a sense, the genetic profile of the genre, putting into words entire histories and cultures. Whether by choice or by chance, such translations, as can be amply demonstrated, are all too often imperfect.

The way many of us today learn about the history of jazz is through texts. There have been, of course, other kinds of sources. Visual media, for example, has been particularly important; documentaries cover nearly every aspect of jazz history, both in a broad sense and with respect to more focused topics.

But the written word has remained at the center of most of our learning about jazz's past, and as jazz has become more firmly established in academic settings, this will likely persist for the foreseeable future. Written texts have been, and continue to be, highly contested spaces featuring different perspectives on who should be included, how the music should be discussed, and whether to emphasize sound or context. Debates such as these have filled the pages of journals and books and resonated through the meeting spaces of conferences and colloquia. At some point, we have to acknowledge a deceptively simple truth: texts are produced by people who make particular decisions about what will be included. How those people, and other people involved in bringing a text into public view, decide on what will fill these pages is the existential *raison d'être* for the modern jazz historian.

There has been a good deal of revisionism in the study of jazz history in recent years, and this work has been a vital corrective to decades of exclusionary practices. The efforts to center and explore the experiences of women in jazz are one significant example. While numerous authors had done crucial work on women in jazz history for a number of years, it has almost certainly been the work of Sherrie Tucker that has brought such issues to the forefront of contemporary jazz scholarship. Tucker's pioneering work on all-woman bands of the 1940s[1] brought a much-needed perspective to jazz historical studies, both in the stories she tells about particular musical communities and in the example her work set for other scholars to follow her lead. In the introduction to *Swing Shift*,[2] Tucker notes the disconnect between "official" jazz narratives and the real, lived experiences of women in these groups. Tucker writes:

> It might sound odd to speak of a dominant swing discourse, yet a quick trip into the library of nostalgic swing narratives reveals a predictable recurrence of hegemonic riffs.... All-woman bands seldom appear in dominant swing discourse, and their existence is therefore denied, first-hand accounts notwithstanding. Or, in texts where one or two of the hundreds of all-woman bands are permitted a type of existence, they are written about in isolation, as if each was a novelty, a gimmick, a dancing dog in a field of real music.[3]

Accounts of such exclusionary practices, as summarized here by Tucker, are a well-known topic in jazz historiography. There is perhaps a debate to be had with respect to the specific mechanics of these practices: was it a result of historians neglecting narratives of women in jazz (the answer is likely "yes") or a function of sexism within the jazz world that prevented women from full participation (the answer is likely also "yes"). But there is, simply put, no debate that such exclusion is real and has had a deep impact on the manner in which jazz's historical narratives have taken shape. In her work, Tucker has been vociferous on this point regarding the exclusion of women in jazz, even to the point that she herself was somewhat surprised to find, during her research, that so many jazz women were "out there," waiting for someone to come asking. Tucker explains:

> When I began my research on all-woman bands of the 1940s nine years ago, I simply hoped that I would find sufficient information to write a short paper on the neglected accomplishments of a few women musicians.... I was astonished when a few inquiries dashed off to newspapers and trade magazines connected me with women musicians eager to give interviews, write letters, fill out questionnaires, and share newspaper clippings, scrapbooks, photos, and other documents, in hopes that their stories would be entered into the historical record. ... Ironically, the reason that I was so surprised when so many women answered my inquiries to such periodicals as *DownBeat*, the *San Francisco Chronicle*, and *Jazz Forum* was not because I hadn't done my homework but because I had... I was an avid reader of swing histories.... I made it a habit to read the major texts on the swing era... which repeatedly presented a story in which all-woman bands either did not exist or were barely worthy of comment. In the worst cases, women's bands were ridiculed.[4]

The women in Tucker's story were, for decades, lost to jazz history; Tucker's project gave them the opportunity to have their voices heard. Yet the kinds of barriers and obstacles scholars like Tucker have been working to overcome over the last few decades have remained stubbornly resilient. By and large, women are still greatly underrepresented in jazz history texts, and while efforts to address this have led to important new perspectives, for the most part, textbooks still largely reflect the "official history" that was critiqued by Scott DeVeaux over three decades ago.[5]

Other constituencies in jazz have claimed (or have had a claim made for them) that they have been overlooked. While jazz studies—and in particular, what has come to be known as "New Jazz Studies"—has been largely receptive to the work of Tucker, Tammy Kernodle, and others engaged in such endeavors, other "revisionist" jazz narratives have been less well received. Richard Sudhalter's 1999 book *Lost Chords: White Musicians and Their Contribution to Jazz, 1915–1945*[6] is one such work. If nothing else, Sudhalter's text is deeply and meticulously researched, but the motivation and ultimate objective of such efforts has been called into question. If Sudhalter were simply to have written a book as a chronicle of the work of these musicians and left it at that, his book might not have generated much of the controversy that it did. Alas, that is not what he did. Sudhalter's underlying contention is that "dominant discourses," to borrow from Tucker, have led to the overlooking or ignoring of White jazz musicians in favor of their Black counterparts. He writes:

> The rage for "multiculturalism" in the arts—as in society at large—has led to the reassessment of, and often elevation of, artistic traditions of non-European and non-white culture. With it has come recognition of many black artists and writers whose achievements long stood hidden from public sight. Applied to jazz history, such thinking has spawned a view of early white efforts as musically insignificant and—particularly in the 1920s and 1930s—vastly oversubsidized. Jazz, says the now accepted canon, is black."[7]

Sudhalter's book came at a particular moment in jazz studies. As Christi Jay Wells notes in an article on Paul Whiteman in racial discourse in 1920s jazz, the field was experiencing "a surge in projects seeking to rewrite a number of 'forgotten' white jazz musicians into the mainstream of jazz historical narrative" that reflected "a tragic consequence of well-intentioned social activism."[8] As Wells writes, Sudhalter's project overlaps with claims of "reverse racism"; such accusations are part of a larger debate over the alleged marginalized status of White jazz musicians that provided the fuel for similar types of racialized rhetoric. I will discuss this idea in more depth in the following chapter.

My intent here is not to offer a detailed overview or critique of the work of Sudhalter and others who are similarly occupied with this topic; the same follows for Sherrie Tucker and others who are attempting to create a more inclusive understanding of jazz. Rather, I wish to demonstrate the various mechanisms through which certain narratives can be "lost" and certain stories "forgotten." To underscore this point, let me relate a story from my own classroom. Several years ago, I was teaching a graduate seminar on the bebop era. At the beginning of the semester, the class had an introductory unit on issues in jazz historiography. In a discussion near the end of this unit, as we were moving into the study of bebop, I posed a challenge to my students in an in-class exercise: make a case that bebop is *not* jazz. Most of the students in the class were either graduate-level jazz studies majors or doctoral-level performance majors with some background in playing jazz; in other words, they had at least a working knowledge of the music. After several minutes of gears turning in their heads, we moved to an open discussion. I was surprised (although I suspect that, in hindsight, I shouldn't have been) that, for the most part, students simply could not do this. They could not conceive of the idea that a genre that is today at the core of jazz's improvisational language (the *lingua franca* of the music, as David Baker put it[9]) was not jazz. After ten minutes or so of going back and forth, I presented my class with the "answer" to this problem: you simply have to accept that jazz ended around 1940, and what came later was a different form of music. After a moment of quiet, one student, a graduate jazz trumpet major, quietly chimed in with, "Prof, you just dropped a bomb on us."

I would like to take most of the credit for such intellectual bomb-dropping, but the reality is that the historical literature of jazz is full of clues that lead to just such a conclusion. The "moldy fig" debates of the 1940s, so effectively chronicled in Bernard Gendron's 1993 essay,[10] John Tynan and Leonard Feather's condemnations of the Coltrane-Dolphy collaborations of the early 1960s as "anti-jazz," Wynton Marsalis's numerous statements on what is or is not jazz . . . all of these—and many more—are examples. These debates have been extensively argued, critiqued, argued and critiqued again, seemingly ad nauseam, and I have no wish to repeat them here. But such assessments, as they have occurred over the years, often have a direct relationship to whose voices are "lost" and whose are heard.

Let us look at one of the major precipitating works of the early 1940s' critical debates: Frederic Ramsey Jr. and Charles Edward Smith's 1939 book *Jazzmen*.[11] Ramsey and Smith's volume is predicated explicitly on the notion that certain forms of jazz (namely the New Orleans traditional style) have been "lost," drowned out by the clatter and noise of commercial swing bands. Ramsey and Smith write in their introduction that many of these artists and their stories have been "forgotten"; *Jazzmen*, presumably, corrects such oversights. A key example is the spotlighting of trumpeter Bunk Johnson, who provides a useful case study of the rescued jazz figure. When Ramsey and Smith first engaged in correspondence with Johnson, they discovered the trumpeter in a less-than-desirable state; this oft-cited story was summarized in a web feature by Hal Smith for Stanford's San Francisco Traditional Jazz Foundation Collection (SFTJC):

> In his prime, Bunk Johnson was considered by most New Orleans musicians to be an excellent trumpeter. He played a wide variety of engagements with brass bands, circus bands, and dance orchestras. Bunk could also play other brass instruments, so [he] did not rely solely upon the trumpet for work. He was also willing to work non-musical

jobs during rare slack periods, including a stint as a policeman in Houston, Texas.

By the mid-1930s, Bunk's teeth were gone, and he was no longer able to play trumpet regularly. He lived in New Iberia, Louisiana, teaching music at area schools, driving a tractor, and hauling rice and sugarcane.[12]

With Ramsey and Smith's assistance, Johnson procured a new trumpet and a set of dentures to replace his missing teeth. Not long after, he began making recordings, which were part and parcel of the larger project that Ramsey and Smith were pursuing. Again, Hal Smith writes, for the SFTJC, about Johnson's legacy:

> The most controversial subject when discussing Bunk Johnson is his ability as a musician. Since his first notes appeared on home-made discs, critics were quick to dismiss the music as being played by an old man, past his prime. When considering Bunk's trumpet playing, the listener should take into consideration the fact that the trumpeter was either 66 or 56 (depending upon which birthdate you choose to believe); had not played trumpet for nearly 10 years and was struggling to play a difficult instrument with false teeth that frequently came loose and/or caused pain.[13]

Indeed, many of Johnson's early 1940s recordings have what might be charitably described as a shaky quality, the sound of a player who was, as Smith notes, out of practice.

If it seems like I am dwelling a bit much on Johnson's story, it's because this particular narrative of falling into and subsequently being rescued from obscurity provides what might be a singularly representative example of the ways that "lost voices" play out in criticism, scholarship, and performance. Jazz had no shortage of great trumpeters in 1942: Roy Eldridge, Rex Stewart, Cootie Williams, and Harry James, not to mention Louis Armstrong himself, plus an emerging player from Philadelphia by way of New York, Dizzy Gillespie. Johnson's sound, to be honest, pales in comparison with such robust players. But some would argue, and perhaps not without some merit, that his playing paled even in comparison to other New Orleans players, both in the 1920s and at the time.

Returning to *Lost Chords*, Sudhalter makes a case that many White musicians have been likewise "lost" and are similarly deserving of greater recognition; others dispute this point. Are the subjects of Sudhalter's book really "lost" in the sense that women in jazz were systematically and intentionally excluded and ignored? Given his comments and those of similarly situated writers like Gene Lees, James Lincoln Collier, and Randall Sandke, Sudhalter would seem to think so. Claims to exclusion can provide a good deal of social capital; the "rescuing" of lost voices by necessity involves bringing them into the spotlight. Among the criticisms of Sudhalter's book were accusations that his selection of artists seemed designed to meet his philosophical ends. As David Sager notes in his review of the book, players like Miff Mole (per the previous chapter) and the Dorsey Brothers are spotlighted, while other players, whose work would not seem to support Sudhalter's thesis, are excluded. Sager also suggests that Sudhalter's "rescuing" of White musicians in early jazz also involves some degree of criticism and marginalization of other (i.e., Black) artists. He points to Sudhalter's characterization of saxophonist Chu Berry's solo style as sounding like it was "being played on ball bearings," while 1920s Black bands were said to be less "aesthetically venturesome" as many of their lesser-known White counterparts.[14] Sager's complaint here is that Sudhalter's critiques work against the creation of a balanced approach to history and are aimed more at comparisons between White and Black artists in which White artists are deemed superior. In closing his review, Sager reiterates this idea, writing, "Where I am disturbed [by the book] lies in Mr. Sudhalter's own use of his ground rules. He comes close to [a] successful exposition of neglected white jazz pioneers and then lapses into the very tendency he was trying to avoid—criticizing non-white musicians. Will the 'noble lie' be righted and will those learning about jazz get a balanced viewpoint?"[15] A "balanced" viewpoint is, of course, a laudable notion. But who defines what this balance entails? Sudhalter apparently believed that his book was just such an exercise, a balancing of the narrative to correct a historical oversight; Sager, for his part, seems to disagree.

Narratives of marginalized communities are often a compelling research subject for historiographers. Musicologists—and indeed, historians in general—have long been interested in stories of figures, works, or artifacts that are "lost" to history; the drive to discover that one figure who languished in obscurity, missing wider recognition due to a particular constellation of circumstances, or that box full of previously unknown outtakes of a John Coltrane recording session or letters from Mozart to his sister. The discovery and rehabilitation of lost figures has a powerful attraction, to say nothing of a certain romantic appeal. Not surprisingly, the restoration of a musician to their "rightful" place in the narrative has driven a fair amount of jazz scholarship over the years. This will likely be the case in perpetuity; the historical record of jazz, or any other genre, comes down to us as the collection of choices made by individuals within particular historical and social contexts and with particular interests and even biases. Those who work with jazz history today, whether as teachers or as authors of historical narrative, must also make such choices, which will themselves continue to echo through the corridors of time.

A Question of Credentials, or Questionable Credentials

In early 2001, the *New York Times* published an account of the late Phil Schaap,[16] a widely known and highly respected figure in the jazz world, having worked in the industry in many different capacities over the years. Schaap's best-known pursuit was almost certainly his hosting of a radio show on Columbia University's WKCR, in particular, *Bird Flight*, which would later lead to production and consulting roles for a number of record labels. Schaap also was an advisor for Jazz at Lincoln Center, where he served as the academic director of "Swing University" and held part-time appointments at a number of schools in the New York area. By any measure, Schaap was considered to be an expert on the topic of jazz history. As Corey Kilgannon writes in his *New York Times* profile, "In a city thick with jazz aficionados, Mr. Schaap is also widely conceded to be its most knowledgeable jazz historian."[17]

It came as something of a shock to many that in 2001 Columbia University, Schaap's home base for many years, declined to hire him for a full-time faculty position teaching jazz history. The *Times* story notes that "many supporters felt that Schaap was a logical choice for such a position. No less than Max Roach, speaking to the *Times* for the article, opined that 'There isn't anyone in the country who knows more about this music.'"[18] Describing him as a "bottomless pit of knowledge," the *Times* piece takes a mostly supportive tone with respect to Schaap, and the article seems, at times, somewhat hagiographic. Nevertheless, the article points to a curious disjuncture between "the academy" and one who might be deemed, without a terminal degree or record of peer-reviewed scholarly publications, an outsider to that community.

L'affaire Schaap underscores the persistence of a gulf between degreed academics, be they musicologists, theorists, historians, or others who have advanced degrees, and others who are "academia adjacent." I realize this is an imperfect term, but to be honest, I have not been able to come up with a better one. In this category, I include many different kinds of people who are involved with jazz and its history but do not enjoy official institutional status. Sometimes such individuals might work as adjunct faculty, teaching an occasional course or two. On the one hand, Schaap was not a "critic" per se, but within the context of an environment in which jazz scholarship is increasingly the province of specialized academic training and credentials, neither was he a professional scholar; he remained a figure who stood somewhat apart from the scholarly jazz world. But to be clear, figures like Schaap are not "amateurs" or "dilettantes"; they are very knowledgeable about the music, in some cases (such as with Schaap), exceedingly knowledgeable. From a strictly intellectual, knowledge-based standpoint, Phil Schaap would seem to have been eminently qualified to teach a jazz history course at any institution one might imagine. But because he did not possess advanced degrees, a full-time, tenure-stream faculty position in a jazz studies or musicology program was likely not in the cards.

The question of which individuals are deemed qualified to engage in the creation and maintenance of jazz's intellectual discourse is certainly not new. Indeed, claims to authority in jazz scholarship have deep roots; Lewis Porter implicitly points to the nature of such a divide in his 1988 essay "Some Problems in Jazz Research." The field of jazz studies, by the late 1980s, had been largely dominated by "individuals who are neither musicians nor academics"[19] and thus presented what Porter felt were a particular set of problems for the field going forward. Porter's essay appeared at an especially important moment for jazz scholarship, situated between the advent of "new musicology," characterized by a more inclusive, culturally informed approach to music history, and the interdisciplinary "New Jazz Studies" project that, like Porter (though he himself has never been fully associated with that movement) sought to wrest control of the discourse of jazz from an older generation of critics. In the noisy, cacophonous space that is the community of jazz scholarship and research, whose voices rise above the din, and whose voices are lost?

When Porter wrote his essay in 1988, jazz scholarship was just beginning to make serious inroads into American academia (due in no small part to his own pioneering work). Central to his argument is the notion that the emerging generation of jazz scholars needed to develop and apply rigorous professional standards as well as a deep commitment to the idea that jazz is, first and foremost, a cultural product of Black communities. In some ways, what Porter described in his essay was a blueprint for like-minded academics who would follow in the coming years. It was also not without some precedent; a half-century earlier, another jazz writer was engaging with some similar ideas, calling for heightened standards through which jazz might be better understood and discussed.

The remainder of this chapter grapples with these kinds of historiographic questions, focusing on two main case studies. In the first, I examine the work of Paul Eduard Miller, whom I obliquely referenced in the previous paragraph. Miller was a prolific writer on jazz in the 1930s, a key figure in the community of jazz critics of the time. Yet today, his work is generally overlooked, and in the course of this discussion, I hope to shine a light on the processes by which such historiographic trajectories are determined. In the second case study, I turn my attention to the place of the "ordinary" musician in jazz history. Drawing on the work of Malcolm Gladwell, I position the figures in the jazz canon as outliers, individuals of extraordinary ability and skill whose work reflects a departure from the vast majority of their peers.[20] And yet, despite their status as, by definition, exceptional figures, their work has formed the core of our understanding of jazz history. In examining these kinds of processes, I consider whether a greater focus on the "ordinary" jazz musician might provide us with a richer understanding of jazz's historical practice.

"THE BEST JAZZ": PAUL EDUARD MILLER AND "VOICE" IN JAZZ HISTORIOGRAPHY[21]

Jazz: Not for Morons Only

Paul Eduard Miller was a frequent contributor to *DownBeat* and other music-based publications in the 1930s and 1940s. Despite this, Miller remains a largely unknown, or at least underrepresented, figure in early mid-twentieth-century jazz writing. He is briefly mentioned in John Gennari's comprehensive work on jazz criticism, *Blowing Hot and Cool*, where he is noted (along with John Hammond and Marshall Stearns) as a "champion of black swing."[22] An obituary appearing in the *Washington Post* in 1972 notes that Miller "became famous as a jazz critic in the 1930s,"[23] though such a statement might seem a bit hyperbolic in retrospect. This brief account of Miller's life fails to note his extensive writing for *DownBeat*, though it does make mention of his editorship of the magazine's *Yearbook of Swing* in 1939. For the most part, the obituary spotlights his post-*DownBeat* work, mainly for *Esquire*, citing his leadership of that periodical's "music department" until 1947.

The most thorough assessment of Miller's work came in the doctoral dissertation on early jazz criticism by Ron Welburn, who writes that Miller's work was explicitly positioned as a corrective to what he often saw as shoddy scholarship. In describing Miller's attitudes toward jazz criticism, Welburn writes:

> Miller, whose writing always displayed a historical perspective, felt that throughout the twenty-year history of jazz its critics had either

maligned it or as the recent crop was prone to do, added confusion, diatribe, and superficiality behind the veneer of good intentions. The failure of these enthusiasts lay in their "inability or refusal," Miller said, to recognize time-honored standards for judging music, and their "indifference to the establishment of a legitimate criterion" for sorting the best from the worst.[24]

Miller's own jazz writing, according to Welburn, was "erudite" and "soberly reasoned . . . asking key questions on the beginnings and developments of jazz."[25] It should not be difficult to see parallels between such sentiments and those expressed by Lewis Porter in his 1988 essay on jazz research and the need to develop a more professionalized approach to scholarship.

Ironically, one of the most fitting descriptions of Miller's writing comes not from a work devoted to jazz but from a book on legendary boxer Sugar Ray Robinson by Wil Haygood. In drawing parallels between Robinson's career and jazz musicians, Haygood writes that "Miller's writing swept across the decades of jazz, remembering how hard a journey it had always been to keep the music alive, how difficult the late twenties and thirties had been."[26] I am drawn to Haygood's description of Miller's jazz writing as having "swept across the decades of jazz," particularly given the fact that the bulk of his writing was done in the 1930s and 1940s. Poetics and (possible) hyperbole aside, this is a fairly accurate description of his approach to the music. More important, however, was Miller's insistence that jazz was changing and that jazz criticism needed to change with it. As the music (at least in some quarters) was becoming more sophisticated and complex, jazz critics could not be content with approaching the music as simple entertainment. This was a particularly pressing issue as jazz, per Miller, was moving toward a higher, more intellectually informed style; it was no longer, as he rather sarcastically put it in a *DownBeat* piece in early 1939, "fit only for morons."[27]

There are two main thrusts within Miller's critical philosophy as articulated in his writings during this period. First, as alluded to previously by Gennari, jazz is, fundamentally, Black music. Second, the musical nature of jazz was becoming increasingly complex and intricate, which required a more sophisticated critical understanding so that listeners would be able to discern "good jazz" from "bad jazz." In fact, these two perspectives frequently overlapped in Miller's writing. An illustrative example of this can be seen in his April 1937 column in *DownBeat* titled, in the awkwardly racialized parlance of the time, "Roots of Hot White Jazz are Negroid." Miller begins his essay with an observation on the relative knowledgeability of swing audiences:

The present interest in swing music, unfortunately, is a microscopic one. By that I mean that Rhythm Club members and other such neophytes are prone to regard swing music solely in terms of what their limited judgments conceive it to be. Not so for the initiate: he looks upon swing music as a fad, and prefers to take a telescopic, long-range view of hot jazz, which embraces not only swing music, but also more than a quarter century of constant improvement upon the ragtime of Buddy Bolden.[28]

Miller, in his characteristically undiplomatic language, chastises young swing fans for not appreciating where jazz *really* came from; more seasoned fans (like himself, presumably) are more likely to take a longer view and are thus more likely to see swing as being intimately connected to earlier Black traditions.

In 1940, Miller left *DownBeat*[29] (along with several other writers) to assume the editorship of another periodical, *Music and Rhythm*, a magazine that covered not only jazz but popular music broadly; according to Ron Welburn, this exodus was the result of "some editorial dissension,"[30] but no further details are provided. This seems reflective of the shift in American popular entertainment during this period; Miller's 1943 edition of his annual *Yearbook* (now under the auspices of *Esquire*) was titled *Miller's Yearbook of Popular Music*. No longer was jazz or swing at the center of the conversation, at least not outwardly. Nevertheless, jazz remained an important part of Miller's work. In the preface to the 1943 *Yearbook*, he engages in what might be seen as a bit of early jazz historiography, citing works by Abbe Niles (1928), Charles Edward Smith (1930), Robert Goffin (1932), and Roger Pryor Dodge (1934) as important examples of "the literature on hot music."[31] Miller continues tracing the growth of what he terms "jazz history" through the works of Winthrop Sargeant, Ramsey and Smith's *Jazzmen*, and Wilder Hobson's *American Jazz Music* as well as Benny Goodman's autobiographical *The Kingdom of Swing*; Miller also includes his own 1939 *Yearbook* in this discussion.

More importantly, however, Miller seeks a work that is, for lack of a better term, more scholarly. Continuing in the preface to the 1943 *Yearbook*, Miller laments the current state of jazz writing:

Throughout the bulk of this literature persisted a tendency to romanticize, to poeticize, to argue about the merits of one soloist as against another. Particularly from European sources, where the writers based their judgments on hearsay and depended on phonograph records for their idea of what American jazz sounded like, the resulting literature was usually without the *true perspective* . . . . I have come to realize more and more that a book of *factual information*—of which there existed none—was more sorely needed than another critical survey, of which there had been an abundance.[32]

I have highlighted two passages from the above extract that I feel are worthy of further discussion. First, when Miller writes of existing literature lacking a "true perspective" on jazz, one senses that this is a shot across the bow at critics who he feels are allowing personal judgments to interfere with what he views as a more objective, scholarly approach. Second, his claim to presenting "factual information" again positions him in opposition to other writers whose work lacks such clear, objective approaches. Thus, Miller explicitly positions his approach as one which might be seen as being more historical than critical, more detached than personal. This is certainly, on the surface, a laudable goal. The question that confronts us, then, is this: to what degree did Miller's own work reflect these ideals? How did his "voice" convey such principles, and perhaps more importantly, was it heard?

The Historiographic Road Not Taken: Paul Eduard Miller's Jazz History Texts

In addition to his critical writings for *DownBeat*, Miller aspired to complete a larger-scale work, a book-length manuscript that would be, in essence, a broad study of the history and nature of jazz. Miller's writings are archived at Columbia College Chicago as part of the collections of the Center for Black Music Research, and among the various materials included in this collection are typescripts of two unpublished book manuscripts.[33] The documentation for the collection describes Miller's efforts thusly: "[T]here are versions of Miller's attempts to write a canon-defining book on jazz: 'Testimonial to Jazz,' (1936) and a later undated typescript 'The Best Jazz' in which Miller discusses and rates musicians and recordings."[34] As someone interested in issues of canon and historiography, I am most interested in the *Testimonial* manuscript, as this represents Miller's most pointed attempt to construct a cohesive historical account of jazz's development. Nevertheless, Miller's *The Best Jazz* is also instructive in that it lays out, in great detail, his criteria for assessment and evaluation. It should be noted that both manuscripts are incomplete in terms of both Miller's work itself and with respect to the holdings in the CBMR collection.

I would now like to turn to an overview of Miller's work, beginning with the 1936 *Testimonial* manuscript, which provides some clues as to what the field of "jazz history" might look like in 1936. For the most part, Miller's narrative emphasizes jazz's early history, and this would, of course, make sense, as recorded jazz was only about twenty years old. Miller was writing at the cusp of the Swing Era; Benny Goodman had only been the "King of Swing" for about a year, the recordings of Count Basie's Old Testament band were just being made, and Duke Ellington's landmark Blanton-Webster Band was still a few years away. While swing was popular, it had not yet peaked, commercially or musically. The story was still being written, and as one might expect, swing does not merit extensive coverage in Miller's manuscript.

In fact, Miller's first departure from the New Orleans/Chicago-centered narrative comes with his discussion of George Gershwin's *Rhapsody in Blue*. Miller openly questions the value of such a piece in jazz discourse, comparing it to what he considered to be more valuable efforts by African American artists:

> In this welter of indiscrimination, what is to be singled out as the representative music? Broadly speaking, the best jazz is Negro jazz. Its best compositions and finest renditions are mainly the work of the Aframerican. It is the music of Ellington, Morton, Oliver, Henderson, ~~Armstrong~~, Handy, Garland, and ~~Hopkins~~ ["Redman" is written above Hopkins]. Long before the Whiteman uplift movement, Negro jazz was making musical history.[35]

I would point to several things here. First, I am fascinated by the strikethroughs of Armstrong and presumably Harlem pianist and bandleader Claude Hopkins. While one could certainly argue that Don Redman might be a better representative of the music than Hopkins, the strikethrough of Armstrong, probably the best-known jazz musician in the world at the time, is curious, to say the least. On the following page, Miller makes what can only be regarded as an anti-modernist statement:

> Modernity in music, as in painting, admits of many characteristics and much bathos[36] .... It is a farcical courtroom in which nothing is justly tried upon its merits. It is a Broadway stage on which the cast of characters ranges from an Irish lout of an apartment house manager to a gilded countess. Above all, it is the neurosis out of which has grown the shallow sophistication of the multitude.[37]

Such attitudes would seem to place Miller squarely within the context of the so-called "moldy figs" of jazz criticism (as discussed in Gendron's article).

But Miller was largely absent from such debates, and indeed, what counts as modernism in his work is not exactly clear. And given Miller's extensive (and effusive) discussion of the music of Duke Ellington, whose band Miller refers to as "the most extraordinary of all jazz bands" and whose work was certainly very "modern" in comparison to earlier artists (the same might be said for Henderson and Redman), one senses that relative musical progressiveness is not the critical factor. Rather, Miller seems to conflate "modern" with "White," and, to a lesser extent, with commercialism. There is, in fact, very little discussion of swing as a musical style; rather, Miller critiques the use of the term as being imprecise, and it is here that his emphasis on the establishment of a set of studied evaluative criteria comes into play.

If there is one complaint that Miller makes regarding many of his pro-swing peers in jazz's critical communities, it is that they are largely amateurs, in essence "superfans," who were more concerned with the meaning of jazz for its audiences than in assessing the actual music. Miller praises European critics for their studious attention to recorded jazz; American critics, on the other hand, seemed to be more concerned with the "frenzied publicizing of opinions."[38] A more serious, professional class of critic was needed in order to properly assess and interpret jazz for the masses, and Miller seemed to be making a case that he might be just such a figure. In his discussion of the various manifestations of jazz at the end of the first chapter of *Testimonial*, we see such perspectives beginning to come into play. In this discussion, Miller identifies both the "forms" and "felonies" of jazz. The former refers to what Miller feels are more authentic manifestations of the style (including much of the "hot jazz" of the time), while the latter includes theater music, popular song, symphonic jazz, and other efforts that have a connection to jazz but whose relationships could be considered as somewhat suspect.

What Miller does not do, and this is a point that I wish to emphatically stress, is claim that anything is *not jazz*. Be it popular versions of the music, *Rhapsody in Blue*, the Original Dixieland Jass Band, or Duke Ellington, all of these can be considered under the rubric of jazz. Thus, Miller's approach could be considered a predecessor to what John Gennari would refer to as the "liberal consensus" view of jazz, epitomized in the 1950s by writers such as Marshall Stearns (a contemporary of Miller at *DownBeat*), in which jazz exists as a broad, stylistically inclusive category.[39] What delineates one type of jazz from another in Miller's conception of the genre is, rather, based mainly on a qualitative judgment. It is, in short, the difference between "good" and "bad" jazz. Such attitudes might seem at odds with a scholarly approach, but this leads us directly to Miller's emphasis on the development of clear strategies of assessment. The core problem facing jazz, Miller argues, is that listeners (and likely critics themselves) simply do not possess the skill to tell the "good" from the "bad." As a result, they were just as likely to see Rudy Vallee as a significant jazz artist as they might Duke Ellington.

Over the course of the next several years, Miller's efforts to advance a more specific system for evaluating jazz began to take shape. Despite the fact that *Testimonial* was not published, we can see his belief that jazz scholarship needed a precise, intellectual approach articulated in his writing for other publications throughout the late 1930s. In September 1936, for example, Miller writes, in a *DownBeat* column with the provocative title "Blind Critics Add Confusion to Jazz," that current jazz criticism was lacking, echoing his arguments from *Testimonial*. He writes:

> [Critics'] very enthusiasm has led them into a maze of generalities and contradictions, with the result that the interested public has no more satisfactory a conception of jazz now than it had back in the days when sweet jazz reigned supreme. This failure of the recent self-named critics-of-jazz lies in their inability or refusal to recognize the standards which have always been the basis for judging music generally, and in their indifference to the establishment of a legitimate criterion for sorting the superior from the ignoble in the realm of jazz music.[40]

This essay, published at nearly the same time as the dating of the *Testimonial* manuscript, is in some ways, a summary of the longer text. I would suggest that it may have been an effort to get his views into the public discourse in light of the book not being published. If this is the case, that this *DownBeat* article was a "summary" of his ideas in *Testimonial*, then the end of the piece points to Miller's second manuscript, *The Best Jazz*, to which I shall return later.

Continuing in his 1936 *DownBeat* essay, Miller suggests that jazz can be classified into three main categories: symphonic jazz, sweet jazz, and hot jazz, a scheme which he acknowledges is "nothing new." Symphonic jazz, as we might expect, features works such as those by Gershwin, Grofé, and their peers. Sweet jazz is described as "popular music in 4/4 tempo" and a "crass music," citing Guy Lombardo as one example. Hot jazz, meanwhile, is also in 4/4 time but is "genuine music as well." He elaborates:

> [T]he point in which [hot jazz] differs from sweet jazz is not in its form but in its musical quality. Just as Beethoven's *Eroica* is superior to Tschaikowsky's [sic] *Pathétique*, so in jazz Ellington's "Saddest Tale"

is the peer of "Goody Goody" and "Bugle Call Rag." And while "Bugle Call Rag" may be accurately classed as hot jazz, it has neither the emotional depth nor the intelligent treatment found in "Saddest Tale." It may be said, then, that there are degrees of quality even within the confines of hot jazz.[41]

It is, once again, an explicit emphasis on quality that is the point here, not necessarily stylistic distinction (although these are not completely absent). The newly emerging swing style complicates such a narrative, but Miller uses such ambiguity to his advantage, as a way to illustrate his call for more precise and rigorous standards:

> Hence an orchestral interpretation of "The Dixieland Band" (an inferior selection) by Benny Goodman's orchestra may be termed swing music, while Duke Ellington's version of "Mississippi Moan" (an example of really good jazz) is also swing music. The former is simply a cheap melody with monotonous and uninteresting variations; the latter meets the demands of superior music.[42]

Take note of the distinction between Goodman, whose music "may be" swing, and Ellington, who is not only jazz but *also* swing, with no "may be" qualification. Miller provides some general rationale for this assessment, but the most obvious difference between the Goodman and Ellington groups was that one was White while the other was comprised of musicians of color. And while such a distinction is not made explicitly in this piece, it certainly echoes Miller's emphasis on the primacy of Black authorship of jazz forms expressed in *Testimonial to Jazz*. It is no accident, I would suggest, that Miller chose these two groups for such a comparison.

Miller's emphasis on the development of critical standards and methods for jazz is continued in his subsequent writings; in order to be considered a great art, jazz required educated, knowledgeable critics to interpret it for an audience that no longer could be considered simply as "morons." In this context, I would like to briefly consider Miller's second attempt at a jazz textbook. It is not clear when Miller stopped working on *The Best Jazz*, but given the dating of some of the recordings included, it must have been completed (as far as it was completed) in the early 1960s at the earliest. That said, I would speculate that much of the writing of *The Best Jazz* was completed earlier; in fact, many of Miller's arguments track closely with those of his late 1930s *DownBeat* columns, particularly those that sought to establish clear criteria for critical evaluation. The document in the CBMR collection is, it would seem, the result of a process of writing over as long as twenty years, though I acknowledge that this is speculation.

In a draft preface to *The Best Jazz*, Miller makes his project of creating a highbrow discourse for jazz explicit, writing that he has "compiled a Rated Recordings list which, though stringently selective, ranges in time over four decades." Here again we see Miller's dual purpose made manifest. His aim was to create not only a "stringently selective" set of criteria for assessing the music but also a broad approach to the music that treats it as a unified whole rather than a series of disconnected genres and traditions. In conceptualizing jazz's historical narrative, Miller is an unabashed evolutionist, writing that "it is well to remember that the 'new' in jazz, or in any art form, is not a sharp, neurotically amnesiac break with the past; rather, the art moves forward persistently with the traditions of the past—in a natural way, like everything else in the universe."[43] I would wager that many contemporary jazz scholars would, of course, take exception to such a characterization, instead favoring an approach to jazz's history that eschews a "natural" approach in favor of a narrative that is more disjointed and chaotic. That said, Miller's emphasis on the smooth, natural development of the music resonates with the perspectives of many jazz historians of the time, and this would become a core tenet of jazz historiography.

The establishment of clear assessment standards and well-defined narratives would seem to have the benefit of placing jazz on a level similar to that of the classical tradition, as Miller explicitly notes that "it becomes startlingly evident how the emotional range of jazz compares most favorably with that of classical music—a point which classical music lovers have gone out of their way to deny."[44] Such overtly classicist connections would be echoed by other writers of the time, perhaps most notably Marshall Stearns and Gunther Schuller. In this context, Miller's second text appears to be in dialogue with his first. In *Testimonial*, Miller argues that jazz need not be so sharply delineated into particular styles but rather should be assessed by what is "good" (or not). In *The Best Jazz*, Miller advances a critical framework for doing just that. The combination of these two texts, had they appeared as a single work in, say, the 1940s, might have provided a clear and comprehensive approach to the study of jazz in a historical context. But this is moot, as the publication of these texts never happened. While Miller's approach to the creation of a systematic way of evaluating jazz may be admirable, he ultimately couldn't make it work, at least in terms of producing a publishable text. Like his one-time colleague Marshall Stearns, Miller was, for a time in the 1930s, poised to take his place as one of jazz's leading critical and scholarly voices. Why then, given his position at *DownBeat* and his reputation among jazz writers as well as his well-documented desire to create a more professional class of jazz writers, didn't this happen? What Miller perhaps couldn't do, and what Marshall Stearns seems to have been more successful at, was to cultivate a sense of detachment, at least in terms of its surface-level discourse. With Stearns, there is little in the way of an overtly expressed agenda. That is not to say that Stearns did not have deeply held opinions on the nature of jazz and its origins, and indeed, those perspectives often tracked with Miller's own. Rather, Stearns was able to construct his argument in such a way that he appeared to be a more neutral voice (it is worth noting that Stearns also held a PhD from Yale, albeit in medieval literature). Miller did not position himself in such a way (nor did he have similar scholarly credentials), and I would suggest that this might go a long way toward explaining why his work has largely been overlooked.

Commenting on Miller's writings, Paul Lopes writes, in his 2002 book *The Rise of a Jazz Art World*, that Miller's work represented an effort to bring jazz to a "highbrow" audience.[45] Lopes's commentary on Miller is instructive if we consider Miller's efforts as a parallel to those described in Lawrence Levine's *Highbrow/Lowbrow*,[46] in which elite artistic culture in America is positioned as a product of specific efforts and initiatives in the late nineteenth century. In such a scenario, we might consider Miller as occupying a role similar to that of John Sullivan Dwight, the nineteenth-century Bostonian who would become, arguably, America's first truly influential music critic. In an editorial published in the January 1, 1881, issue of *Dwight's Journal of Music*, he notes the publication's "high tone" in its treatment of the contemporary music scene.[47] Miller's work seems to strive for a similar standard. Indeed, in one passage from the *Testimonial* manuscript that discusses Paul Whiteman, Miller notes that the bandleader's statements on jazz often "make an apology for the 'lowbrow' jazz of the second decade of the century."[48] Still, Miller's approach is not one that simply attempts to create an elite, privileged cultural space for jazz. Miller's approach to jazz as can be observed in the title of his 1939 *DownBeat* essay reflects a curious dialectic between highbrow and lowbrow approaches to the music. It is not that jazz is not appropriate for morons, but not *only* for morons, who it seems can still enjoy jazz as they did before. While Miller is attempting to establish jazz's highbrow bona fides, its lowbrow identity does not disappear. And indeed, such a dialectic remains at the core of much jazz discourse, then and now.

Issues such as these are essential to understanding the ebbs and flows of jazz writing over the decades. It is a relatively simple exercise to look back at Miller's work eight decades later and make a determination that his work was perhaps focused too heavily on criticism and the determination of what was "good." Such an approach, while grounded in a desire to make jazz criticism less "partisan,"[49] might have limited his works' usefulness as a broad account of the music's development. And thus, it would be Marshall Stearns rather than Miller who would rise to assume this mantle, that of the pioneering figure of postwar scholarship in jazz history. For his part, Miller continued writing in jazz and popular music and remained active in Chicago as a jazz radio host and presenter. We are left with what might have been had he been able to complete and publish these manuscripts. How might we understand jazz differently if he had assumed a more prominent role in postwar jazz discourses? What would his voice in this conversation have been? We can only guess the answers to such questions. But his work does, at any rate, provide an interesting look at a possible alternative historiography.

LOUIS ARMSTRONG AND CHARLES JOHNSON: THE GENIUS AND THE JOURNEYMAN[50]

Most serious jazz fans, musicians, and writers are familiar with a short film made by Louis Armstrong in late 1933. Shot on a soundstage while touring Scandinavia,[51] Armstrong's "Hot Harlem Band" recorded three selections, "Dinah," "I Cover the Waterfront," and "Tiger Rag." The filmed performance of the first of these, in particular, has achieved legendary status in jazz circles. Ben Ratliff notes, writing in the *New York Times*, that the film represents "a short and efficient answer for why [Armstrong] was and is important."[52] Discussing his PBS documentary on jazz[53] with Wynton Marsalis and Charlie Rose, Ken Burns describes the Armstrong film, telling Rose, "I remember Geoffrey [Ward] showed this to me . . . the hair on the back of my neck stood up . . . Louis Armstrong changed my life, not just as a filmmaker, but as a person . . . . This is a man on the level of the Wright Brothers, Freud, Einstein, Picasso, Stravinsky. He is rearranging the molecules of jazz and American music in that moment."[54] This film has long been used to demonstrate the greatness of Louis Armstrong; an article by Mike Springer on the Open Culture website captures the general consensus about Armstrong and the film's role in establishing his singular "genius." He writes that "Armstrong is brilliant in the film. His exuberant showmanship and virtuosity are striking, and his unmistakable genius for phrasing—the way his trumpet and voice sound like two sides of the same distinctive instrument—remind us of why many people still consider Armstrong the greatest jazz musician of all time."[55]

I wish to take a slightly different approach to this film. At the end of Armstrong's vocal turn on "Dinah," another trumpet player rises to begin a solo. His playing is competent, solid, if not spectacular. Midway through his chorus, the film abruptly cuts to a shot of the "audience"[56] as Armstrong scoots to the side of the stage. When the band is seen again, we are suddenly listening to a saxophone soloist. In discussions with colleagues and students, this trumpeter has often been described as "that other trumpet player in the Louis Armstrong film," a role that he seems to have a hard time escaping. But a question arises from the juxtaposition of these two men, one a major star at the height of his popularity and creative activity, the other a relatively anonymous sideman for whom this performance might represent his lone appearance in the jazz canon. Which of these men is a better representation of the community of jazz musicians in the 1930s—the star or the sideman? It might suffice to acknowledge that Armstrong was simply better than his second trumpeter, but such simple assessments of "better" or "worse" do not satisfy the requirements of the larger project of canon-building that has been at the heart of so much jazz writing for many decades.

(Re)Considering Genius in Jazz Historiography

Jazz seems to have a lot of geniuses. From Armstrong to Ellington to Parker to Coltrane, jazz has had, if one is to believe critics, scholars, and fans of the music (to say nothing of musicians themselves), a plethora of individuals who can be described in such terms. Even a cursory glance at the vast literature of jazz reveals this fascination with genius. Take, for example, Stanley Crouch's volume of collected writings, *Considering Genius*. What is perhaps most surprising about Crouch's work, given the book's title, is how little he talks about the nature of genius itself.[57] There is no case to be made that particular artists are geniuses—they simply *are*. Consider, for instance, the following passage, in which Crouch argues that "[n]either Miles Davis nor Max Roach, *each man a genius*, could have imagined just how clearly the events of [Davis's first Carnegie Hall concert] summed up much of the music and the social texture that had come into being since they both performed with Charlie Parker on 52nd Street fifteen years earlier."[58] Later, in discussing Charlie Parker's death at the home of the "Jazz Baroness," Pannonica de Koenigswarter, Crouch writes, "A statistic of his own excesses, the *innovative genius* had been nursed round the clock not by a Jewish princess but by a Jewish baroness."[59]

All this is not intended to single out Stanley Crouch. But his use of the term "genius," without critical comment or explanation or any need to justify its usage, provides a fair illustration of the ways it is often employed.[60] The designation of an artist as a genius is a common feature, in fact, in many book or essay titles. Multiple works on Louis Armstrong demonstrate this, such as James Lincoln Collier's *Louis Armstrong: An American Genius* and Gary Giddins's *Satchmo: The Genius of Louis Armstrong*.[61] A number of books seek to explore the "life and genius" of other artists. Leslie Gourse approaches Thelonious Monk in such a way in the book *Straight No Chaser: The Life and Genius of Thelonious Monk*. James Lester's book on Art Tatum, *Too Marvelous for Words: The Life and Genius of Art Tatum*, and John Edward Hasse's *Beyond Category: The Life and Genius of Duke Ellington* provide further examples.

This is not to say that there have not been some attempts to explore the idea of genius in jazz more critically. Bob Yurochko articulates (perhaps inadvertently) a problem with the jazz genius discussion:

> If the creative act can be relegated to one word, it would be genius. Throughout the history of jazz a handful of geniuses came forth and were responsible for the evolution of the art form .... Louis Armstrong, Duke Ellington, Charlie Parker, and Miles Davis were geniuses because of their original contributions to jazz .... There are many stars and super-stars in jazz, but only a few can be considered geniuses of the creative process.[62]

In juxtaposing so few geniuses with so much evolutionary process, Yurochko reiterates the idea that jazz has been driven by a few individuals whose work, resulting from genius, has influenced the entire course of the music.

Gabriel Solis has provided an extremely thoughtful and important meditation on the nature of jazz genius and its impact on historiography and teaching, noting that genius reflects "a feeling that is widely held by people in the jazz scene ... that there are greater and lesser musicians in the music's history,"[63] and that this has been a primary force in shaping our understanding of the music. Solis's essay reflects a deep historiographic discomfort (which, as a teacher of jazz history, I share) about the canon, while at the same time recognizing that it is a useful tool for conceptualizing the music's history. Solis does not attempt to explicitly define the nature of genius or talent in his essay, nor is that his intent. What is important here is that the idea of genius, of "great" musicians, is not only a function of jazz historiography and criticism but one that often arises from artists themselves, based on assumptions about performance ability: some artists are simply seen as being better.

This emphasis on the unquestioned greatness of certain musicians, often attributed to an inherently indefinable sense of genius, presents enormous problems for jazz historiography. These musicians are, because of their perceived genius, by definition, exceptional figures in the jazz world. At the same time, these figures form the core of the jazz canon, the basic narrative of the music's history. The exceptional, it seems, has become the standard; the iconoclast has been retrofitted as the icon. With the emergence of the "New Jazz Studies" in the last two decades, such perspectives have increasingly been called into question, but not without spirited debate and, in some cases, vitriol. Take, for instance, a spirited exchange between Krin Gabbard and Lawrence Gushee in the journal *American Music* between 1989 and 1990. In reviewing James Lincoln Collier's *The Reception of Jazz in America*, Gabbard seems to defend the author from criticism by other jazz writers. As Gabbard writes:

> Collier is especially vulnerable to those jazz writers who still regard their function as primarily hieratic . . . [Collier's biography of Ellington][64] has been repeatedly and gratuitously attacked by jazz critics in the popular press.[65] There is no question that this reflects more on the current state of jazz writing than it does on Collier. In spite of the attacks, Collier continues to work among the handful of scholars who are more interested in writing an accurate socio-cultural history of jazz than in preserving the comfortable pieties that have long characterized the work of many jazz writers.[66]

Implicit within Gabbard's defense of Collier is a critique of hero worship that he sees in much jazz writing. In closing his reply to Gushee's letter criticizing the review, Gabbard writes, "If the study of jazz is to come of age and thrive as a discipline, criticism of canonical masters must be tolerated, or at the very least, received without rancor."[67] This closing statement cuts to the core of issues of canonicity, genius, and the supposed heroic nature of many jazz artists.[68] The invocation of genius in jazz discourses often serves as a way to stop critical arguments in their tracks; how, after all, can one question genius? Our collective idolization of jazz geniuses as heroes limits our ability to look beyond common assumptions about the music, its history, and the pervasive influence of canonical discourses.

Jazz and the Outlier

A more useful framework, one that situates these individuals within the context of their own communities and social groups, can be drawn from Malcolm Gladwell's 2008 book *Outliers: The Story of Success*. Gladwell writes that outliers[69] are individuals who do things that are out of the ordinary and who reflect the experiences of "geniuses, business tycoons, rock stars, and software programmers."[70] What distinguishes these individuals from others in their communities depends on a number of things, of which talent is only one. The "great men" (and women) in Gladwell's story are those whose success is the result of a constellation of factors, many of which are deeply dependent on the contexts of a person's community and life. In other words, outliers are not simply "geniuses," at least in the conventional understanding of the term, but products of specific environments and circumstances whose talents were developed and focused through intense study and practice, and in some instances, luck or privilege.

We can see some elements of Gladwell's argument in the narratives of major jazz figures. Of particular interest is his emphasis, and some might say overemphasis, on the "10,000-hour rule," that in order to achieve greatness or to develop one's talent to its full potential, one must put in 10,000 hours of practice or work, citing as an example the Beatles' apprenticeship in Hamburg in the early 1960s, where the band played a relentless schedule of club dates, amassing the theoretical 10,000 hours in the process. All jazz performers (presumably) practice to some extent, and, indeed, practicing seems to be a fundamentally important activity for musicians at nearly all levels. Accounts of the obsessive practice habits of jazz musicians, like those of innate genius, are a common trope in jazz writing; occasionally, such stories become part of the mythology of certain artists. Consider the following account from Gene Ramey of Charlie Parker's time at a resort in the Ozark Mountains in the summer of 1937:

> We would sit in the park practicing all night long. In the summer of 1937, Bird underwent a radical change musically . . . he got a job with a little band led by a singer, Georgie Lee. They played at country resorts in the mountains. Charlie took with him all the Count Basie records with Lester Young solos on them and learned Lester cold, note for note. When he came home, he was the most popular musician in K.C.[71]

Arguably the best known of these narratives of intense practice is that of John Coltrane, whose rigorous practice routines have become the stuff of jazz lore. As Lewis Porter notes, Coltrane showed a remarkable affinity for practicing even in the early stages of his career:

> There is absolute agreement that Coltrane practiced maniacally. Granoff[72] says he would arrive at the school early and wait for it to open, then stay until evening. Several people say that he even liked to practice long into the night, just the fingerings, without blowing

air into the instrument, so as not to wake anyone . . . there is often a suggestion that Coltrane's practicing was obsessive."[73]

It is not difficult to see the resonance between these stories and those outliers described by Gladwell. Like the Beatles, who played a constant schedule of gigs during their time in Hamburg, Parker, Coltrane, and other "virtuosic" jazz artists paid the requisite amount of "dues" in the form of practice and performance.

The 10,000-hour rule, which Gladwell adapted from a 1993 research study authored by K. Anders Ericsson, Ralf Krampe, and Clemens Tesch-Römer, has been the topic of continued controversy. Ericsson et al. examined the practice habits of advanced-level violinists at a conservatory in Berlin, concluding that professional-level performance generally required students to put in a certain amount of what they termed "deliberate practice."[74] While the study did not attract much notice at the time of its publication (outside of academic and research contexts), Gladwell's use of this theory thrust it into the public discourse. Criticism of Gladwell and the original authors has sometimes been fierce in both academic and general interest publications. A number of research articles have found fault with the original study; one such piece appearing in the journal *Royal Society Open Science* in 2019 argued that the findings of Ericsson et al. could not be replicated, though the benefit of practice was, as the authors conceded, "substantial" even if "considerably smaller" than in the original study.[75] In the general media as well, the theory has come under attack. The *Royal Society* study was the springboard for an article on Vox, a website known for its frequent "explainer" articles. Author Brian Resnick writes, "I find these debunkings of the 10,000-hour rule to be a complete relief. Because implied in the rule (at least, to me) is a deeply self-deprecating message: that if we fail to achieve greatness, it's our own damn fault."[76] For his part, Ericsson seems to lay at least part of the responsibility for such reactions at Gladwell's door. In an interview with David Burkus on the internet podcast *Radio Free Leader*, Ericsson states:

> Malcolm Gladwell came up with this idea of a 10,000-Hour Rule. He emphasized the almost magical aspect, that when individuals have spent 10,000 hours [practicing something] they are then able to make contributions . . . . He was citing our work, but unfortunately, he misread it a bit . . . . We agree with Gladwell that the most talented have spent a large number of hours actually training. [But] he was not counting hours of practice; he was counting the number of hours the

Beatles had been playing in front of audiences. What we were talking about is deliberate practice.⁷⁷

Ericsson thus joins the pile-on that began almost immediately upon the book's publication; such criticisms of Gladwell's work are not unique to *Outliers*. As Eric Levinson notes in *The Atlantic*, "Gladwell backlash is nothing new."⁷⁸ For his part, Gladwell has defended his adaptation of the 1993 study, writing in a 2013 essay in the *New Yorker*:

> In cognitively demanding fields, there are no naturals. Nobody walks into an operating room, straight out of a surgical rotation, and does world-class neurosurgery.... [T]he amount of practice necessary for exceptional performance is so extensive that people who end up on top need help. They invariably have access to lucky breaks or privileges or conditions that make all those years of practice possible [which Gladwell notes is a major theme in *Outliers*].⁷⁹

One problem with this debate—and to be clear, much of the responsibility for this rests with Gladwell's fairly literal articulation of the idea—is a sense the two sides may be talking past each other (which Gladwell himself suggests in his *New Yorker* essay). Whether the amount of practice is specifically 10,000 hours is likely beside the point. Deliberate practice is but one of a number of factors in determining success.

Many jazz musicians, not just the central figures of the canon, practiced or played a great deal, probably well in excess of the theoretical 10,000 hours, and other factors are certainly at play in their development, a point which Gladwell has himself repeatedly emphasized. Luck, in particular the circumstances of when or where one was born, also can play a role in the formation of an outlier within a community. Like the clothing merchant of lower Manhattan who was born into a particular community or the ice hockey player whose birthday came early in the year (two of the case studies cited by Gladwell), jazz artists who were born in particular locations or whose families moved to such locations would often have an advantage. Would Charlie Parker have been a "genius" had he been born somewhere other than Kansas City? Would Thelonious Monk have emerged as he did if his mother had decided to keep the family in North Carolina instead of moving to San Juan Hill in New York when he was a child? Of course, this also speaks to the influence of the music community of the time, but again, being born into that community itself could rightly be regarded as something of a fortuitous event. The same might be said of significant community institutions like Crispus Attucks High School in Indianapolis, Westinghouse High School in Pittsburgh, or Miller and Cass Technical High Schools in Detroit, schools that produced many well-known jazz artists. Young, developing artists in these contexts were afforded experiences and opportunities based on where they lived. It was, in terms of the musical development of many jazz artists, a matter of being in the right place at the right time.[80] None of these factors alone can explain the seeming "genius" of an Armstrong, Parker, Coltrane, or other artists. But what all of these individuals share is that they were, relative to others in their communities, *outliers*, through a combination of talent, effort, and personal circumstance, establishing a sense of difference from most of their peers. It is this very sense of difference that sets them apart from others. One could make a case that Parker was, in fact, exceptionally *un*representative of bebop. He was the tip of the iceberg, standing head and shoulders above the crowd, a figure who would almost certainly qualify as an outlier relative to his peers.

Outliers must be measured in relation to the sample. But what is that sample? If we are to understand the "genius," we must also understand the "ordinary." There are numerous jazz artists whose identities would neither be defined by a seat at the table of the jazz canon nor by historiographic obscurity. Sonny Stitt provides an instructive example. Stitt was widely (and remains today) recognized as an outstanding saxophonist, a contemporary of Parker and the bebop/hard bop generation. Criticized by some earlier in his career for supposedly imitating Parker's style (a criticism which surely could be leveled at many, if not most, saxophonists of the time), Stitt had, by the mid-1950s, established himself as a highly respected performer on the jazz scene, recording with many well-known artists as well as under his own name. Still, despite his reputation as a fine performer, Stitt's profile has never reached the level of jazz's main canonical figures. As Gabriel Solis notes in his book *Monk's Music*, Stitt is but one example of numerous "fabulous, distinctive players and composers whom musicians admire and who have inspired others but have not made the leap from the lists of an individual's favorite musicians into the canon of great musicians."[81] Are artists such as these "ordinary"? Are they outliers? In reality, they are probably a bit of both. At times, their identities are even linked to discussions of genius. Preston Love refers to Stitt's own "individuality and personal genius"[82] in setting him apart from other musicians of the time. In other instances, however, genius is what separates artists like these from the canonical masters. As Scott Yanow notes, "Stitt's alto playing was often identical to Charlie Parker's, although without the genius."[83] One cannot be both "genius" and "not genius," and such disparities underscore the often indefinable and contested nature of just what genius means.

But there have been other jazz musicians whose efforts did not place them in the upper echelons of jazz performance communities, who seldom appear on "favorite musicians" lists as noted previously by Solis, or whose brushes with "greatness" were more fleeting. Unlike the figures at the center of the canon or those intermediate artists who often moved in a close orbit around them, this last group of artists occupied spaces on jazz's periphery. Whitney Balliett writes in a profile of trombonist Benny Morton:

> One of the persistent beliefs in jazz is that the byways of America are peopled with unknown geniuses. But the world of jazz is small, it has an almost telephonic grapevine, and touring musicians who at one time or another play most of the general-store towns have notably curious, open ears. Another belief is that jazz contains a sizable population of excellent but underrated musicians who, because of mischance, the winds of faddism, or retiring personalities, exist in a permanent twilight, and this is true.[84]

The "permanent twilight" that Balliett references may not adequately describe the career of Stitt or of similar sub-canon jazz artists such as J. J. Johnson, McCoy Tyner, Lee Morgan, and their peers, often achieving notoriety through a combination of their own individual efforts and frequent associations with better-known artists.[85] In the "permanent twilight" were those musicians who perhaps aspired to greatness but never quite achieved widespread renown, acclaim, or influence. This is not a criticism of their musicianship per se—many were, as Balliett suggests, excellent players. But they have largely been forgotten in jazz discourses, relegated to tangential discussions in which musicians are not celebrated for their typicality but for their departure from it. They were, in other words, ordinary, everyday working musicians whose efforts often were ignored or dismissed. On occasion, such artists would emerge from obscurity, stepping out of the "permanent twilight" on the fringes of the jazz world, making a brief appearance in the annals of the music.

Establishing a Sample: In Search of the Ordinary Jazz Musician

I return to the 1933 film I discussed at the beginning of this section. The second trumpeter in question is not actually anonymous, though sorting out his identity is no small feat. He is credited in most sources as Charles

D. Johnson, though other sources have credited him as Charles S. Johnson. The root of this discrepancy is not clear, but I would speculate that it might have something to do with the fact that the "D" and "S" keys are adjacent to each other on a standard typewriter or keyboard. Just who this Charles Johnson was (D. or S.) is not entirely clear. Johnson—not to be confused with renowned bandleader Charlie Johnson—is virtually absent from jazz history. Tom Lord's *Jazz Discography*[86] credits him with only two recordings, both performances in Europe with Armstrong.[87] But the situation is even murkier. As Eugene Chadbourne notes in the *All Music Guide*, this was a common name, and "[a]n entire band could be worked up out of the pool of musicians named Charlie Johnson or Charles Johnson."[88] Citing John Chilton's *Who's Who of Jazz*, Chadbourne notes that a trumpeter named Charles Johnson, who made earlier recordings with Ellington in the 1920s and died in 1937, is not the same Charlie Johnson who led a series of successful bands in Harlem at around the same time. Whether *this* trumpet-playing Charles Johnson is the same as the "Ellington" Charles Johnson is not entirely clear, but he may well have been.[89]

It would seem, at any rate, that Charles Johnson's half-chorus of notoriety had come and gone with the Armstrong film. But it was not quite over. The following month, Armstrong and his band performed at a broadcast concert from The Hague, and once again, Johnson can be heard. What is most notable about his solos on these recordings is that they are not "bad"; rather, they are technically competent, accurate improvisations, which are probably superior to his work the previous month and which display a highly syncopated rhythmic approach, wide range, and fleet technique (including some very intricate, fast eighth-note runs in the second A section of "Dinah").[90] Still, Johnson seemed to disappear from jazz's historical narrative relatively quickly. For his part, Armstrong was simply better, it seems. In fact, Johnson's playing has served as something of a pedagogical measuring stick that places Armstrong's superior performance into sharp relief; one can hear just how good Armstrong is because such comparisons are apparent relative to Johnson. But one can also imagine that a musician like Johnson might better represent the everyday "working" musician who generally played whatever jobs came along and occasionally was able to hitch their wagon to a major figure like Ellington or Armstrong. What advantages of circumstance, what talent, what work ethic Johnson might have lacked relative to Armstrong are not immediately apparent. What is apparent is that Armstrong is the outlier, and the juxtaposition of his playing with that of the more typical Johnson brings this into sharp focus.

Musicians such as Charlie Johnson have always lurked just beneath the surface of jazz's accepted history, occasionally popping up when their paths crossed those of more established musicians. Another such figure is the late alto saxophonist Dave Schildkraut. Most casual jazz fans have probably never heard of Schildkraut, and indeed, his recorded output consisted mainly of sideman dates. But there are some curious intersections that marked his career. Schildkraut was by no means an amateur; he was, in fact, a veteran of the Stan Kenton organization and also played with such artists as Tony Bennett and George Handy. But his most significant appearance in the jazz canon was a date with Miles Davis in April 1954, rounding out a quintet that included Davis, Percy Heath, Kenny Clarke, and Horace Silver. The resulting album, *Walkin'*, represents Schildkraut's most significant brush with greatness, one that unfortunately did not lead to bigger and better things. And indeed, the trail of Schildkraut's later career seems to go cold; Herb Geller laments that "I don't know what happened [to Schildkraut], but he just seemed to stop playing and started working for his father, who had a grocery store and didn't like jazz musicians."[91] Grego Applegate Edwards, writing on his "Gapplegate" blog, sums up the conventional wisdom concerning Schildkraut's place in the narrative of jazz by writing, "To me he epitomizes the 'falling off the face of the earth' syndrome. What happened? There are reasons. He apparently turned down some key opportunities, to record for Norman Granz, etc. Why that was I do not know."[92] Schildkraut was definitely a competent performer, and such descriptions are often used to explain his presence on Davis's recording of "Solar," where he follows the trumpeter's solo with his own that seems to be something of a cross between Charlie Parker and Lee Konitz. This begs the question: which of these musicians—Charlie Parker or Dave Schildkraut—stands as a better example of the everyday, lived experience of jazz musicians in the early 1950s? Is it Charlie Parker or those "ornithologists" who followed him? Schildkraut was likely representative of many "typical" musicians, mostly following trends rather than setting them, playing like Charlie Parker because if an artist wanted to get a recording date with Miles Davis in 1954, that was what they did. For every Charlie Parker, there were undoubtedly dozens of Dave Schildkrauts. And thus, Parker may not be the best representation of what the jazz scene was at the time; he may represent only a small sliver of it, with the rest occupied by musicians who constituted the backbone of the community. As Thomas Greenland writes in a study of "journeyman" jazz musicians in the contemporary New York scene, such players are critical to the "establishment and maintenance of [jazz] community."[93] I suggest the same is true from the standpoint of historiography;

ordinary, everyday musicians must be seen as a critical component of the communities from which outliers emerged.

John Coltrane's music, like Parker's, has become a model for both pedagogical practice[94] and historical narrative; his influence on contemporary practice and the jazz canon cannot be overstated. That does not mean it was representative, however. We can examine this issue through another recording, a 1957 date with Coltrane and tenor saxophonist Paul Quinichette, released in 1959 under the title *Cattin' with Coltrane and Quinichette*. When the session is addressed in Coltrane scholarship, it is rarely given the attention that Coltrane's other recordings receive. Ben Ratliff describes the session:

> [*Cattin'* was] a wan little record made with forced-march rhythm section accompaniment; at its most expansive moments, which are Coltrane's solos in "Anatomy" and "Vodka," Coltrane nearly sounds as if he's practicing alone, squeezing diminished scale patterns to the limit of their usefulness. Mal Waldron . . . plays as if he's got mittens on, grinding short gray phrases around middle C into the keyboard.[95]

Similarly, Carl Woideck points to a disparity in style between the saxophonists: "On a two-tenor date with Lester Young man Paul Quinichette, for example, Coltrane's superimposed chords and sixteenth notes create the illusion that he's speeding along at twice Quinichette's tempo."[96] Quinichette himself was, like Schildkraut, not a "star" by any means but a fairly well-known player on the New York scene, nicknamed the "Vice Prez" for his uncanny—some might say derivative—similarity to Lester Young (who supposedly referred to Quinichette as "Lady Q"). He had played in the 1940s with the bands of Jay McShann, Benny Carter, and Sid Catlett, but the date with Coltrane is what he is best known for today. And like Schildkraut, Quinichette was an artist whose reputation was measured in direct relationship to another, more established player, Lester Young. Unsurprisingly, it is Coltrane's star that would continue to rise. Quinichette, by contrast, apparently found the challenges of the jazz world tough going. Like Schildkraut, his later career dimmed, and by the late 1960s he had, according to Bill Crow, "disappeared from the jazz scene,"[97] re-emerging in the mid-1970s; the intervening years were filled, in part, with work as a TV repairman in New York.

SIGHT-READING, VIRTUOSITY, AND IDENTITY

Big Bands and Race in Jazz Education

INTRODUCTION: READ THIS!

In 1967, the premier jazz lab band (big band) at what was then called North Texas State University recorded the first of what would become a series of annual albums that continue to the present day. Directed by Leon Breeden, the "One O'Clock Lab Band," so named due to its daily rehearsal time, included in this session a piece that was specifically commissioned for the recording. This itself was, of course, not unusual. What *was* unusual was that the band sight-read the track on the session in a single take. The fact that such a high-level group would undertake an endeavor such as this illuminates a number of important issues with respect to the practices of jazz in American higher education, which themselves are intertwined with discourses of race, class, and the complicated histories of the discipline. I'll return to a discussion of this recording later in this chapter.

This emphasis on reading, and sight-reading in particular, is one that resonates with my own experience as a student at North Texas in the 1990s; sight-reading was a skill that was highly prized. Horn auditions for the many Lab Bands were, first and foremost, a sight-reading audition, which assessed students' abilities to read—at sight—parts from various arrangements played by the groups. A subsequent audition was used to assess students' improvisational abilities.[1] A post about the band on the *UNT University Union* blog underscores this kind of experience. Describing the audition process, the article states:

> Players are expected to play anonymous charts in a way that demonstrates their ability to interpret and stylize the music. "For the

trombone audition, my professor will pull out three big band charts. They usually take the name off of them, so I don't have a reference." One O'Clock [t]rombonist, DJ Rice, said, "It'll just be one or two pages of music that I have about 30 seconds to look at. Then they go 'okay go, here's tempo.' And you just have to be able to nail it."[2]

Separated by more than two decades,[3] this experience seems to track almost exactly with my own. Sight-reading was not simply a function of the audition process but was woven into the very fabric of the ensemble itself. During rehearsals, students were expected to be able to sight-read at an exceptionally high level. This was especially true in the One O'Clock Lab Band, in which rehearsals nearly always included a significant amount of sight-reading. I can still recall the first time hearing the band in person. Standing outside Stan Kenton Hall,[4] I could hear the sounds of an exceedingly high-level big band coming from inside the room. When I opened the door, I expected to see the band setting up while a recording was playing; instead, I saw the band itself, sight-reading a new chart. I began to understand why sight-reading was such a central part of the audition process. Neil Slater, the director of the group during my time in the program, would regularly call numbers seemingly at random from an enormous folder that contained—literally—hundreds of charts. It seemed to me at times that the only real "rehearsal" came in preparation for a specific performance or in preparation for the annual Lab recording done in the spring semester. Students were expected to not only play the "correct" notes on the page, but with the correct phrasing, interpretation, and so forth. To say that this experience was stressful was an understatement. But it was also exhilarating, as this band played at an exceedingly high level—it is still, to this day, possibly the consistently finest ensemble I have played with on a regular basis.

Jazz education's history runs as a parallel stream to broader historical narratives of jazz, intersecting at various points with nonacademic developments. In the remainder of this chapter, I wish to explore how experiences such as those I have described above have their roots in particular histories, practices, and perspectives, which themselves are intertwined with issues of race, class, and identity that emerge largely from outside the academy. The emphasis on a highly technical skill such as sight-reading in assessment within jazz education illuminates how disparities in access to economic capital and resources are manifested in a seeming lack of representation in jazz education programs. They are also the product of particular influences and individuals whose views on race might have, even if unintentionally or indirectly, led to the creation of a kind of exclusivity within the field, which reinforced—and was reinforced by—particular inequities of access to the kinds of tools that were needed for success in such a setting.

THE FUTURE OF JAZZ: STAN KENTON AND EARLY JAZZ EDUCATION

One area that has been relatively unexplored is the connection between jazz education and the musical scenes on the West Coast in the 1940s and 1950s. Two developments are particularly noteworthy in this regard. First, the West Coast had, by this point, become an important center for the studio recording industry, which would, in turn, exert a significant influence on the developing field of jazz education. While mainly focused on developments outside the West Coast, the historical literature of jazz education does contain scattered references to the Westlake School, an institution established after World War II in Los Angeles. Like Berklee, Westlake was centered on the work of theorist Joseph Schillinger and enjoyed a close relationship with the Hollywood studio scene. Michael Spencer, in an article in the *Journal of Historical Research in Music Education*, fills in many of these gaps, connecting Westlake directly to the nascent West Coast jazz scene as well as the Hollywood studios. Spencer notes David Baskerville's recounting of the school's formation, in which he worked with Westlake founder Alvin Learned to put together "a curriculum that would serve the needs of musicians seeking careers in the Hollywood studios."[5] Spencer's study is useful in his positioning of Westlake as an integral component of both the studio music world and the LA jazz culture at the height of the West Coast scene's popularity. Unfortunately, Westlake would not survive in the long run, closing its doors in 1961, but its influence could still be felt in jazz education in a number of ways.

One Westlake student in particular points us toward another link between jazz education and the West Coast studios—Bill Holman, a saxophonist and composer/arranger who was a student at Westlake in the late 1940s and early 1950s. Although he would later collaborate with Buddy Rich, Woody Herman, and Doc Severinsen, among others, Holman is best known for his work as one of the core arrangers for Stan Kenton in the mid to late 1950s, exactly the moment when Kenton was beginning to take an interest in the burgeoning jazz education scene. Holman's arrangements and compositions for big band remain very popular with collegiate (and some high school) jazz ensembles around the country. As one of the most influential figures to emerge from the 1940s LA jazz scene, Kenton himself had a fairly close relationship with the LA studios during this period as he had been active in the studio system in his early career. Michael Sparke quotes Kenton in his biography of the bandleader, titled *This is an Orchestra!*:

> I decided that I wanted to be something important around Hollywood, and I realized that if this was going to take place I had to be able to school myself to be an all-around piano player—a good utility pianist—someone who could play all sorts of music and all kinds of things, so that I could work myself into the studios and radio stations, and that's what I was pursuing.[6]

Kenton's ambitions to work in the Hollywood studios would not come to fruition, though his connection to the LA studios remained intact through the 1950s as many of his sidemen had been active in that scene. But the ideal of the studio player shaped Kenton's worldview in profound ways; I would suggest that it never completely left his consciousness. Longtime LA musician, producer, and record industry executive Harvey Kubernik recalled that studios often had a dim view of jazz musicians, with some notable exceptions: "All the Stan Kenton men could really play, read music well, and were not junkies or juice-heads, which was the perception and vibe the big studios felt some of the time when they heard the word jazz musician in conjunction with potential movie work."[7] It may not be that much of a stretch to imagine that the "junkies or juice-heads" to which Kubernik refers were, at least in the view of the studios, predominantly Black. And the juxtaposition of such players with Kenton's (at the time) all-White band is striking; these were musicians who "could really play" and "read music well."

Reading, and sight-reading in particular, has frequently been positioned as a significant skill within the studio scene, and it is not difficult to understand why. Film scores were (and still are) often completed near the end of the production process, and recordings of this material are often done on exceptionally short notice. Frank Hayde, writing in his biography of renowned West Coast drummer Stan Levy, noted that Levy, upon "[deciding] to reinvent himself as a full-time studio musician" in Hollywood, "resolved to hone his sight-reading ability and become a finished musician."[8] Hollywood was not the only location where the ability to sight-read music proficiently was a prized skill. Trombonist J. J. Johnson recalled how his "sightreading savvy had to improve" when he played in the New York studio scene in the 1960s.[9]

Johnson's experience here is instructive, as "reading" has often been seen as a barrier to Black musicians' acceptance into the relatively lucrative world of studio playing. Dick Weissman and Frank Jermance write that:

For years, black musicians had trouble breaking into studio work, which was and is mostly unionized and lucrative. Jazz critic and composer Leonard Feather often exposed this problem in his *DownBeat Magazine* articles. In defense of their practices, some musical contractors claimed that black musicians didn't read music well enough to cut the studio gigs, or that they didn't double on various instruments.[10]

The idea that jazz musicians, and Black musicians in particular, possessed inferior abilities in terms of reading has often been expressed in the literature of jazz. In his book on contemporary big bands in New York, Alexander Stewart quotes trumpeter Eddie Allen addressing this point: "There are a lot of rehearsal big bands out there, and I don't know if they assume that black musicians don't want to play in them, or we can't read well enough, but we wouldn't get the calls. And now they see this big band there and say, 'Oh, OK. I didn't know he could read.'"[11]

Stan Kenton's penchant for technically skilled, and by extension, tight, precise ensemble performance, undoubtedly carried over into his extensive advocacy for jazz education. Among the nascent jazz programs he patronized, none was more prominent than that of North Texas. Kenton became enamored of the band on hearing them at the Notre Dame jazz festival in 1960, and he would continue to be the program's major patron until his death in 1979. I'll return to the discussion of Kenton and his relationship to jazz education later in this chapter.

Clams, Anyone?

Let us now return to the recording I mentioned at the start of this chapter. By the late 1960s, the top lab band at North Texas had begun to achieve some measure of fame and influence. It was within this context that Leon Breeden decided to conduct his experiment, to sight-read a chart on a recording session. For their 1967 album, Breeden commissioned an original composition titled "Clams, Anyone?" The title is, of course, a tongue-in-cheek reference to incorrectly played notes ("clams"), which it was assumed the listener would hear as the band sight-read the chart on the recording with no rehearsal. Breeden offers an extended introduction at the beginning of the recording:

> This is Leon Breeden, director of the North Texas Lab Band. The noise you hear in the background is that of music being passed out to the members of the lab band, music which they have never seen before, and which they are now being challenged to read at sight. We believe

that music education suffers when any group works throughout an entire school year to perfect a few numbers to take to a festival or contest in order to try for a first-place rating. Our lab band has commissioned Mr. Larry Muhoberac, a brilliant young composer, to write a number for this band to sight-read on this album. He was given absolutely no restrictions and was told only to satisfy his own musicianship. We hope that this will serve as an inspiration and challenge to young musicians everywhere. Larry has given this number a title which is certainly appropriate. Since musicians call a wrong note a "clam," Larry calls this composition "Clams, Anyone?"[12]

The performance itself, it should be noted, is mostly free from the kinds of "clams" to which the title refers. There are, to be sure, some wrong notes, as one can hear at around twenty-five seconds into the performance (1:30 or so on the track, when a trumpet player seems to make an early entrance). But for the most part, the band sounds very together, very "tight." The chart itself is a medium swinger in the spirit of someone like Neal Hefti, Quincy Jones, or Sammy Nestico, and one is perhaps most impressed at the level of energy throughout the performance (driven in no small measure by drummer Ed Soph, who would later become the program's jazz drum set instructor). This is not simply an "accurate" reading of the chart (which it largely is), but the band's interpretation is, shall we say, quite "swinging." Several years later, in 1973, Breeden and the lab band took this a step further, performing an entire live concert of charts that the band read at sight. Recounting the performance in his memoir, Breeden notes that it "prove[d] an important point to our students."[13]

Breeden's emphasis on reading is also apparent in a brief piece published in *Music America* in 1977. Part of a feature on "The Future of Jazz Education" (which also featured contributions by Jack Wheaton and Rayburn Wright), Breeden's piece articulates many of the same ideas expressed in the recorded reading session a decade earlier. Insisting that jazz students will more likely be successful, Breeden writes, "IF students will recognize the need to learn to *READ* well instead of relying upon a good ear or a natural ability to improvise, and will accept the fact that much hard work goes into the preparation for a successful life as a performer and/or teacher of jazz music."[14] I want to pull out a few ideas from this passage that I think are telling. For instance, Breeden makes a delineation between reading and improvisation, or more specifically, a "natural ability to improvise." Two things strike me about this passage. The first is the way that Breeden seems to place reading and improvisation in opposition to each other. While he does not treat these as mutually exclusive, the framing does seem to imply that these exist as different types of musicianship. This leads to a second point, the correlation of improvisation with "natural" ability. Nowhere in this discussion does there seem to be an allowance for improvisational skill that is the result of studied, deliberate practice. This might be simply a matter of wording, but as the leader of one of the largest and most visible jazz programs in the world, Breeden's words undoubtedly carried a good deal of weight. And whether intentionally or not, the implicit separation of reading and improvisation is firmly established.

Breeden's intent in this exercise is certainly admirable, to suggest that student ensembles move beyond the perfection of those pieces that they might play at a contest or festival. But there is, to be sure, no small amount of showing off here as well. Breeden seems to take pride in the fact that his band can sight-read at such a high level. These are the skills, it is implied, that young musicians need to possess in order to succeed as professionals. Such skills were undoubtedly appreciated by many big band and commercial bandleaders of the time, and Breeden is, at least indirectly, signaling to them that his students are ready to go. It is worth noting that the roster of musicians in the 1967 version of the One O'Clock Lab Band contains many familiar names, including drummer Ed Soph as well as future *Saturday Night Live* and *Blues Brothers* saxophonist Lou Marini, who is heard soloing on "Clams, Anyone?" (fellow *SNL* bandmate Tom "Bones" Malone would also pass through the North Texas program a short time later).

It is *also* worth noting that this band was, as it would be when I was a member of the same group precisely three decades later, comprised almost entirely of white men.[15]

Sight-reading, and more technical aspects of musical performance in general, are often situated as being an objective form of assessment that is based entirely on musical skill and one that is race-neutral. But assessment in educational settings is always inextricably tied to broader currents in cultural and community contexts. Sight-reading is a particularly resource-intensive activity. It requires a substantial library of musical scores to avoid repetition and often is supported by individual private study. In his book *The World of Jazz Trumpet*, Scotty Barnhart speaks to what he sees as the importance of sight-reading for aspiring jazz musicians:

> Sight-reading is an area of musicianship that is extremely important regardless of the level of talent. The ability to read new music while in practice and especially performance can determine the success of a musician. All of the professional musicians I have ever worked with have the ability to sight-read new music as fast as it is put in front of them.[16]

He points to his own particular musical education as a major factor in his development of such skills: "I realize how lucky I am to have had a high school instructor who always gave us new music to read and play. However, I did not wait to get to school to sight-read new music. I used to scan the hymnals during church services before I even began to play the trumpet and read every music book I could find."[17] Barnhart's comments are instructive for several reasons. His emphasis on being "lucky" to have a high school teacher for whom reading "new music" was important is striking, and one senses that Barnhart recognizes that this experience may not be widely shared. Additionally, Barnhart's comments seem to suggest a high degree of personal motivation to develop this skill. Both of these might be seen, in some sense, as outliers in the education of young musicians, especially when considered in relation to underresourced communities.

It also should be noted that Barnhart's statements come with a couple of significant qualifiers. First, his perspectives, as expressed in his book, are based mainly on the importance of sight-reading as a function of big band playing, as exemplified by the central place the Count Basie Orchestra occupies in the narrative. Further commentary on this topic emphasizes the playing of ensemble parts as opposed to other aspects of playing jazz. Second, Barnhart is himself a product of higher education, having earned a degree from Florida A&M University. Finally, he holds a professorship in Jazz Studies at Florida State University. Barnhart is, then, speaking not simply as a Black jazz musician working in the "real world" but also as part of jazz education's institutional structure. None of this is intended as a criticism of Barnhart as either a performer or a teacher; he has clearly excelled in both roles, and his perspectives on the importance of sight-reading articulate why such skills are important in jazz musicians' overall development. But his perspectives must also be placed within the context of his very high-profile work with one of the premiere large jazz ensembles in the world today and his professional identity as a faculty member in a well-regarded jazz studies program. Barnhart's experiences, in other words, may not reflect the typical career path of a contemporary jazz student. Would young jazz musicians in underresourced educational contexts have the same opportunities as Barnhart? Would they be as "lucky" to have a teacher who was trained and/or committed to the development of sight-reading or to have regular access to "new music" with which to practice sight-reading?

The emphasis on sight-reading as part of assessment in higher musical education is but one component of the larger problem of inequity when it comes to establishing standards for musical performance and assessment. In a 2008 article in the *Philosophy of Music Education Review*, Julia Eklund Koza notes that music school admissions also can be seen as a site where what is typically viewed as "neutral" evaluative criteria could actually be anything but. Koza suggests that current audition requirements and expectations of knowledge for incoming students place students of color at a particular disadvantage. She writes of her experiences as a faculty member in music education, noting that students face an "access conundrum" in which a series of barriers, themselves often regarded as objective, have the effect of narrowing the pool of applicants to an "elite" group and one in which minority students are vastly underrepresented. These barriers might include things such as SAT/ACT scores, but they can also include value judgments with respect to what is or is not an acceptable level or type of musical skill. Noting the increasingly high skill level that is expected of incoming students, Koza writes:

> The changes in applicants' musical knowledge and the increased technical quality of audition performances, I argue, are effects of a widening affluence gap in the U.S. Families that can afford to provide their young children with a range of privately enhanced educational opportunities are, in effect, raising the admissions bar at my institution and so far, my university has not responded sufficiently to this challenge. Because the affluence gap has a racial pattern, this access conundrum has racial implications, too. Under these circumstances, the current admissions process becomes a racially discriminatory practice that exacerbates persistent race-equity problems.[18]

Koza continues later in the article by addressing repertoire, and in particular, what she sees as an emphasis on *bel canto* singing styles in vocal auditions. The question of whether such a vocal technique and repertoire are "race-neutral" or not presents a particular dilemma in the development of assessment and evaluation strategies. For Koza, such techniques are decidedly not neutral; indeed, this speaks directly to what kinds of music, and by extension, what kinds of people, are "acceptable" within the academy. I quote Koza at length on this point:

> Skeptics may argue that the audition list is color blind because the rules apply regardless of the race or ethnicity of the applicants; they may claim that specifying acceptable genres helps all students "choose the right song," to borrow a phrase from the popular television singing contest, *American Idol*. They may counter that racism laces the assumption that people deemed non-White either cannot or are not

interested in singing European/American high art music, and they may point out that the repertoire specifications also have ramifications for some White applicants. For example, Broadway musicals and country music, which primarily appeal to White audiences, also fall outside of the boundaries of acceptability. Understanding how the audition repertoire list accomplishes de facto racial and ethnic discrimination begins with the recognition that racial exclusion and domination can be achieved "without making any explicit reference to race at all." Even though the audition specifications do not explicitly refer to race, they discount genres having deep roots in non-White musical traditions and, more importantly, reject the styles and genres that non-White people in the U.S. currently are more likely to enjoy.[19]

It should not be difficult to see how an emphasis on sight-reading in jazz education programs, or even on relatively complex and technical big band performance, might have a similar effect. As a skill that necessitates extended technical study, sight-reading might too be regarded as an element of the "access conundrum" that Koza highlights. While such practices are damaging enough within the context of a curriculum that focuses mainly on Western art music, it might be especially troubling when applied to a genre that has deep historical roots in African American cultural and musical practices.

The notion that jazz musicians were (and are) "ear" players set in opposition to classical musicians' dependence on the written score holds great sway in jazz writing. Yet jazz musicians by and large have been, and continue to be, adept at reading. Charlie Parker was able to read sufficiently well to play in several working big bands in the early 1940s; Miles Davis completed roughly a year of classical study at Juilliard; John Coltrane was known to dive deeply into method books and technical studies. All of these activities required competence in reading. Such links between reading and jazz performance can be traced to the beginnings of the music. Clovis Seemes notes that reading ability among Black musicians in the early twentieth century was not simply a marker of professional skill; it was also an important marker of class identity. Writing about the Regal Theater, a mainstay in Chicago's "Brown Belt" from its opening in 1928, Seemes argues that reading ability among African American musicians who comprised the members of the house orchestra formed "a fundamental part of a small but growing Black middle class."[20] Led by prominent Chicago musician and critic Dave Peyton, these groups "valued the skill of reading music"[21] and were considered to be among the elite of the Black musical community in Chicago at the time.

Similarly, David Chevan, writing in *Current Musicology* in a 2002 essay, underscores the importance placed on reading among early jazz musicians, both as a means of functioning within the professional music world and as a marker of professional identity and even pride. The most successful players, Chevan suggests, were those whose technical skills, including reading, were balanced against a high level of aural ability.[22] Reflecting on the implications of his study with respect to race, Chevan writes, "Race has not played as large a role in this story as I had initially expected it would. There were African American musicians who placed a high value on reading and those who did not. The same could be said of white musicians. Musicians who wanted or needed to learn how to read found a way, no matter how many obstacles they encountered."[23] In questioning the notion of an inherently racialized dynamic with respect to reading ability, Chevan's comment brings up another question: where *do* such assumptions come from? Continuing to reflect on these ideas, he implies an answer to this question:

> What remains striking, however, is the emphasis placed on non-reading musicians by white music critics and writers of the 1920s and 1930s. One of the earliest examples of this is Charles Edward Smith and Frederic Ramsey's *Jazzmen*, which opens with a quote from Bunk Johnson that identifies the Bolden Band as the first jazz band because "it did not read at all." The book continues in the same vein with a strong emphasis on the inability of the first jazz musicians to read music. Historian Kathy Ogren has identified "primitivism" as one idea central to these writers. She states that "white readers *believed jazz* performance could transmit the values of a simpler past into the furious present." I would suggest that for these writers the disregard of musical literacy helped add to that sense of primitivism, thereby affirming these values.[24]

Could it be that the latent identification of Black musicians as *nonreaders* is, in essence, a holdover from the critical "moldy figs"[25] of the Dixieland Revivalist era? And if so, what are the implications of this on our understanding of jazz education today, an endeavor in which reading ability has long been highly prized? No one, myself included, would argue that sight-reading is not a valuable skill for a professional musician to have. But should it be positioned as a barrier skill for musicians in jazz education programs? Or, more to the point, should it be privileged over other skills more attuned to the creation of successful improvised performance? Does it really matter, in the grand scheme of things, whether Louis Armstrong or John Coltrane was a good sight-reader?

A Long, White Shadow:
Stan Kenton and Race in Postwar Jazz Education

In his essay on jazz's critical "wars" of the 1940s, Bernard Gendron recounts the decline of big band swing and the emergence of modernist critics like Leonard Feather and Barry Ulanov. Instead of a bebop-centered jazz scene, as is common in today's "official history," the post-swing world of the modernists was "characterized by a profusion of different and increasingly adventurous experimental approaches," whose practitioners included not only the radical pioneers of bebop but bandleaders such as Stan Kenton as well.[26] History—or at least historiography—seems to have had its say with respect to which artists are today deemed to have been of greater import, but at the time, the jury, so to speak, was still out.

This might simply be another way to emphasize the idea that Kenton, in the late 1940s through the 1950s, was a figure who had to be taken seriously. And there is little question that he was, at least as far as the press (jazz and mainstream) and entertainment industries were concerned. Frequent appearances on television programs—including a 1950 appearance on *The Ed Sullivan Show* that spotlighted a young trumpeter who had recently arrived from Montreal named Maynard Ferguson—cemented Kenton's reputation as one of jazz's foremost public figures. Kenton's demeanor on these broadcasts was not simply that of a bandleader but someone who was a sort of jazz sage, especially when weighing in on the topic of jazz's future. For Kenton, the future of the music would likely traverse several different paths. But more than anything else, Kenton held that jazz's future lay in its "progressive" nature, of an ever more challenging genre based on larger scale compositions. At the same time, his band never lost its core identity; the mid-1950s groups featuring players like Lennie Niehaus, Maynard Ferguson, Carl Fontana, Mel Lewis, Frank Rosolino, and Pete Candoli, to name a few, as well as the arrangements of Bill Holman and Bill Russo, made some of the finest big band music on record to that point. But Kenton's sense of upward mobility (that some would call pretention) would see his late 1950s and 1960s efforts take a different direction, culminating in his "neophonic" work in the 1960s, featuring a massive ensemble and compositions by Clare Fischer, Allyn Ferguson, and a then up-and-coming composer, known mostly for his television work, by the name of John Williams.

The second of Kenton's ideas about the future of jazz was that it would be centered mainly on college campuses. Like much Western art music composition of the time, jazz would become the music of the academy, to be nurtured, preserved, and disseminated in particular ways. In a sense, he followed the lead of fellow West Coaster Dave Brubeck, who, since the early 1950s, had seen the campus as a potential market. Brubeck began making inroads into the college market in the early 1950s and, by 1954, was releasing albums taken from live recordings on college campuses. As artists like Brubeck increasingly brought their music to campus, student ensembles became increasingly active throughout the country.

In South Bend, Indiana, in 1960, these ideas would converge. It was there, at the second annual Notre Dame Collegiate Jazz Festival (NDCJF), where he was serving on the panel of judges, that Kenton would encounter the lab band from North Texas State for the first time. Kenton's presence at the festival was of great significance, as Joseph Kuhn Carey writes in his history of the NDCJF:

> [F]or the last judging spot, [festival organizers Jim Naughton and Chuck Suber] obtained the services of the musician who was considered by many the biggest professional jazz name in 1960: Stan Kenton. At the end of the Fifties, Stan Kenton was perhaps the most influential musician in big band jazz and, therefore, so were his arrangements or "charts" in high school and college stage band repertoires.... The critics were often intimidated by Kenton's music and his attempts to extend jazz's "legitimacy" by integrating classically oriented sounds into his works (hence the "progressive" label), the dapper articulate bandleader had become a frequent visitor to plush concert halls and college campuses.... Most of all, though, he was an exemplary teacher who (no doubt recalling his own difficult early days trying to pry hints and praise from jazzmen in California clubs) went out of his way to work with aspiring young musicians, eventually going so far as to donate his valuable presence and time to the national stage band camp free of charge.[27]

By all accounts, Kenton was immediately struck by the high caliber of both the playing from the North Texas ensemble and the original writing. Carey writes:

> While challenged by the loose, freewheeling drive of Ohio State and Northwestern's fired-up finals play, the North Texas Lab Band's imaginative, complex arrangements, original compositions such as "Powell One" by trombonist Morgan Powell, and rich, deep Kenton-like sound stole the show. Taking time to glance over at Stan Kenton during the Lab Band's finals set, judges' chairman Charles Suber noted the look on the bandleader's handsome but ordinarily road-weary face

as "transcendent." "He didn't look tired anymore," detailed Suber. He could see a new crop of [Buddy] Childerses, [Maynard] Fergusons and [Conte] Candolis right before his eyes."[28]

Kenton likely heard in the North Texas band the fusion of the two ideas mentioned previously, his penchant for complex, "progressive" works and his interest in jazz on college campuses. The event would forge a lasting relationship between Kenton, Director Leon Breeden, and the North Texas program, as Breeden recounts in his memoir:

> When the awards were announced the following night, we learned that we had won "Best Big Band" and "Best Jazz Group" of the festival. Stan Kenton rushed up to greet us and told me that we had renewed his love of music—he also invited me to come to his suite which was on the campus. We had a long visit, and his interest in our program was intense. He asked me if there was anything he could do to help us with our jazz program, and I told him that our greatest need was MUSIC. He patted me on the knee and said: "That's solved, what ELSE do you need?" I did not know it at the time, but he had decided to send his entire library which he was using on his road trip to us immediately after his tour was completed. He later sent $50,000 worth of music to my office! An unbelievable man and musician—a dear friend from that day on![29]

A few years later, in a program broadcast on ABC, Kenton appeared with Breeden and the NTSU band and linked their efforts directly with his broader vision for jazz:

> A year ago on a panel discussion, I made the statement that jazz is dead. What I meant by the statement *jazz is dead* was that it has taken on a new sound. Is it a now sound, is it a swing sound? It's not a tranquilizing sound. It's the new sound that we call *neophonic*. Some have referred to jazz as America's only original art form; perhaps it is. Whatever it is, the group we have with us on this program plays it brilliantly.[30]

Kenton's connection to the NTSU program in the early 1960s seems to be more than simply a function of the band being "good." It assuredly was, but so were many other bands. Rather, it was that Kenton saw something in the band that reminded him of himself; recall Carey's description of the band as "Kenton-like." For Kenton, the North Texas band became something through which he could work to enact his own particular vision of what jazz ought to be. And certainly, these ideas left their mark on Leon Breeden as well, who, throughout his career, cited Kenton as a significant influence on the program. But how, exactly, did his influence show itself? What would characterize a "Kenton-like" approach to jazz education, in which the bandleader's experiences, perspectives, and other factors would all come into play? The shape and character of the program were aligned with Kenton's overall philosophy, which made any collaboration that much easier. An emphasis on sight-reading and technical skill predated Breeden's tenure at North Texas; founding director Gene Hall, in his 1944 master's thesis that would become the blueprint for the North Texas program, notes that "the dance musician is expected to read at sight the music of the band with which he hopes to work."[31] Kenton's emphasis on highly skilled "reading" musicians thus resonated with ideas and practices that were already in place at the school, initiated by Hall and that continued under Breeden. For Kenton, such a relationship would seem to have been a natural fit as both a bandleader and an influential patron of jazz education.

And on this point, we must also take into consideration Kenton's identity in the jazz world with respect to race and consider how Kenton's worldview might overlap with jazz education's own fraught racial discourse. Kenton was a figure whose views on race were, to be diplomatic, somewhat questionable. Some of these ideas are well documented. Probably the most notable of these concerns Kenton's reaction to the failure of *DownBeat* to award him first place in their poll for best band of 1956. Upon hearing of the results of the poll, Kenton fired off an angry telegram to the editors of *DownBeat*, decrying the results (the Big Band poll was topped by Count Basie, while Black artists took thirteen of fifteen top spots in the Established Artist category).[32] The September 5, 1956 telegram read as follows: "JUST SAW YOUR FOURTH JAZZ CRITICS' POLL. IT'S OBVIOUS THAT THERE IS A NEW MINORITY GROUP, WHITE JAZZ MUSICIANS. THE ONLY THING I GAINED FROM STUDYING THE OPINIONS OF YOUR LITERARY GENIUSES OF JAZZ IS COMPLETE AND UTTER DISGUST."[33]

Leonard Feather, one of jazz's most visible critical figures, wrote an open letter in response to Kenton, which was published in the magazine a few weeks later:

> I am writing this letter more in sorrow than in anger . . . . Unlike many musicians and critics who have discussed you so often among themselves, I have bent over backwards to give you the benefit of the

doubt on your racial views.... With your telegram to the editor published in the 5 September *DownBeat*, I am afraid all possible doubt was removed.... [Y]our telegram was so painful to read, so hard to believe, and has already lost you so many friends among your fans and so much respect among your fellow musicians, that I wish I could believe it was a hoax, sent in viciously by somebody else under your signature to besmirch your name.[34]

One of the most intriguing things about Feather's letter is the implication that accusations of racial animus toward Kenton were not new. This seems to reflect a lingering belief among many observers in the jazz world that Kenton harbored racist views, which his telegram to *DownBeat* only seemed to confirm. For Feather's part, there is some attempt at diplomacy, but he was certainly disturbed by what he had read.

Many observers have taken the Kenton telegram incident to be *prima facia* evidence of the bandleader's hostility toward Black musicians. Others have cast it more as an uncharacteristic act borne of a moment of frustration. In either case, the incident was an important point in the contentious narratives of race in 1950s jazz. Kenton's comments on the "new minority" of White jazz musicians are in keeping with a racialized discourse in jazz that was sometimes referred to as "Crow Jim," a bit too on-the-nose of a descriptor for what today might be termed "reverse racism." If matters had ended there, Kenton's place in this discussion might be more secure. But others have accused Kenton of harboring more sinister views that go well beyond dissatisfaction with a critics' poll.

Kenton's supposed flirtation with far-right-wing politics has hovered like a dark cloud over his legacy since the 1960s. There have been, it should be noted, a number of right-leaning jazz musicians over the years. Lionel Hampton, for example, was a noted supporter of Republican political candidates and causes. But no right-leaning jazz figure's political sympathies were as pronounced—or as problematic—as Kenton's. During the 1964 presidential campaign, Kenton aligned himself with the campaign of Barry Goldwater, the conservative senator from Arizona who would be the nominee of the Republican Party. While Goldwater's campaign was ultimately a failure, winning only a handful of Deep South states in addition to his home state, its long-term effects were profound. Indeed, Goldwater is often regarded as the pioneering figure in the modern conservative movement, paving the way for later political figures like Ronald Reagan, whose campaigns in 1976 and 1980 (in which he succeeded to the presidency) fully embraced his identity as a follower of Goldwater.

Kenton's support of Goldwater has been the subject of curiosity for many jazz writers. The bandleader's political leanings are often treated as something of an aberration within jazz communities; Steven B. Elworth, for example, cited Kenton as "one of the few jazz musicians to publicly embrace the right-wing politics of Barry Goldwater."[35] Goldwater himself was a somewhat enigmatic figure; despite his massive influence on conservative politics, his beliefs might be more accurately classified as *libertarian*, which emphasized a limited governmental role in peoples' lives (particularly on social issues, which frequently placed him at odds with many of his Republican colleagues). Unfortunately, this "laissez-faire" attitude also extended to federal initiatives intended to secure basic rights for people of color, and as such, his refusal to support civil rights legislation in 1964 is often (and I would suggest rightly) seen as a stain on his political legacy. The fact that Kenton lent his support to Goldwater's campaign has often been read by critics as a reflection of his own seeming ambivalence—or even outright hostility—toward racial justice and civil rights, an attitude that, it is often suggested, is manifested in his musical worldview.

While Kenton's backing of Goldwater might possibly be chalked up to a fundamentally libertarian sensibility that espouses (at least in theory) a "race-neutral" perspective, it is much harder to understand his support of a political figure such as George Wallace, whose career through the 1960s was defined in large measure by his overt support of racial segregation. It was Wallace, for example, who made national headlines by attempting to block the enrollment of African American students to the University of Alabama in June 1963 by literally standing in the "schoolhouse door."[36] Wallace made several presidential runs, the first in 1964 as one of the last of the "Dixiecrats," then again in 1968 as a third party candidate, when he managed to garner forty-five electoral votes by winning segregationist strongholds such as Georgia, Mississippi, Alabama, Arkansas, and Louisiana (in addition to running fairly close in a number of other states).

In the companion book to Ken Burns's *Jazz* documentary series, Gerald Early's essay on Whiteness in jazz, focusing on Kenton and Keith Jarrett, takes a deep dive into the bandleader's politics, racial and otherwise. Kenton, whom Early refers to as the "apotheosis of white jazz,"[37] does not fare well in Early's telling of the tale. In discussing Kenton's closeness to Wallace, Early writes:

> It can be assumed that [Kenton's] politics were not simply conservative but far right-wing. It can also be assumed that Kenton did not think much of the civil rights movement. A jazz record producer told me that Kenton's records still have enormous appeal to the members of the NRA [National Rifle Association].[38]

In another passage from the essay, Early draws attention to a rather odd coincidence regarding Kenton's fan base, writing, "One finds occasional articles about his bands' appearances in the black press in the 1940s and 1950s, but it isn't likely that many blacks joined the Stan Kenton fan club in those days; it put 'KKK' on all its letters, which stood for 'Keep Kenton Kicking.'"[39]

While Goldwater might be seen, in a charitable reading, as someone whose opposition to federal civil rights laws was based on a principled stand against the expansion of centralized governmental power, Wallace's politics must be read within his long history as an ardent segregationist and trafficker in often openly racist appeals to populist support. In his 1972 presidential campaign, Wallace, perhaps sensing that the mood of the country had shifted, publicly renounced segregation and, incredibly, attempted to cast his previous work as that of a "moderate" on racial issues. These efforts were (and remain) difficult to accept; in 1970, in his successful bid to regain the governorship of Alabama, Wallace openly criticized Democratic incumbent Albert Brewer for reaching out to Black voters, an effort that Jimmy Carter (who was elected governor of Georgia that same year) called "one of the most racist campaigns in modern southern political history."[40]

Over the years, Kenton supporters have exhibited a degree of defensiveness with respect to his political activities, and many have decried the accusations of racism that have been lobbed at the bandleader, noting his hiring of and collaboration with a number of Black musicians over the course of his career.[41] Despite this, as Simon Rentner notes in an NPR profile, Kenton "never fully shook the stigma" of accusations of racial animus.[42] Does Kenton's support of Goldwater and especially Wallace by itself signify that he was a racist? Given the larger discussion of race in jazz and the fact that the peak of Kenton's career came during the most active years of the civil rights movement, this is not something that can be easily overlooked. More important, however, is the question of what, if any, connection there could be between Kenton's political attitudes and the musical aesthetic that defined his work during this period. And given his support for and patronage of the emerging field of jazz education at the same time, how might these ideas have influenced the manner in which the field would develop from the 1950s to the 1970s?

It is all too tempting to draw a straight line from Kenton's defensiveness about White musicians, expressed in his telegram to *DownBeat*, to his support of right-wing, even segregationist politicians several years later, to his propensity for fielding all White or at least nearly all White bands to the rather large imprint he left on jazz education, a field that was also having its own problems with respect to racial inclusion. To do so would be an oversimplification of a complex process. Whether or not Stan Kenton was or was not a racist is not the point, and indeed, no one, aside from Kenton himself, can ever really settle this question definitively. The point, rather, is to consider how these various historical and cultural currents influenced the development of the field. As he was a major influence—perhaps *the* major influence—on the development of jazz education in these early years, it is crucial that a full accounting be given to the forces that shaped this relationship.

What we do know is this: Kenton long faced accusations of reluctance to include more Black musicians in his bands. The same is true for the main beneficiary of his patronage, the jazz program at North Texas, which itself has long faced criticism for what has been seen as a lack of Black students in its program. And to be clear, such criticisms are not without merit, as they are for many (if not most) jazz education programs across the country. Comments about inequity and a lack of inclusiveness are not new with respect to the North Texas program. In a 1970 article in the *NAJE Educator*, Bryan Lindsay links critiques of jazz education's Whiteness with other "problems" in the field:[43]

> Then there's the Crow Jim–Jim Crow conflict. Leon Breeden is especially sensitive to this. "I've been backed into a corner and confronted too many times with 'Why don't you have any black cats in the band?'" [Breeden] says. "The answer, whether they believe me or not, is that I've had at least a dozen in the lab band program and none of them had any musical problems at all. They flunked out of school on things like English and math. To a man they were great players but I couldn't save them. Now, I have a couple more and it looks as if they are going to make it."[44]

In invoking the phrase "Crow Jim," Lindsay inverts accusations of discrimination against Black jazz students, redeploying them as accusations of discrimination *against* White students. Despite such defensiveness, such perspectives were often couched in "colorblind" or "race-neutral" terms. When asked about this issue by Lindsay, Kent State's jazz director gave what might be regarded as a standard response: "I don't have any white cats or black cats in the band; just musicians."[45]

To be sure, the lingering effects of statutory segregation, having only been breached a few years before,[46] might well be expected to impact the program in the years that immediately followed. By the 1970s, however, to say nothing of more recent years, such explanations tend to ring hollow. There is no particular evidence that suggests Breeden sought to exclude Black students, and indeed, we should keep in mind that public school desegregation, particularly in the Deep South (including Texas), moved at a glacial pace in the 1960s. Educational disparities that resulted from decades of funding and resource inequities left their mark on the first generations of students of color who attended southern colleges like North Texas. Breeden's comments about "English and math," while appearing dismissive, might have some truth in actual practice, a result of persistent disparities in public education. Still, Breeden's comment might be interpreted as deflecting responsibility or, at the very least, displaying a lack of concern for the unique and pervasive structural obstacles that confronted Black students. At any rate, the end result remained largely the same, an overwhelmingly White group playing music from an African American tradition. And the question may still be asked, what kinds of barriers might Breeden and his peers, even unknowingly, have put into place that would give many White students a marked advantage in achieving success in collegiate jazz programs? And how might such ideas continue to impact the experiences of students and educators in the field?

A Kentonian Postscript: Big Bands, Odd Meters, and "White Jazz"

In an essay in *Jazz Perspectives*,[47] Fritz Schenker argues that the trends toward "Balkan" influences in jazz may serve as an expression of "realness" and racial authenticity for many White musicians in the 1980s and 1990s, spearheaded most visibly by trumpeter Dave Douglas. And in an interesting parallel, Schenker traces the roots of this trend to another academic institution, New England Conservatory, and specifically to the Contemporary Improvisation program directed by Ran Blake. Schenker writes:

> The musical marker of this sense of "realness" is most conspicuously Balkan rhythm, a point of fascination for most devotees of music from Southeast Europe. While most dance musics in the U.S. feature meters of 2/4, 4/4, or 3/4, with even subdivisions of the beat, Bulgarian, Macedonian, and other Balkan dances commonly feature additive meters, where two and three beat pulses are added together to create asymmetric meters such as the 5/8 paidushko horos (2+3), 7/8 ruchenitsas (2+2+3), and 11/8 kopanitsas (2+2+3+2+2), among other combinations.[48]

So-called "odd meters" are, of course, not specific to Balkan music, nor are they unknown in jazz; a notable example is Dave Brubeck's composition "Take Five." But they are, to be sure, among the less common types of jazz meter. Another jazz figure who made frequent use of these kinds of metrical constructs was Hank Levy, a composer and saxophonist who also served as the director of jazz studies at Maryland's Towson University. Levy collaborated with many big bandleaders who were active through the 1960s and 1970s. Among his best-known works is "Whiplash," a piece written for Don Ellis that features prominently in the film of the same name (discussed in chapter five). But Levy was likely best known as a frequent associate of Stan Kenton, contributing other odd-meter works to the band, such as "Time for a Change," a piece in 9/4 time that was recorded by Kenton's band on the album *Kenton '76*. Levy's works, as one might suspect given his role as a college jazz educator, have been particular favorites of school jazz groups; during my tenure as a graduate student at North Texas, Levy's charts (especially those that had been played and recorded by Kenton) were frequently performed by the lab bands. Kenton, citing his fellow bandleader Ellis as an innovative force in jazz, praises Levy at the start of his performance (and later recording) at the University of Redlands in 1970:

> We have with us a composer that has walked arm in arm all the way with Don Ellis so far, and we have asked him to bring some of his music to us. We're going to ask him to conduct it this evening. Before we introduce the composition, we'd like to introduce him. His name is Hank Levy, from Baltimore, Maryland.[49]

Kenton then explains to the audience the complex, intricate nature of Levy's writing before launching into Levy's composition "Chiapas," which features a shifting metrical structure that is quite difficult to play. Kenton would perform or record over twenty of Levy's pieces during the 1970s until the bandleader's death in 1979.

Did Levy's charts, with their emphasis on odd meters, perhaps serve to provide a sense of racial authenticity for White performers in a manner that was similar to that of Balkan music for some White musicians a decade later? Might the same have been true for listeners who were attracted to Dave Brubeck's odd-meter works in the 1950s? Brubeck, like Kenton, was also a passionate advocate for jazz education, performing (also like Kenton) frequently at college campuses across the country. Did Brubeck, Ellis, Levy, Kenton, and others set out to create a space for "White jazz" within college and university jazz programs? I would suggest, at least on a direct level, that this was probably not the case. But they did not need to be direct or even conscious of such things in order for this to be the end result. By choosing to emphasize certain musical gestures and traditions, this result was, if not inevitable, at least predictable. And as nothing succeeds like success, as the saying goes, it should be no surprise that these issues linger in jazz education to the present day, particularly given the outsized shadow that Stan Kenton cast over the field.

PRIMAL SCREAM: MAYNARD FERGUSON AND JAZZ EDUCATION'S CULT OF VIRTUOSITY[50]

There was a large crowd gathered in the gymnasium at a rural high school in northern New England on a spring evening in April 1989, maybe more than had ever been in that space before for a basketball game or a pep rally. They were there to hear the latest stop on legendary trumpeter Maynard Ferguson's tour with his fusion-driven "High Voltage" combo. High school jazz students from across the region had packed into school buses for the trip, and there was a decided air of excitement and anticipation. Before Ferguson's set, the crowd was treated to an opening act, the host high school's jazz ensemble. A recipient of many awards at the regional and national level, the group's hosting of Ferguson was, in some ways, its crowning achievement to that point. Their director was himself a trumpeter who had grown up idolizing Ferguson, and the ensemble had played numerous arrangements that had been recorded by his band. After winding through a set lasting around a half hour, it was time for the main event. As Ferguson and his band took the stage, a roar went up from the crowd. The members of the high school band got front-row seats, but the real treat had already come when they were joined by the legendary trumpeter to play one of his signature charts, Jay Chattaway's arrangement of "Gonna Fly Now," better known as the theme from the film *Rocky*. As the band raced through the arrangement, Ferguson's trumpet soared overhead in characteristic screeching fashion. When the band finished, Ferguson gave them a deep bow and applause and embraced the director in a bear hug. It was, for these musicians, the greatest gig of their lives.

After the show, one of the members of the band made his way down to the school's Home Economics wing at the other end of the building. Ferguson was encamped inside one of the classrooms. The young musician waited patiently for a glimpse of his idol. Finally, after what seemed like an eternity, he emerged, and the young musician's eyes lit up. Noticing the young man's tuxedo and gig bag slung over his shoulder, Ferguson quickly deduced that this was one of the players in the high school band. He came over, extended a hand to the student, and complimented him on his playing. Then, almost as quickly, he exited through the side door, boarded his tour bus, and rode off into the night, presumably to repeat the whole thing at another school a night or two later.

This story is an important one for me because it is, in fact, my own. On that night, in the hallway outside the sewing room at Nokomis Regional High School in Newport, Maine, I met the musician who had been, through four years of constant rehearsals, solitary practice, freezing road trips on modestly heated school buses, and the development of a premature addiction to coffee, nothing less than my hero, my idol, the musician I would listen to first thing in the morning and as I got ready for bed at night. Ferguson's *MF Horn* was one of the first three CDs I bought when I got a Sony Discman as a Christmas present in 1988, along with a gift certificate to the local Sam Goody's (Miles Davis's *Kind of Blue* and U2's *The Joshua Tree* were the other two). Meeting one's hero, especially at a young age, can be disorienting. When I saw him up close, Ferguson looked older than I'd imagined him to be. I was used to the pictures I saw in magazines or on record jackets or the occasional VHS cassette of a live performance that would come my way, with his wild mop of silver hair dripping sweat, jacket and shirt open to reveal numerous chains and pendants, and most of all, his characteristic swagger and bravado. Yet, in that moment, he seemed like, for lack of a better term, a regular person, not the larger-than-life personality I was used to thinking about.

Age, and many years on the road, will invariably take their toll, and for Ferguson, this was no exception. By the time our paths crossed, he was arguably past the best playing days of his career, though to be sure, he was still a formidable performer and would be for some time to come. But what shaped my mental image of Ferguson were the recordings he made from about 1970 through the early 1980s, when he was at the peak of his career both in terms of his playing and with respect to his impact on the contemporary jazz scene. There were arguably few musicians in jazz who had as much popular appeal as Maynard Ferguson at the time. And yet, his reputation in jazz is somewhat suspect. His engagement with popular music, in particular, has led many "purists" in jazz to dismiss his 1970s work as pandering to the demands of the pop audience. To be fair, there is probably some truth to this; Ferguson did indeed make recordings that were meant to *sell*. But sell they did, and the positionality of his work with respect to his audiences speaks to a number of important issues that impacted jazz education then and now. In the remainder of this section, I'll explore Ferguson's work during this period, and in particular, his relationship to both the jazz-pop divide and the fast-growing jazz education movement. I suggest that Ferguson's success in this period was the result of several interrelated factors: an intense, virtuosic style of performance, an aggressive, physically demonstrative stage manner, an open embrace of pop music and culture, and an appeal to adolescent and young adult men who, like myself, were involved with school jazz programs.

From Hollywood to Millbrook and Beyond

Ferguson was born in Montreal in 1928, the son of two professional musicians. He took up the trumpet at the age of nine and, within a few years, was attracting a good deal of attention in Montreal as well as at the Canadian Broadcasting Corporation (CBC). As a young adult, he had set his sights on joining the band of Stan Kenton, and in 1948, he finally made it across the border, just in time for Kenton to disband his group at the end of the year. The late 1940s were a very challenging time for big bands, and Kenton's organization was certainly no exception. During the year-long hiatus, Ferguson occupied himself with whatever work he could find; most notable in this period are several dates with Boyd Raeburn and Charlie Barnet, two other "progressive" bandleaders who, like Kenton, had the ambition to create what they saw as a more cerebral, intellectually challenging form of jazz. Barnet, in particular, would feature Ferguson in a prominent role, and like Kenton, his band was loud, brash, and brass-centric. His 1949 recording of the standard "All the Things You Are" is perhaps Ferguson's first real showcase on record. Screaming high above the band, Ferguson's playing on this recording would serve as a template for much of his subsequent work.

By January 1950, Kenton had restarted his organization, with Ferguson joining his trumpet section, in the form of his newly expanded "Innovations in Modern Music" orchestra in a concert on January 30. The following month, the group entered the studio for the first of a series of sessions for Capitol Records that would continue late into the year. The resulting album, *Stan Kenton Presents*, thrust Ferguson into the spotlight; among the sides released was a June recording of bandmate and fellow trumpeter Shorty Rogers's composition titled "Maynard Ferguson,"[51] which would catapult the young trumpeter to new heights, figuratively and literally. Over the lush strings of the Innovations orchestra, Ferguson soared into jazz legend, showing himself to be not only adept at high range-playing but also a very capable improviser who was well versed in the contemporary bebop style. "Maynard Ferguson" would become a staple of Kenton's live performances over the course of the next several years; a notable example can be found in Kenton's previously mentioned appearance on *The Ed Sullivan Show* on CBS in December 1950, the bandleader's first appearance on the still-nascent medium. Returning to the standard big band format (and dressed in rather garish matching plaid blazers), Kenton's band powered through three arrangements. The second of these was "Maynard Ferguson"; in introducing the tune, Kenton brought Ferguson out to the front of the stage to be greeted by Sullivan before ripping through Rogers's chart. The middle section, done in a medium up-tempo on the original recording from June, was now blazing fast, allowing Ferguson to fly over the top of the band. Sullivan, usually known for his stoic demeanor, seemed to be quite impressed with the spectacle.

It is, by any account, a remarkable performance, one that shows Ferguson in fine form not only as a trumpeter but also foreshadows his own idiosyncratic stage manner and presence as a bandleader in his own right. Ferguson's affect is very animated compared to the relatively static positioning of most of his bandmates (drummer Shelly Manne is a notable exception). At several points, Ferguson punctuates entrances with a dramatic downbeat motion as if conducting the band with his trumpet. His posture shows a slight backward lean, particularly in the higher range. He often releases notes in dramatic fashion. A good example of this occurs at the transition from the first ballad section to the swing section; upon reaching the high B♭ at the end of the line (on the downbeat of the new tempo), Ferguson seems to jump up slightly as he approaches the note, timing the downbeat to the moment he comes back down. He then pulls the trumpet from his face very abruptly, bouncing his head in time to the new tempo as he prepares for his next entrance. For Ferguson, playing the trumpet seems to be an intensely physical expression, one that is part physiology of brass playing and part bodily performance.

In 1953, Ferguson signed a contract as a player with Paramount Studios that, among other things, restricted his ability to perform live. As a result, he ceased touring with Kenton but would remain with Kenton's recording band during its mid-1950s heyday, contributing to some of the band's best-known work. He would leave Kenton for good in 1956; his last recordings would be made in February of that year in a pair of sessions that would result in one of Kenton's best-known and most highly regarded albums, *Kenton in Hi-Fi*. Throughout his time with Kenton, Ferguson had also made a handful of recordings under his own name. Sessions in 1950 and 1952 featured bands comprised mainly of Kenton veterans, while sessions in 1954 and 1955 featured small groups and an octet. But in 1956, he would step up into a higher profile role as a leader when he joined Morris Levy's Birdland Dream Band; the band's gig at the titular nightclub did not last, but the musicians in this group would go on to become the core of Ferguson's working band through the mid-1960s. While his band may have been overshadowed by figures such as Ellington, Basie, and his old mentor, he remained a visible and relatively popular presence on the jazz scene, recording a number of critically well-received albums and appearing at major jazz festivals and clubs.

All this began to change in the mid-1960s. At some point, Ferguson became acquainted with Timothy Leary, the infamous psychologist who was best known for his fervent advocacy of psychedelic drugs. As Leary recounts in his autobiography, his first encounter with Ferguson was sometime before 1962; in his memoir, Leary recalls meeting Ferguson and his wife Flo:

> Enter Maynard and Flo Ferguson, intrepid ontologists visiting me for the weekend. They were easily persuaded to follow [Michael] Hollingwood out where no other humans had been before. Docilely they swallowed a heaping tablespoon out of the famous mayonnaise jar. Thirty minutes post-launch, [Flo's] face radiated that glow you see in Giotto paintings.[52]

Leary recounts several more encounters with the Fergusons during this period; how deeply they were into LSD is not well documented, but they did, for a time, relocate to Leary's Millbrook estate, as daughter Lisa explains:

> It was at that time [late 1963] that my parents had had a spiritual awakening with psychedelics and made a decision to give up their more materialistic lifestyle, and go on the transformative journey of spiritual "seeking"... the big adventure. This was when they decided to move our family into Tim's Millbrook commune. One of the beautiful things about Millbrook was how much they were all immersed in the study of [E]astern religions and philosophies, because these [E]astern philosophies paralleled exactly what they were all experiencing and learning first-hand during their LSD experiences.[53]

I want to draw attention to Lisa Ferguson's comments about the links between LSD and her parents' "spiritual awakening" and "[immersion] in the study of [E]astern religions and philosophies." Ferguson maintained an active schedule of live performances and recordings through 1964, but by 1965, there was a noticeable drop-off in his professional activities. By 1967, he had moved his family to Madras, India, where he would remain off and on for about two years. He would make occasional live appearances and recordings during this period, but for the most part, he remained somewhat distant from the professional jazz scene. By 1969, Ferguson would return to the scene on a more regular basis. Relocating to England, near Manchester, and with a new contract with Columbia in hand, Ferguson would embark on a new phase of his career, one that would place him at the center of the contemporary jazz world as well as at the center of controversy.

Gonna Fly Now: Ferguson and the Jazz-Pop Divide

Ferguson's popularity throughout the 1960s, and especially the 1970s and 1980s, was largely predicated on the "screech trumpet" concept that he had become known for during his time with Kenton. He became something of, and I want to take care in using this term that it does not sound critical, a *novelty*. This is not to say that playing high notes was Ferguson's only skill; he remained, throughout this period, an exceptionally fine improviser. But it was his extended high range that he was best known for that set him and his band apart in the big band world and that made him an attractive figure of emulation for many young, aspiring brass players, especially young men.

While acoustic jazz largely languished in the 1970s, at least in terms of popular reception in the US, Ferguson enjoyed a good deal of recognition, even fame. Beginning in 1970, he began to make a series of recordings, first with an all-British big band and later with a new band on his return to the US a few years later, that established his unique reputation in the jazz world. The first of these recordings, made with a British band and released in 1970, was titled *MF Horn* (later known as *MF Horn I*, following subsequent releases in the series); the album leaned heavily on arrangements of contemporary pop songs as well as Ferguson's characteristic high range style. Of particular note was Adrian Drover's arrangement of "MacArthur Park," Jimmy Webb's famous (or infamous) hit song, which sees Richard Harris's somewhat wobbly vocal replaced by Ferguson's stratospheric, bravura trumpet. Over the course of the next few years, Ferguson would continue in this manner, recording covers of pop songs and film themes such as Isaac Hayes's theme from *Shaft*, James Taylor's "Fire and Rain" and "Country Road," and Simon and Garfunkel's "Bridge Over Troubled Water," to name a few. Ferguson's pop-oriented recordings sold relatively well, at least enough to keep him in the public eye and, more importantly, in the good graces of the record label.

But in 1977, his trajectory would change radically. In keeping with his practice of covering contemporary popular songs, Ferguson recorded an arrangement by Jay Chattaway of Bill Conti's theme for the recent hit film *Rocky*. "Gonna Fly Now," as the song is known on its own, is among the most iconic theme song/pop song crossovers in American music up to that time. The release of Ferguson's single for "Gonna Fly Now" was noted in a somewhat understated report in *Billboard* from January 1977:

> Columbia Records has released a single—"Gonna Fly Now (Theme from Rocky)"—from the forthcoming album *Conquistador*. This is an appealing, melodic and well-produced song. There is a short but

effective conga and horn break, and the tune sounds like it could have been taken from his last album.[54]

The "last album" mentioned in this passage was Ferguson's *Primal Scream*, which had generated a good deal of critical debate upon its release in 1976 (though the album was recorded in the fall of 1975). *Primal Scream* likely marks the commencement of Ferguson's "disco period," in which the trumpeter made a series of recordings that intentionally forged links to the emerging and increasingly popular disco scene.

Upon *Conquistador*'s release, Columbia began to heavily market both the album and the single. An advertisement that appeared in *Music America Magazine* in May 1977 described the album with typical hyperbole:

> [Ferguson has] continued to redefine the boundaries of progressive music with each successive album. His last album *Primal Scream* became the talk of jazz clubs, discos, and households all over America—earning Maynard the distinction of becoming one of *down beat*'s [sic] top big band artists. Now he's back with *Conquistador*—a new album in which Maynard leaves no barriers unbroken, and every listener amazed. Share the thrill of Maynard's victory.[55]

Conquistador's climb up the *Billboard* charts was illustrated in a post on the Jazz LPs blog, a website devoted to close examinations of jazz recordings with a particular emphasis on chart performance. The post carefully traces the album's move up the charts in 1977 from its first appearance on April 2, where it came in at #159 on *Billboard*'s album charts and #157 on the parallel chart from *Cashbox*. The following week, the album climbed to #121 and #127 respectively, while also entering the bi-weekly *Billboard* jazz album charts at #18. From there, *Conquistador* rose steadily on both charts, cracking the top 100 on *Billboard* on the April 23 chart (when it was also at #3 on the jazz chart). A significant moment in the album's steady ascent was on June 11, when it reached the #1 spot on the jazz chart (and #26 on the main album chart). *Conquistador*'s rise culminated with its climb back to the #22 spot on the main chart two weeks later, on June 25 (dropping to #3 on the jazz chart). Ferguson's next two albums, *New Vintage* from late 1977 and *Carnival* the following year, hewed closely to his disco-infused approach and likewise sold well, although nowhere near as well as *Conquistador*. The "Gonna Fly Now" single, meanwhile, enjoyed similar success, cracking the top 30 on the *Billboard* "Hot 100" chart, a nearly unheard-of feat for a jazz artist (although

Weather Report's recording of "Birdland" also hit the top 30 the same year; true to form, Ferguson included a version of "Birdland" on *Carnival*).

While Ferguson's recordings were attracting a sizeable audience, critics were decidedly split on his work in this period. One review described *Conquistador* as "wretched excess,"[56] while another referred to it as "immaculately performed drivel."[57] Ferguson's live performances did not fare much better among critics; writing for the *New York Times* in 1978, Ken Emerson derided Ferguson's "showboating screeches and whinnies [that] have long borne only a marginal relationship to jazz," noting that his "antics please crowds but not critics."[58] For Ferguson, such critical treatment seemed to have little impact. In a 1976 profile in *The Christian Science Monitor*, Ferguson—perhaps foreshadowing the debates over his music to come over the next few years—places the emphasis squarely on those who are listening: "We're into today's music a lot . . . . Kids identify with the rhythms we get into. Yet our approach is a mixture . . . . It is jazz, it is rock, and it is what pop represents: popularity!"[59] Here Ferguson makes a specific connection between his band's engagement with popular idioms and the increasingly significant role those young listeners were playing in his audience. And this should probably not be a surprise; throughout the 1970s, he had worked to cultivate a loyal audience among students in school jazz programs. Kim Ferguson, the trumpeter's daughter and manager, notes this in a 1984 profile of Ferguson for the *Boston Globe*:

> Music education in the schools has kept it alive and so strong for Maynard . . . . He's become a hero in the schools. There are so many stage bands and marching bands across the country and music education has grown so much that the jazz lovers of yesterday have become today's music educators . . . . We're on the road nine months out of the year . . . and 70 percent of the shows are in junior high schools, high schools and colleges. Most of those concerts are promoted by the band directors at the schools. The parents bring in food for our band members. We carry our own sound, and the high school musicians are the stage crew.[60]

Ferguson himself spoke directly to the centrality of jazz education to his success. Leonard Feather writes in a 1977 profile that "Ferguson credits his chart vaulting primarily to the upsurge in jazz education. 'We have to be very thankful for the 30,000 stage bands at schools and colleges, and for the music directors who make sure that big bands are not conceived in terms of a nostalgia trip—after all, *how can you impose nostalgia on a 14-year-old?*"[61] I'd like to focus on this final passage, which I've highlighted here. Ferguson seems acutely aware of young listeners, whom he recognizes as a core component of his audience. They needed to be met where they were, and where they were was often as musical consumers who were deeply connected to contemporary popular music. For Ferguson, his pop-based pieces could stand side by side with a "pure jazz" work such as the band's arrangement of "Airegin."[62] They come for "Rocky," but they stay for Sonny Rollins.

The Ferguson Effect: Virtuosity, Identity, and the Spectacle of Excess

Pop songs are one thing. But for Ferguson, the connection that young musicians seemed to feel with him might flow from something else, namely, a demonstrative, physical approach to playing the trumpet, which translated into a signature stage presence and persona. Ferguson's style of performance is based first and foremost on his startlingly virtuosic facility in the high range of the trumpet. But the impact he had on audiences goes beyond the nature of the sound itself. John Seery provides a vivid description of what we could call the Ferguson Effect:

> [Every] Maynard song features Maynard working up to and eventually hitting a high G above triple C.[63] When he gets there, it is a sonic spectacle to behold. The audience roars in approval, and Maynard milks the applause for all it is worth. Usually Maynard appears in concerts in an orange full-body jumpsuit with a scarf around his neck, and he jumps to center stage displaying an innovation that he introduced into the musical world which he calls the pelvic thrust. When Maynard hits his high note, simultaneously he arches his back and juts out his pelvis, presenting it to the audience as a visual gift of sorts. Maynard is a man's man.[64]

In Ferguson's performance aesthetic, instrumental virtuosity becomes a spectacle, both in sonic and visual terms. This idea is not without a good deal of precedent. Commenting on virtuosity's effect on audiences in the nineteenth century, Hoppe et al. make clear the connections between virtuoso performance and particular invocations of power:

> The appearance and performance of the *virtuoso* is stage-managed as a real event striving for a specific *effect* on the listeners: the *effect* of

a "*virtuosic* moment" at a particular performance needs the perception of an *audience* which—through its reception—transforms the event into a virtuosic one and the performer into a virtuoso. At the same time, the virtuoso has a certain power by creating sounds which capture the audience.... There is a reciprocal power dependence between both the audience and the virtuoso ... [the] prominent position of the virtuoso performer in the spatial arrangement which puts his expressive and emotive manner of performance and his own "private" feelings on public display invites the audience of the early nineteenth century to a hitherto unknown identification, and forces them at the same time to give up their personal feelings, to surrender with all their senses and submissively concentrate on the listening event.[65]

The reference here to the early nineteenth century, of course, conjures up images of the legendary virtuoso performers of the period, most notably Nicolo Paganini and Franz Liszt. Known for their exuberant, charismatic performance styles, to say nothing of their unparalleled virtuosity, Paganini and Liszt stunned audiences with abilities that were often described in otherworldly terms. Paganini's aura was linked to supposed associations with dark, supernatural forces. With respect to Liszt, his performances in the 1840s were sometimes described as having produced a profound response, especially in young women. Dana Gooley, writing in his book *The Virtuoso Liszt*, recounts these appearances as an example of what was referred to as "Lisztomania," a particular effect that was caused by exposure to Liszt's performances, thought by some observers to be the function of electrical disturbances brought forth by his astonishing technique.[66]

The relationship between virtuosity and masculinity has been explored in depth, both in musicology and in its allied disciplines. Ivan Raykoff points to a direct connection, noting that the word "virtuoso" itself stems from the Latin term for "man" or "hero." Raykoff's description of Liszt, who is characterized as "virile—masculine, potent, vigorous, forceful, physically dynamic," could easily be used to describe Ferguson, at least from the perspective of his audience.[67] In applying this to educational contexts, Clare Hall notes that virtuosity's associations with masculinity can serve as both a reification and a disruption of traditional gender roles: boys engaged in activities that are traditionally identified as "feminine" often can employ virtuosity to mitigate such a reception.[68] Ferguson's style and manner similarly enabled adolescent boys to engage in a nonsports activity that was still physical and athletic and deemed to be "masculine," at least within the context of school music programs; his assertive virtuosity became a model, musically and socially, for countless young men (I do not exclude my adolescent self from that cohort).

While Ferguson's playing might not have led to crowds of young women being overcome by the intense energy of the moment, his virtuosic style does have important connections to physicality, notions of energy and power, and an implicit genderedness that have resonances with other accounts of a particular "virtuoso effect." In jazz performance, artists often orbit around the two particular poles. On the one hand, virtuoso performance is often highly prized as a sign of artistic achievement; at the same time, musicians are sometimes assessed with respect to subtleties of performance, of interpretive nuance that is seen as distinct from technical facility. Miles Davis and John Coltrane, standing side by side while recording "So What" in early 1959, provide a particularly striking example. Davis's solo is characterized by an understated and introspective approach that—at least in terms of trumpet technique—is relatively simple. Coltrane's solo, meanwhile, is squarely based on his "sheets of sound" approach, featuring startlingly dense, virtuosic passagework. Yet with respect to the reactions of audiences, both trajectories might be seen as leading to a similar goal: the creation of a type of *out-of-body*ness, a sense that the performer is striving to reach a space that is beyond the realm of everyday lived experience.

As Ferguson noted in a *Christian Science Monitor* feature, "I approach the instrument very physically."[69] This is illustrated in an appearance at a performance and clinic at the Canadian Stage Band Festival in 1977, where he offered a detailed explanation of his approach and the physical nature of his playing. Comparing himself to a weightlifter, he explains to the audience, comprised largely of young musicians:

> It's important that I talk about the particular technique that works for me. Now when you watch the way I do this, compare me with any good weightlifter you've ever watched. If you give the weightlifter my trumpet and ask him to lift it [Ferguson lifts his trumpet over his head], he'll just keep right on talking to you because there's no energy demand. But as soon as there's a heavy challenge on each side of this, then all of a sudden, he has to pay attention to his air stream, his air power, and coordinate all of his body. Which means first of all he's got to plant his feet [Ferguson demonstrates] so that they're equally balanced, right? There's aren't many one-legged weightlifters [laughs] that aren't in the hospital. So, when we talk about me in relation to all that, because of course a weightlifter with weight has to do this, right?

[Ferguson leans back and pushes the trumpet overhead as if it were a barbell] And that's the classic pose.[70]

This is a familiarity here with statements about virtuosity that emphasize skill and athleticism. David VanderHamm writes, drawing upon Bruno Nettl:

> This model conceives of virtuosity as superlative skill, implying measurability and competition. Bruno Nettl equates the "athletic view of music" with "the expectation of virtuosity," and although he attributes this attitude to "lovers of the Western classical tradition," he admits that ethnomusicologists also hold virtuosity as a value and have often chosen to study traditions that seemed to require the most impressive musical technique.[71]

Ferguson proceeds to demonstrate the connection of his physical approach to the production of sound, working up from a low C (concert B♭) over the course of an octave. At this point, Ferguson notes:

> The first slight energy demand, you'll notice that I start to bend my knees a little. That's the first thing to bring in, all your back muscles ... once again, it's just your way of reminding yourself that you're going to use more and more of your body, and more and more of your air stream, *not* what everybody seems to want to do, more and more hand pressure and more and more pinching of the lips.[72]

At this point, Ferguson steps back from the microphone, resets the trumpet to his embouchure, and begins working up from middle C (concert B♭), climbing to G, and then to a high C. As he does so, he arches backward in a pronounced manner, "bouncing" a bit on the attack of each note. Ferguson continues with a more pronounced attack on a high G before concluding after a brief pause with a double C, which he signals with his trademark drop of the horn at the point of attack. After sustaining this pitch for several seconds, Ferguson finally rips the horn away from his mouth with a dramatic open-arms gesture, and the crowd responds with enthusiastic applause. Ferguson's demonstration is both clinical and visceral, appealing to both the audience's intellect, with a detailed explanation of his approach and the physical spectacle of his sound and stage presence. In this sense, mind and body are unified, an idea that resonates deeply with Ferguson's own spiritual practices.

Much of the reaction to virtuosity on the part of Ferguson's audience comes from a sense of transcendence, of bearing witness to something that seems beyond reach. A common reaction among my peers to hearing Ferguson's high range-playing in my youth was laughter, not because we thought there was anything particularly humorous but because it was, in some ways, ridiculous, a spectacle of excess that is simultaneously absurd and wondrous. David VanderHamm notes the idea of virtuosic excess, using a similar comparison to sports:

> Although measurability is central to much of the discourse of virtuosity as sport, the reason for exultation in viewing sports often has little to do with its measurable characteristics. When a basketball player leaps high into the air and displays some kind of acrobatic skill while dunking the ball, the crowd will go wild. But they are not cheering simply because the act results in two points, nor because of the exact height that the player reached. What is valued here is not the measurable outcome of a properly executed goal, but the unmeasured, indeed the unnecessary, effort and skill deployed. The difficulty in understanding virtuosity, then, is that different ends and values—some easily measurable, some not—exist alongside one another.[73]

As Ferguson's explanation to the workshop attested, his approach was not some well-guarded secret; it was, in fact, widely understood and emulated by young brass players (as even a glance at the hornline of a contemporary drum and bugle corps will demonstrate). His statements about breathing support, power, and posture are well known and widely disseminated. And yet, there is still the sense of awe of both the spectacle of excessive "skill" and its "social meaning."[74]

Brass playing can certainly be a physically intensive activity. Players and teachers spend a great deal of time discussing and debating the physical aspects of playing various brass instruments. The idea of learning "correct" ways of playing involving posture, jaw placement, embouchure, breathing, and so forth occupies a significant portion of pedagogical interactions. Let me give a particular example. As a high school trombonist, one area of my playing which preoccupied me was playing in the higher range of the instrument (which I'm sure was due in part to Ferguson's influence). As was the case with many inexperienced players, I would tend to "tense up" when I was trying to play higher notes; unfortunately, this is more or less the opposite of what one should do. One particular technique I would employ was to position my tongue high in my mouth, which resulted in an airstream that was more focused, which in turn "pushed" on the inside of my lips and embouchure. This practice is a "quick fix"—it allows one to hit higher notes but at the expense of fullness of sound and tone. When I went to my first trombone lesson as a freshman in college, my teacher, a highly experienced and well-respected classical trombonist, quickly recognized this and began the process of deconstructing and rebuilding my entire approach to playing. He worked with me to lower my tongue position, to play in a more relaxed manner, and to avoid the tendency to "tense up." What I noticed after a few weeks was that my core sound did indeed improve; it was a bigger, warmer sound than I had been used to. The tradeoff was that it cut about half an octave off my upper range because the muscles that *are* required for higher-range playing had not been fully developed. It took me over a year to finally get to a point where I was comfortably playing in the high range again. But I was, without question, a stronger player after having undergone this process. It was very hard work, and at times it was extremely frustrating, but ultimately it paid off. And more to the point, it was a process that is very common among younger players who move on to more advanced professional-level study.

Why do so many young players learn "bad technique" as part of their development? There are, I think, a few reasons for this. One is simply that many high school-aged players simply don't have the resources, time, or interest to engage in focused private study. In my own case, I did have the opportunity to work with a very fine local teacher and player, but our interactions were somewhat haphazard. But another factor is, I think, the nature of school ensembles. What matters most in some of these contexts is the end result. If a lead trombone part goes to a high D♭, then the lead trombonist needs to be able to hit that note. There is a good deal of pressure that is applied, and I'm not simply referring here to what's going on inside someone's mouth. Particular methods and "tricks" which can be used to achieve that goal, regardless of whether they are a function of "good technique," are very tempting for younger players, not to mention their ensemble directors.

Is Ferguson's physical approach an example of such a "trick" or "crutch"? Is it another shortcut to the upper range? There are those who would answer this question with a firm "yes." It is certainly not in alignment with what might be regarded as the "correct" way to play. But does it matter, in the final analysis? Probably not.[75] The point is that Ferguson's idiosyncratic approach, conceptualized and performed as a cogent, fully theorized performance practice, is understood in a visceral way by many of his fans. They *feel* his performances. In a segment on Billy Taylor's jazz program on National Public Radio, Ferguson and Taylor discuss the physical nature of his playing: "Maynard reminds musicians that the craft is physical as well as mental and emotional. Ferguson puts his whole body into playing; he tells Dr. [Billy] Taylor, 'when I'm playing correctly, my socks are soaking wet when I'm through.'"[76]

What interests me the most about this is that for Ferguson, physicality is not simply a means to an end, a way to get into the "screech" range. It is, rather, a performance in and of itself. We can see this in an appearance on *The Dinah Shore Show* in 1976. Dressed in a white leisure suit not unlike that made famous by John Travolta in *Saturday Night Fever*, Ferguson performs an arrangement of the Beatles' "Something." As Shore sings the final passages of the song, Ferguson plays a blistering cadenza, culminating in a trademark shake figure with his trumpet in his right hand while he conducts the band with his left. At the end of the performance, Ferguson conducts the band through a concluding rubato passage, ending with an abrupt lowering of the trumpet from a raised angle to a relatively level position as if signaling a downbeat. From here, Ferguson arpeggiates an open intervallic pattern from high C to high F, then finally to a loud, sustained double C; here, he repeats the downbeat gesture, physically preparing himself for the effort required to sustain the note. After holding the note for approximately five seconds, during which Shore first seems to chuckle in disbelief before turning to the audience, Ferguson abruptly rips the horn away from his face, throwing both arms into the air in a triumphant "touchdown" gesture, followed by an exaggerated cutoff.[77]

Such ostentatious displays of instrumental skill are not unlike other kinds of virtuosic displays. Overt (or perhaps overdone) virtuosity has long had its critics and detractors, and the arguments they put forth have, in some cases, a striking resemblance to contemporary voices on this point. Writing over a century ago, J. N. Burk suggests of ballet dancers that "[p]eople are getting more and more inclined to yawn at those unhuman creatures in pink tights that, with a superlative skill acquired by life-long practice, perform balancing feats which are entirely inane and uninteresting."[78] Extending these arguments to music, Burk continues:

> In that more pretentious world of the concert-halls, which maintains a more hushed and dignified sense of its own importance, there are acrobats, too, acrobats of the piano and violin, with a remarkable skill acquired in exactly the same manner, but the magic spell of culture calls them "virtuosi," and their skill, "technique," with the help of which distinguished passwords the same human need for diversion goes under the name of high art. The most essential difference between the two forms of entertainment is that the one public is disillusioned as to the tricks, and looks elsewhere for something not so entirely devoid of sense as skill for skill's sake, while the other public flocks to the lure of billboards and world renown, pays enormous sums, and

beholds, in puerile wonderment and delight, feats which dazzle, and leave in their wake little more than a tingle of stupefaction.[79]

Burk also cites what he refers to as a "physiological ruse" in concert performance, in which solo artists play

> ... cadenzas of scales, arpeggios, glissandi, or harmonics, while the great orchestra sits as patiently as may be with their instruments idle, and ready to lend volume to a closing flourish when it is all over. It is not at all unlike the other acrobats' way of erecting a final symmetrical structure of arms and legs, shooting off two pistols, and unfurling an American flag with their feet, that the audience, both awake and asleep, may be aroused by patterns, patriotism, and noise, to reactionary applause.[80]

But virtuosity has its proponents and defenders. One argument often invoked in favor of overtly virtuosic performance is that it forms a connection between the artist and their audience. Sudip Bose advances just such an argument in a piece published in 2005 in *The American Scholar*. Bose writes that the disdain for virtuosity goes hand in hand with the shift to a more "serious" approach to the world of classical performance in which the interpretation of the composition is of paramount importance:

> The virtues of virtuosic music began to lose their appeal in the second half of the 20th century. At one time a violinist could fill an entire program with flashy numbers and bonbons; the personality of the artist mattered most, even more than what the composer had written on the page. The idea was to play to the crowd, to make people swoon and cheer, even sweat. But by the 1960s, such recitals were out of fashion. Seriousness was the order of the day; fidelity to a musical score would later become sacred .... Ours is a more serious musical culture because of this attitude, but it is a bit poorer, too. What I am beginning to realize is that virtuosity is not something distanced from or subservient to art, but a legitimate expression of the musical impulse in and of itself.[81]

One might question some of Bose's conclusions, namely that a canonical view of the sanctity of a composition is a function of the late twentieth century (as opposed to taking hold much earlier). Nevertheless, there are, I think, some important considerations to take from this. Whatever else virtuosity may represent, it is generally a crowd-pleaser, and in Ferguson's case, crowds were certainly pleased even if critics were not. For Bose, the disdain for virtuosic display among some critics runs in parallel with a broader disdain for music that elicits certain reactions and that connects with an audience in certain ways. Too much virtuosity risks tainting the purity of musical expression. The same might be said, and indeed frequently was, about pop music.

Reflecting on Ferguson's career shortly after his death in 2006, David Von Drehle writes that "adolescence and masculinity" were two major factors driving Ferguson's appeal:

> Ferguson lit up thousands of young horn players, most of them boys, with pride and excitement. In a world often divided between jocks and band nerds, Ferguson crossed over, because he approached his music almost as an athletic event. On stage, he strained, sweated, heaved and roared. He nailed the upper registers like Shaq nailing a dunk or Lawrence Taylor nailing a running back—and the audience reaction was exactly the same: the guttural shout, the leap to their feet, the fists in the air. We cheered Maynard as a gladiator, a combat soldier, a prizefighter, a circus strongman—choose your masculine archetype.[82]

Von Drehle's description resonates with Krin Gabbard's discussion of jazz trumpet playing and masculine sexuality in his provocatively titled essay "Signifyin(g) the Phallus." Ostensibly concerned with representations of the trumpet in Spike Lee's *Mo' Better Blues*, Gabbard cites Ferguson as a "trumpet jock" who contrasts with "the Signifyin(g) black artist" and that Ferguson "simply plays as high as possible in order to establish his power unself-consciously [*sic*] and without irony."[83] Gabbard's description of Ferguson is, admittedly, somewhat dismissive, but there is a certain truth to what he writes, at least in terms of Ferguson's reception among his core audience and critics alike. Power was, in Ferguson's own description, a key element of his approach to brass playing. Gabbard extends this idea in his subsequent work on jazz and race in cinema, writing about the 1955 film *Blackboard Jungle*, remembered today primarily for popularizing Bill Haley and the Comets' "Rock Around the Clock." Gabbard describes one particular scene in the film in which a "nerdy" teacher in the midst of a "masculinity crisis" proposes playing Kenton's "Invention for Guitar and Trumpet" for his students; Ferguson's playing on the recording is, in Gabbard's description, "hyperphallic."[84] While my peers and I did not necessarily regard Ferguson or his music as specifically being "phallic," much of this tracks with my own experiences with (and admittedly, reactions to) Ferguson's music as a teenage jazz student. Listening to Ferguson's recordings on a long bus trip to a performance or festival would elicit excitement, astonishment, awe, even reverence from my fellow (generally male) Ferguson fans. Ferguson gave us what we wanted: music that we knew (as in many cases we had played it ourselves in our school ensembles) combined with a sense of transcendent spectacle.

One final anecdote underscores this point. Over the course of these same three albums—*Conquistador* (1977), *New Vintage* (1977), and *Carnival* (1978)—Ferguson made a trio of recordings of themes from prominent science fiction works: the themes from *Star Trek*, *Star Wars*, and *Battlestar Galactica* respectively. Ferguson's cover of the "Trek" theme (from an arrangement by Jay Chattaway) was, like his cover of "Gonna Fly Now," based squarely on disco, which was on its way to dominating the pop music charts. Ferguson's showcase comes in the final minute and a half, with the trumpeter shooting into the high register over a propulsive Latin disco beat. With Ferguson's recording of the *Star Trek* theme hitting hi-fi systems around the country at almost exactly the same moment that *Star Wars* was beginning its takeover of the box office, a cover of John Williams's epic theme for the film would seem to be a logical choice for his next album. Recorded in July 1977, *New Vintage* largely followed the basic script of Ferguson's previous album, with its combination of covers and arrangements of jazz classics; again, Jay Chattaway would provide most of the arrangements. Leading off the album is his version of the *Star Wars* theme, which follows a similar pattern as the previous arrangement for *Star Trek*; given its proximity to the release of the film, the arrangement was quite popular as a 45rpm single release, while Chattaway's arrangement was published and widely played by school jazz groups.

Following a similar script, Ferguson's next album, *Carnival*, appeared at about the same time as the premiere of Glenn Larson's *Battlestar Galactica* on ABC in 1978. A number of television programs would appear in the wake of *Star Wars* that sought to capitalize on the film's massive success. For example, NBC would attempt to revive the Buck Rogers franchise in 1979. But none of these generated more discussion, or more controversy, than *Battlestar Galactica*. Following the exploits of a "rag-tag" fleet of human survivors of a devastating war with the robotic Cylons, *Galactica* faced allegations of plagiarizing the *Star Wars* universe from the very beginning. Similarities to *Star Wars* could not, it seemed, rescue the series from derivative plotting and writing, and the show was canceled after one season. But the premiere of *Galactica* would provide yet another opportunity for Ferguson to explore the world of sci-fi. With an arrangement by Nick Lane (also a trombonist with the band), Ferguson's *Galactica* theme may be the most unusual of these recordings. Among the odd features is the responsorial exhortation of "Galactica" by a group of backup singers preceding the introduction of the main melody. Ferguson's *Galactica* theme remains today something of a curiosity among Ferguson fans who are not prepared to criticize their idol but still find the recording to be rather odd.

Considering Ferguson's popularity among young men in school jazz groups and the similarly situated target audiences for popular sci-fi, we may ask: was the decision to record arrangements of the theme songs to three of the most popular science fiction franchises of the time a coincidence? At the risk of engaging in some speculation, I would suggest that it was not. I can speak to this a bit anecdotally from my own experience as a Ferguson acolyte in the 1980s. In my own world, the overlap between Ferguson-loving high school jazz players and "Trekkies" was fairly substantial. Jazz band and sci-fi were both outlets for students whose identities perhaps did not align with the stereotypical All-American image of the football or basketball star. However, I would also add that these spaces were not only overwhelmingly male but also overwhelmingly White. Both sci-fi and jazz education have historically had difficulties with inclusion, and the present discussion is certainly no exception. Ferguson's band was, like that of his mentor Stan Kenton, composed almost exclusively of White musicians (with some notable exceptions). So too were jazz education programs, particularly since the early 1970s; more robust and widespread among White-majority suburban schools, all-White school jazz ensembles were all too common from junior high to college level. Similarly, women have found both jazz education and sci-fi communities to be often unwelcoming spaces, as has been well documented elsewhere. These are legacies whose effects are still being felt today. In particular, Ferguson's extroverted style resonated with a particularly performative masculinity not unlike that of guitar-centric rock bands of the day. Though not hyper-sexualized in the same manner as artists like, say, Gene Simmons or Ted Nugent, Ferguson's brass playing was very often interpreted in terms of stereotypically masculine qualities: extroversion, power, forcefulness, aggression, and a pronounced physical demonstrativeness, often placed in direct opposition to tropes of "playing like a girl." And this might be the most ironic legacy of Ferguson's dabbling with sci-fi; in an effort to cater to the core audience for his music, Ferguson may have, in retrospect, contributed to an even greater sense of exclusion in jazz education programs, centering young White men with, if I may be pardoned for using this expression, a laser-like focus.

It is certain that the immense popularity of Ferguson's band had a profound influence on jazz education in the 1970s and 1980s. We can hear this from a musical perspective as the charts played by his band would very often find their way into the rehearsal folders of many school jazz groups. But what of the more intangible influences? When a White jazz student saw Ferguson's band, they very likely saw themselves reflected in the band's membership. But would a young Black student have the same reaction? Would they, looking at an all or mostly White group, feel the same kind of kinship? Would they take as readily to Ferguson's music? While Ferguson's influence as a musician is clear and quite easily observed, the more subtle message that was sent by Ferguson, Kenton, by the bands from North Texas and similarly situated programs was that school jazz was a "White thing." I'm quite sure that Ferguson never intended to send such a message (and indeed, Ferguson himself enjoyed close relationships with jazz musicians across the racial spectrum). But intent is not really at issue here as much as impact. When we observe that school jazz groups tended to be disproportionately populated by White male students, we need not go far to find an explanation as to why nor to understand its legacy.

Chapter 4

UNDERSTANDING JAZZ EDUCATION'S "RACE PROBLEM"

INTRODUCTION

In the previous chapter, we examined case studies in which two White jazz artists with close ties to jazz education and learning are centered. I am not unaware of the irony that this represents within the broader context of jazz learning, especially in consideration of long-standing debates and discourses with respect to racial representation in the field. Simply put, jazz education has been, for most of its history as an institutional entity, largely associated with White educators and students and housed in White-majority schools, colleges, and universities. Everyone in the field, it seems, is aware of this, yet it remains a topic of much contention. A recent exchange over the seventy-fifth anniversary of my alma mater's storied jazz program provides an illustrative example. In its February 2022 issue, *DownBeat* published a brief feature by Frank Alkyer recounting the anniversary of the UNT program.[1] Typical of such works, it was a general, more or less celebratory essay, not delving into significant historical detail nor into any terribly contentious topics. The following May, the magazine published a letter from Tracy McMullan, a saxophonist and jazz scholar who is a professor at Bowdoin College in Maine and herself a UNT alum. Taking exception to *DownBeat's* characterization of the program and in no small measure with the legacy of the program itself, McMullen is unsparing in her criticism, writing, "If *DownBeat* is committed to recognizing that Black Lives Matter (and I will presume that it is), then the magazine needs to tell the truth about jazz history. The jazz program at North Texas began when the school was a whites-only, Jim Crow-segregated college."[2] She continues, "The segregated nature of North Texas supported a jazz curriculum and method tailored to white men's perspective and comfort. This university professor would argue that the dearth of Black students and women in jazz programs today traces back to this segregated lineage."[3]

McMullen articulated a number of long-held complaints about the role (or lack thereof) of women and students of color in the field; such ideas were commonly expressed even during my time there, which was shortly before McMullen attended. Her letter solicited a response, published in the July 2022 issue, from drummer and long-time UNT faculty member Ed Soph, himself an alum of the program in the 1960s. Soph takes issue with many of McMullen's points. In particular, he bristles at the claim of "a jazz curriculum and method tailored to white men's perspective and comfort."[4] Soph also emphasizes the opposition that the jazz program faced in its early years from classical faculty as well as the student-centered nature of the program under Leon Breeden. He ends pointedly: "You do a great disservice to a program that was and continues to be progressive and tolerant and welcoming."[5] Whether Soph is referring to *DownBeat* or McMullen by "you" is not clear; most likely, it's both. I address this dust-up at length because it stands in some ways for the broader discussion of race (and gender as well) in jazz education. Critiques are launched, defenses are erected, and all too often, little changes on the ground. A significant challenge in this debate is that it is often waged in the arenas of emotion and perception rather than with objective information. Emotion and perception are powerful forces for guiding social action, and I have no desire to discount them, but institutional change often requires something more concrete. One of the biggest obstacles to changing the contours of this debate has been the lack of an easily accessible, easily comprehensible set of data that demonstrates the very kinds of inequities to which McMullen and many others refer. Let me try, in my own abjectly amateur role as a statistician, to attempt a modest rectification.

One of the most profound positive contributions of the paving of the information superhighway is that raw numerical statistics and data are remarkably more accessible than they have been at any other point in our history. Take as an example the website called "Data USA," a joint venture between the accounting firm Deloitte, MIT, and Datawheel, a company devoted to the dissemination of data on the web. Wikipedia describes Data USA as "a free platform that allows users to collect, analyze, and visualize shared U.S. government data,"[6] and indeed, this basic description generally gets to the heart of what the platform does. Data USA facilitates access to a mind-boggling array of statistics emerging from government databases related to nearly every conceivable topic. This includes, as luck would have it, jazz studies.

I came upon the Data USA report for jazz studies quite by accident while engaged in one of my regular internet searches for a topic that I'm confident was not related to statistics on jazz studies. My surprise, then, upon landing on this page, was even more pronounced than it might have otherwise been. Drawn from US Department of Education annual statistical surveys of colleges and universities throughout the United States, the data presented for jazz studies reveals some interesting things about the field. The page begins with some basic data collected between 2012 and 2019 concerning the relative size of programs and features a rough ranking of private and public schools. But what is by far of greatest interest here are the statistics concerning the awarding of degrees and program completion, which are further broken down by demographic categories, including race and gender. From this data, we can see, for example, that between 2012 and 2019, students who identify as Black consistently earned less than 10 percent of all jazz degrees awarded; the highest percentage during this period came in 2013 when 9.28 percent of all jazz degrees awarded in the US went to Black students. The lowest such percentage during this period was in 2016 when the percentage was 5.79 percent. In general, Black students during this period earned between 7 and 8 percent of jazz degrees. Meanwhile, at only one point during this period (2016) did White students comprise less than half of all jazz degrees; in general, White students could be expected to earn somewhere between 50 to 60 percent, although the last few years of this stretch of time saw figures closer to the 50 percent mark. Other categories in the reporting of this data problematize these figures a bit. For example, one category, "non-resident alien," makes no reference to race; some of these might be White students from Europe, while others could be Black students from the Caribbean, still others from Japan, and so on. Hispanic/Latin students likewise are not aligned with particular racial identities, despite the fact that some might also identify as Black or White. Nevertheless, one must acknowledge that the disparity between White and Black students does indeed seem to be quite profound, with White students outnumbering their Black counterparts by a factor of seven or eight, exceeding the factor in the general population of roughly five to one. But as jazz is a musical form that has grown largely from Black communities and pioneered largely by Black performers, one might expect such disparities to be narrower.

This admittedly brief and surface-level foray into statistics is important, I think, because it demonstrates that claims about Black students being underrepresented in jazz studies are not simply assumptions; the data would seem to support the contention that this is real, and it is persistent. What would a "racially balanced" jazz education look like? Should it reflect the population as a whole? Or should it be expected that more Black students would be present in such programs, given the cultural history of the music? The answers to such questions are the topic of fierce debate. But a solid foundation from which to proceed with such work is necessary; statistics such as these might well provide the basis from which efforts can finally begin in earnest. Statistics are a valuable tool in the reorientation of institutional systems, and if my brief wade into the numbers helps move things along even a modest amount, then I will consider that to be a success. But what happens in the meantime? Or more to the point, what *has* happened in the meantime? What kinds of efforts and initiatives have emerged to address and correct these problems?

The present chapter will attempt to address these questions. In the first part of this discussion, I examine the stories of the Kashmere High School and Malcolm X College jazz bands, focusing on their experiences in the world of school jazz contests in 1972. Both groups were imbued with the spirit and conviction of the Black Power movement, and both institutions had deep links to the surrounding communities. The experiences of these students and teachers in engaging jazz education's historically White institutions stand as an important moment in the field's history, coming at precisely the same time that the Black Power movement was arguably at its zenith. In the subsequent section, I examine the development of the Essentially Ellington program. Under the leadership of Jazz at Lincoln Center and its director Wynton Marsalis, Essentially Ellington has grown into the most visible and prestigious interscholastic jazz competition in the US, attracting entrants from across the country. After an extensive process of screening recorded entries, twelve finalist bands are selected to travel to New York to compete in the final round of competition. I posit that Essentially Ellington's growth has, in large measure, served as a counternarrative and corrective to a jazz education system that was seen as being dominated by White teachers and students, to say nothing of big band composers and arrangers, a fact that was readily apparent at existing festivals and contests through the 1990s. The centering of Ellington in this endeavor serves to ground the program historically, aesthetically, and philosophically within the Black experience in America, an idea that is at the core of JALC's overall mission. At the same time, the program must be situated within the context of the place of JALC—and Marsalis—as highly visible and contentious entities within the contemporary jazz scene. For some critics, the program is simply another manifestation of JALC's markedly conservative aesthetic but aimed more directly at a younger and more malleable audience and with decidedly mixed results.

CRASHING THE STAGE (BAND): WHITE BANDS, BLACK BANDS, AND JAZZ CONTESTS THROUGH THE 1970S

Before the decline of the steel industry in the US began in earnest in the 1970s, Gary, Indiana, experienced something of a boom. A historical magnet for migrants in the preceding decades, due in part to the significant job opportunities afforded by the GaryWorks and other mills as well as its proximity to Chicago, Gary was, by the early 1970s, becoming one of the most prominent "majority-minority" cities in the country. Gary's status in contemporaneous Black culture was such that its demographic identity was immortalized in Parliament's classic recording "Chocolate City." George Clinton's shoutout to Gary, coming in 1975, was certainly influenced by events during the previous few years. None of these would be more important nor more vital to Gary's place in the Black Power movement than its hosting of the National Black Political Convention in 1972. Attracting in excess of 10,000 attendees, the NBPC's purpose was to address the relative lack of political power held by African Americans and to develop strategies for continued action to redress this. The convention would release a document that became known as the Gary Declaration, which outlined significant challenges facing Black communities around the country and served as something of a blueprint for Black political action arguably to the present day. The spirit of the Gary Declaration can be perhaps best summarized in one particular phrase: "We must seize the time, for the time is ours."[7] This philosophy would also be the impetus for a number of changes in American higher education. The rise of the Black Power movement coincided with the creation of the first academic programs in Black Studies, beginning in 1968 at San Francisco State University. Other programs would follow suit in colleges and universities across the country. Similar developments occurred with respect to the study of Black music. Most notable of these was likely the establishment of the Black Music Center at Indiana University; jazz studies director David Baker was deeply involved with its founding and early programming.[8]

It is, I would suggest, not an accident that such developments occurred in parallel with the growth of jazz education, positioned (often grudgingly) as a way in which schools of music could diversify their curricula and programming. But these developments too often occurred within the context of musical institutions in which people of color were still vastly underrepresented, a problem that, as noted previously, is stubbornly persistent. The same year that the NBPC was held in Gary, two student jazz groups—one from a high school in Houston, the other from a community college in Chicago—would make their own particular contributions to the fight against White-dominated cultural spaces. The Kashmere High School Stage Band and the Malcolm X College African American Jazz Ensemble would burst into what was commonly regarded as a White space, namely, the worlds of competitive high school and college jazz band festivals. In both cases, these bands interrupted a long process of exclusion, going precisely where they were not necessarily wanted, not understood, and most certainly not expected.

The school jazz band movement had grown considerably by the early 1970s, as explained by Charles "Chuck" Suber, the former *DownBeat* publisher who took a leading role in both documenting and developing jazz education in the 1950s and 1960s. In one of his numerous essays and articles on jazz in schools, Suber notes in a 1962 piece in *Music Journal* that "6,000 high school stage bands" are set to begin the new school year, while "as many as 1,500 additional stage bands will be newly organized."[9] This substantial growth, according to Suber, was a direct result of "a series of chain reactions stemming from a vacuum," as he told the *New York Times* in 1964:

> The vacuum was produced by the almost complete disappearance of big jazz bands in the years immediately following World War II. . . . A result of this vacuum, according to [Suber] . . . was that many big band musicians turned to teaching in elementary and high schools. . . . They became known generically as "stage bands" because the term "jazz band" or even "dance band" raised too many parental hackles.[10]

It's worth a moment, I think, to take a slight detour into a discussion of terminology, especially with respect to the nomenclature used to refer to school jazz groups. Reviewing the early literature on jazz education, one is struck by the fact that such groups are more often than not referred to as "stage bands." The circumstances surrounding the adoption of the term are somewhat murky. In their encyclopedia of jazz in the 1970s, Leonard Feather and Ira Gitler suggest that the term came about as "a euphemism coined in the Baptist southwest to avoid the sinful aspects of dancing and jazzing."[11]

While Feather and Gitler position the term as a euphemism to obscure the actual nature of what these ensembles were doing, it's clear that the term itself had a much longer history. Writing in the *Journal of Band Research* in 1978, for example, R. M. Longyear notes the history of the "banda sul palco" (band of the stage) in nineteenth-century French and Italian opera; Linda Tyler similarly expands on this topic in a 1990 article on the "stage band" in Verdi's middle period.[12] By the early 1920s, the term seems to have been in relatively common usage as a reference to modestly sized jazz and pop-oriented orchestras, often associated with musical revues and Vaudeville-style variety shows. A 1924 news brief in *Variety* noted that just such a group had recently been involved in a labor dispute in Davenport, Iowa; while the term "stage band" was used in the headline, the text of the article identifies the group as a "10-piece jazz orchestra" led by Walter Davison under the name "The Louisville Loons." Thus, it would seem that the use of the term "stage band" to refer to high school big bands was a continuation of a relatively common designation for such groups. This is not to say that Feather and Gitler did not have a point about the term muddying the waters with respect to identifying jazz, but it does not seem to be correct that the term originated as a "euphemism coined in the Baptist southwest."

Whether they were intended for "jazz bands" or "stage bands," school jazz contests would share one notable characteristic: the bands that tended to have the most success were more often than not those that hailed from more affluent, Whiter school districts. This seemed to reflect a broader trend of inverse participation and representation between White and Black students. Such disparities in the field were a frequent topic of discussion among the leadership of the National Association of Jazz Educators (NAJE), established in 1968 as an offshoot of the Music Educators' National Conference (MENC). NAJE was the brainchild of a group of educators who, in early 1967, worked to establish the structure and constitution of what they felt was a critical need in the field. In his 1979 dissertation on the history of the group, David Herfort highlights the work of eight individuals who would serve as NAJE's founders. These individuals brought to this effort a wide array of experiences and backgrounds in jazz performance, music education, arts entrepreneurship, and educational administration. There were two main things that these men shared: 1) they were all committed to the growth and development of jazz education, and 2) they were all White men.[13]

It's easy to criticize NAJE and its founders for, perhaps inadvertently, reinforcing the sense that jazz education was a White endeavor. And certainly, this was a topic of concern for the group's leadership. Herfort notes that even then the disparities between Black and White students were well known in the field. Such concerns were recognized as a particular challenge, as he writes:

> [M]any black student musicians have not been attracted to the curricula of jazz and popular music. As [Berklee president] Lawrence Berk has stated, the personnel of America's high school jazz ensembles have been "almost exclusively white...." Some educational as well as sociological reasons have been offered for this seeming enigma. For

example, Allen Scott has observed that many blacks have rejected the "regimented" big-band image of jazz education, particularly at the high school level.[14]

Along with concerns over student participation, NAJE's leadership was also mindful of the relative dearth of Black jazz educators; this was a subject of discussion at an early NAJE board meeting:

> During the Board's recapitulation of NAJE participation in the MENC National Convention of 1972, a need was indicated for "more black and other subculture involvement." The Board also considered several reasons for some music educators not joining NAJE. Two of the most pertinent explanations cited were NAJE's overemphasis on large instrumental jazz ensembles and "racism . . . both ways (real and/or imaginary)."[15]

Several years later, racial disparities were still a topic of discussion for the NAJE board:

> The Board also resumed its ongoing discussion concerning the lack of black members in NAJE. Earlier in 1974, Edward Meadows (Chairman of the MENC Black Music Caucus) had expressed "deep concern" about the lack of black participation in jazz functions at MENC meetings and a similar noninvolvement of blacks in NAJE. During a convention panel discussion on December 16, 1974, jazz trumpeter Clark Terry commented on the relatively small number of black students involved in jazz education programs and suggested that NAJE members seek ways to "combat this imbalance."[16]

Perhaps the most striking piece of information uncovered by Herfort in his research on the NAJE was this statistic offered by Matt Betton, one of the group's founders: out of a membership of 2,500, the organization claimed only ten Black members.[17] NAJE understood that there was a major problem, but despite an expressed desire to correct such imbalances, its lack of real institutional clout limited what it could do. What was needed was something or someone with real influence who could bring about significant change and who could circumvent the usual corridors of institutional power that all too often stand in the way of real progress.

While NAJE's leadership wrung its hands over the state of the field, competitive festivals were an increasingly important outlet for many school and college bands; as discussed in the previous chapter, the meeting of Stan Kenton and Leon Breeden at the Notre Dame festival in 1960 arguably changed the course of the entire field. By the end of the 1960s, there was substantial interest in establishing truly national level contests for high school and college-level jazz groups. One of the highest-profile of these was the American College Jazz Festival. The ACJF consisted of a series of regional preliminary festivals held around the country, which would serve as a qualifying round for bands that would eventually appear in the final round of competition. The intent was to have the finals of the festival held in Washington DC at the as-yet unopened Kennedy Center. The first two national finals (1970 and 1971) were instead held on the campus of the University of Illinois (Urbana/Champaign). In 1972, the festival moved to its planned permanent home in the nation's capital. Alas, the first festival at the Kennedy Center would turn out to be the last, as the contest was discontinued the following year. Some of the various regional festivals would continue. Probably the best known of these is the annual festival sponsored by Elmhurst College in Illinois. Still, the event attracted a good deal of attention, even in the national press. John S. Wilson, a prominent jazz writer for the *New York Times*, wrote a feature on the festival in May 1972. Wilson gives a general description of the festival, noting the entrants from various institutions. Of note are Wilson's accounts of two particular student performers. One of these was a quintet from Memphis State led by a pianist named James Williams, who, by decade's end, would occupy the piano chair of Art Blakey's Jazz Messengers and would later become the director of jazz studies at William Patterson University in New Jersey, a post he occupied until his death in 2004. The other was a young bassist from Los Angeles Valley College named John Clayton, whose group showed up late, forcing the young bassist to improvise a while the crowd waited, which Wilson described as a "charming bit of virtuosity."[18]

Young, Gifted, and Black: Malcolm X College and the Notre Dame Collegiate Jazz Festival

One particular collegiate case study from this period is worth examining in more depth. In his historical retrospective *Big Noise from Notre Dame*, Joseph Kuhn Carey notes the efforts of 1972 festival chairman Bob Syburg, then a Notre Dame junior Black Studies major, to increase the participation of Black students in the festival:

> Seemingly the result of Syburg's own concern with the history of black literature and related cultural developments, as well as the CJF's

own history of black collegiate participation (stretching back to the first festival in 1959), the '72 CJF would feature more black musicians, bands, and combos than any other year in the past. Among these groups in 1972 was a large band from Chicago's Malcolm X College, a Chicago Art Quartet Plus One, and, as a guest band, the massive Alvin Batiste-led Southern University Jazz Band Jaguars from Baton Rouge, Louisiana.[19]

I want to take a moment to focus on the band from Malcolm X College, described by Carey as having given a "swinging, bongo-energized" performance.[20] Carey notes that their appearance at the Notre Dame festival in 1972 was very well received; the group received an "Outstanding" designation from the panel of judges, and band members Bill Howell and Sonny Seals earned outstanding musicianship awards (another award recipient at this festival was Jim McNeely, then a student pianist at the University of Illinois).[21] A recording of the ensemble at the festival reveals a band that plays with joyous bombast, tight, precise ensemble work, and exceptionally talented soloists.[22] There is relatively little historical record of the Malcolm X College band beyond the account of their performance at Notre Dame, although George Lewis, in his landmark study of the AACM, points to the school—and the band—as having close links to the politically active South Side community. Carey indicates that the band made a return appearance at the CJF the following year, but no subsequent record of them attending after this can be found. Charles Walton, the band's director, was himself a well-known jazz drummer on the Chicago scene in the 1960s and had also taught in Chicago public schools. Lewis notes that Walton "was recruiting the best of Chicago's South Side musicians" for the program, which surely helps to explain the high level of skill they exhibited. Among Walton's students at Malcolm X were Mwata Bowden and Sabu Zawadi, both of whom would later join the AACM.[23] Walton was also well known in Chicago for his work on "Bronzeville Conversations," an oral history project that documented the jazz and blues scenes in the city.[24]

The Malcolm X College band is a fascinating case study of the intersection of school jazz bands and the broader aims of the Black Power movement. The college was part of the City Colleges of Chicago, a network of community colleges serving the Chicago area since 1911. Originally founded as Crane Junior College, the campus would change its name in honor of the late Black nationalist leader in 1968. The school was, in the spirit of its namesake, dedicated to the education and development of the city's Black communities, especially the South Side; the school's jazz band was engaged directly in these efforts. The same year that the band made its successful appearance at the Notre Dame Festival, they recorded a studio album that weaves together music and social commentary from the college's president, Dr. Charles Hurst. In the album's introductory track, Hurst explains the goals of the institution as African-inspired hand percussion plays in the background, echoing the contemporary spoken word recordings of artists such as Gil Scott Heron and the Last Poets:

> We come to Malcolm X to find a way. A way of changing the life of people who have suffered endlessly under the yoke of oppression in this country.... It's a different kind of college because it exemplifies, or it attempts to exemplify, all that we would like to see this society become.... Its charge is to re-humanize people who, by the nature of their existence, have been de-humanized; to de-colonize people who have by the nature of their existence lived under a colonialistic yoke.[25]

The remainder of the album features the band playing several jazz-funk arrangements (including the arrangements of "Music for Gong Gong" and Deep Purple's "Hush" heard on the Notre Dame festival recordings), the ballads "With These Hands" and "My Funny Valentine," before closing with an adaptation of Nina Simone's "Young, Gifted, and Black," following another "short message" from Hurst (which, at nine minutes, is actually the longest track on the entire album).[26] The Malcolm X College record is a remarkable document. No recording in jazz education, to my knowledge, so directly links an ensemble with the mission of an institution, particularly one so squarely focused on racial and social justice as Malcolm X College was. It was, in its own way, the clearest expression of the goals of the Black Power movement as manifested in jazz education.

Such ideas were certainly not lost on the handful of Black jazz educators who were active in the NAJE, concerned with the underrepresentation of Black students and teachers in the field, and in particular those who were affiliated with predominantly Black institutions (as Malcolm X College was). This would provide the impetus for the creation of the Black Jazz Music Caucus, an interest group within NAJE that advocated for a greater emphasis on Black music, and Black people, within the ranks of the organization. Established at the 1977 NAJE conference, the group was largely the result of the efforts of Anderson White, a school orchestra teacher in Detroit, and Larry Ridley, a well-known bassist who also directed the jazz program at Rutgers University. The purpose of the group was "to increase the representation of African American Jazz artists and educators within the larger body of the

Jazz Educators Association [the NAJE] which originated as a spinoff of the Music Educators National Conference (MENC)."[27] Renamed the African American Jazz Caucus in 2001 (in conjunction with the parent group's shift to the "International Association for Jazz Education"), the group continues to advocate for greater inclusion and visibility for African Americans in jazz education. Among the initiatives undertaken by the AAJC was the organization of an "AAJC/HBCU Student All-Star Big Band," designed to spotlight the oft-underrecognized role of historically Black institutions in the history of jazz education. Created explicitly as a response to the largely White world of the NAJE/IAJE specifically and jazz education more generally, the AAJC has served as perhaps the most active and visible manifestation of these initiatives. In 2001, the IAJE, in cooperation with the AAJC, began sponsoring the HBCU band, which first performed at the 2002 convention under Ridley's direction. Alas, the eventual downfall of the IAJE in 2008 would derail such efforts. Since the demise of the IAJE, the AAJC has operated largely as an independent group, but it does maintain an affiliate relationship with the IAJE's successor, the Jazz Education Network (JEN), though the AAJC/HBCU band does not seem to be active at present.

Thunder Soul

Much of the discussion of jazz education through the 1960s has focused on developments at universities and colleges. But at the same time, jazz education was beginning to make inroads into public school music programs, particularly at the high school level. Ironically, high school programs, as Suber argued in the introduction to David Baker's treatise on jazz pedagogy, seemed to face much less resistance to the inclusion of jazz. Without a well-established, classically oriented old guard to oppose them, high school teachers, in the words of Suber, "had the advantage of being the only instrumental instructor[s] on the faculty, with no musical colleagues to turn up their noses at teaching jazz to young people."[28]

The conventional wisdom of jazz education has generally held that developments at colleges and universities drove the growth of jazz education during this period, with the impetus flowing "down" to high school programs. Suber's account, by contrast, suggests that this relationship was reversed, that high schools were the driving force behind the growth of the field, and that developments among college programs "were a direct result of pressure from the high schools."[29] While he does not provide any specific data or other evidence to support his claim, from a practical perspective, this idea does make some sense; presumably, many students moving from high school to college who had played in jazz groups wanted to continue in such activities, whether part of their course of study as music majors or as cocurricular/extracurricular programs. Establishing performing jazz ensembles as well as courses devoted to other aspects of jazz (i.e., jazz history, appreciation, etc.) would seemingly help to meet the demands of such students. By the early 1960s, contests for high school jazz groups were also becoming increasingly common around the country. As if anticipating criticism from those who opposed jazz's creep into the secondary school music curriculum, Suber suggests that one benefit of this growth would be to help "'problem' or "unruly" boys become "productive students."[30] As much as it is an account of the stage band scene of the time, his piece serves as something of an advice column for nascent directors in navigating this new landscape.

Suber followed this with an April 1963 piece in the publication *Music Journal* recapping a recent slate of high school and college festivals around the country, noting the ensemble winners and recipients of awards and scholarships (often to the National Stage Band Camp or Berklee).[31] As the regional festivals became increasingly popular, by the late 1960s, there were a number of attempts to establish national-level contests for high school jazz bands. One event in particular attracted a good deal of attention. In 1972, high school groups from around the country gathered in Mobile, Alabama, for the All-American High School Stage Band Festival, an event sponsored by the Mobile Jazz Festival. A May 1972 article in *Billboard* provided a brief preview of the event. Selected high school bands would compete and participate in clinics and workshops provided by a roster of jazz professionals. Hopes were high for the future of the festival; Marion Wickle Jr., the event's director, predicted that the following year's festival would attract participants from "all 50 states."[32] Alas, Winkle's prediction did not come to fruition; the 1973 event had only nine participants,[33] and the contest was discontinued shortly after.

The 1972 festival in Mobile is probably best known today for the appearance of a particular student group. The story of the Kashmere Stage Band has become something of a legend in jazz education. Hailing from a majority-Black community in Houston, the Kashmere band was a prolific group, recording a number of albums and establishing a reputation as a dynamic ensemble, self-described as "Thunder Soul." Between 1969 and 1978, the band would win all but four of over forty contests in which it would appear.[34] And the ample recorded legacy left by the band demonstrates why. This was a top-notch, well-rehearsed group that played with a combination of exceptionally tight ensemble work and an energetic funk and soul-based aesthetic. The Kashmere Stage Band's most enduring triumph would be their appearance at the 1972 festival in Mobile, winning top honors as the festival's "Most Outstanding Band." This result catapulted the Kashmere band into exalted status, particularly among students and directors at similarly situated schools. By winning the Mobile contest, Kashmere had crashed the stage, so to speak. This idea, that a group from a majority-Black school like Kashmere was, despite its success, something of an "outsider" within the stage band community, was understood and deeply felt by jazz students at similar institutions. And this sense of potentially being overlooked and of having something to prove supplied the fuel for the Kashmere band's prolific work in this period.

In 2011, the Kashmere Stage Band was the subject of a documentary film titled *Thunder Soul*.[35] With actor and comedian Jamie Foxx acting as a producer and main patron of the project, the film tells the story of Kashmere's 1972 triumph by way of a reunion concert in honor of the band's director during its heyday, Conrad Johnson, better known to his students as "Prof." In a feature on *Thunder Soul* in the *Los Angeles Times*, Egon Alapatt, president of Now Again Records (which released a compilation recording of the Kashmere band in 2006) describes the world of stage bands that the Kashmere band would face:

> Noting that he has likely heard literally thousands of stage band recordings, Alapatt continued, "Nine times out of 10 if you get a high school stage record from the late '60s, early '70s, generally these guys were playing bad, schmaltzy versions of jazz standards done from charts for stage bands by music publishing houses which in the hands of lesser band directors were just fodder for average music recorded by average kids across the country."[36]

In a segment in the *Thunder Soul* film, Alapatt explicitly sets Kashmere in opposition to a White-dominated stage band community:

> A lot of these high school band directors came out of the jazz era. So, they would fashion these performance bands, stage bands that would record and perform music that was inspired by jazz but was done in a much more pop music sort of way. A lot of it came out being super square.... For every 150 stage band records that you can find from the late sixties and early seventies, maybe one of them will be by a Black band. Maybe two or three of them would be from a mixed band .... It was a White phenomenon.[37]

The larger significance of the band's journey to Alabama was not lost on its members, who understood all too well the deep history of racism and racial terror that was so closely associated with this state. As the Mobile festival was taking place, segregationist Democrat George Wallace was still early in his second stint as Alabama's governor, having recently survived an assassination attempt that left him partially paralyzed. The band's members also understood their own place within the world of high school stage bands. They saw themselves as possessing a distinctive and particular aesthetic borne of their own experiences and histories in Houston's African American community. Put another way, they understood their significance as a *Black* band and the ways in which that identity impacted the way they conceived of themselves as performers. This idea was at the root of Conrad Johnson's approach to leading the group. The Kashmere band would not simply play charts; they would perform. Unlike other high school stage bands, Kashmere would put on a *show*, as Johnson explains: "I felt like the music wasn't enough, because there were people who would listen to the band who were not musicians. It wasn't enough. So I put the show into it, and no one had thought to do that."[38] I want to zero in on Johnson's comment with respect to the "showy" aspects of big band performance, that "no one had thought to do that." Although he does not state this specifically, it's clear that Johnson refers here to other bands, presumably the mostly White bands who populated jazz festivals and contests. Johnson's emphasis on the *show* thus marks the group as having a distinctive approach. It's easy, especially in the world of competitions, to see such gestures as gimmicks, as the kind of thing that a band might do in order to draw attention away from the fact that they might not sound as good as other groups. But this was not the case with Kashmere. This was a band that played at an extremely high level and put on a show as well; in this way, the band's performances recall the efforts of bandleaders such as Cab Calloway and Jimmie Lunceford,[39] for whom visual spectacle was a critical part of their aesthetic. Kashmere alum Earl Spiller expanded on this idea: "We danced while we played, and we grooved. The other bands, they were really good. They was [sic] technically good, but they didn't have the feel. See, they didn't have that soul."[40] For fellow alum Donald Compton, the "show" of which Johnson spoke was something that provided the Kashmere band with a unique identity relative to the other bands on the contest circuit: "When we came on scene and we started dancing, that's what drove the judges wild. It just drove the judges wild, because they had never seen it before . . . . It was a show band."[41]

Despite Compton's claim that the band "drove the judges wild" at the Mobile festival, the actual adjudication seemed to stir up some of the lingering feelings and attitudes about the place of a Black band in a high-level stage band competition. The post-performance judges' deliberation was, for the Kashmere students, a source of great uncertainty and doubt. As band alum Gerald Calhoun explains, "We were getting down to the finish, and there [sic] seemed to be having some problems with the judges." Festival director J. C. McAller elaborates, saying, "The judges went back in the green room. And they said, 'We're just at an impasse.' The two bands that performed in the concert final tonight were equally as good, and we would like to give them each a first-place trophy."[42] For Calhoun and his bandmates and especially Conrad Johnson, the delay sparked concerns that the judges might not, despite the band's raucous reception, choose to select an all-Black band as the festival's winning group. Calhoun continues:

> Prof [Johnson] didn't like this at all. He said, "Just be fair about it. I don't care who you give it to. Just give it to somebody And then, you know, then we'll go." It took so long for them to decide, it actually shook my faith at that time.... And I remember the man's voice, and he said "The winner is ... Kashmere [speaks in a very subdued manner]. It wasn't like "Kashmere!" [speaks excitedly].... And we went ballistic.[43]

Listening to the comments of the various band members, one gets the sense that the larger implications of their winning the festival were not lost on the students. They traveled to the deepest parts of the Deep South to compete in a festival in which they were decidedly going against the norm. The 1972 Mobile festival was probably the peak of the Kashmere Stage Band's run. The band would continue for several more years, wowing crowds, winning accolades, and making recordings, but in 1978, with Johnson's retirement from his position, the group broke apart. And jazz education quickly moved on, returning to the relative status quo in which mainly White groups would dominate the festival scene. Mark Landsman, *Thunder Soul*'s director, is "amazed" at the disparities in arts funding which faced Black majority schools, noting that at his high school "[w]e had a darkroom. We had a film program. We had extraordinary resources at our fingertips largely because we were in a school district with good support.... Those [mainly Black] public schools had to fight tooth and nail for things I took for granted."[44]

In the preceding discussion, I've spotlighted the stories of these two groups because I believe that their experiences run parallel, touching on some similar themes. Of course, what makes these narratives so compelling is the fact that the success of these two bands was unexpected. To put it more bluntly, they were Black bands from Black schools finding success in a competitive world that had been the domain of groups from mostly White schools. As such, they represented an important intervention into the trajectory of school jazz groups in the early 1970s. And it is no coincidence that this occurred in 1972, which as I mentioned previously, was a moment in which the Black Power movement was in full stride. The Kashmere and Malcolm X bands were, in their own ways, a vital part of that same story.

DUKING IT OUT: ESSENTIALLY ELLINGTON AND JAZZ EDUCATION'S "COURSE CORRECTION"

In his capacity as the president of the Jazz Education Network, Todd Stoll wrote a regular series of open letters to the group's membership. In his final letter, published on June 12, 2020, Stoll reflected on the recent developments in American society at large, particularly with respect to racial and social justice. Like so many others, Stoll's comments were made within the context of the tumult spurred by the killing of George Floyd at the hands of officers from the Minneapolis Police Department. Stoll writes:

> [T]**he lack of diversity in our community** . . . is something I have felt strongly about for more than 25 years, and to be perfectly honest, the lack of response from the JEN community was deafening . . . . There were a few private messages from colleagues of color, but that was it. It was a microcosm of what we have seen in our country for generations—people of privilege staying silent in the face of the reality of systemic oppression and racism. And, my friends, *the jazz education community is just as complicit as the rest of America.*[45]

Continuing, Stoll links what he sees as a lack of engagement in these vital social causes from within the jazz education community to the field's lack of engagement with Black music:

> [T]he beginnings of institutionalized jazz education were not about black music. Some of our largest and most lauded jazz institutions still do little to engage black students, black faculty, black audiences, and black music . . . . There are high school and collegiate jazz programs right now whose jazz music libraries consist predominantly of white-composed and -arranged music. Their bands' current folders contain charts by only white composers . . . . Our business is corrupt, racist, and part of the systemic nature of this problem.[46]

His letter was not written in a vacuum. Indeed, the dearth of African American students in school programs was a frequent topic in his communications with the JEN membership. In an earlier letter published the previous July (and which Stoll references above), he shares an account that underscores the problems of race and representation in jazz education:

> In a recent post by a young man I admire, he shared multiple pictures of his band, located in a large to mid-sized northeastern city.... As I looked at the pictures, and remembered my own youthful (and somewhat fumbling) attempts at band leading, I was struck by something—there wasn't **one single** band member of color.... I make a plea for a call to action by all of "us," the jazz community of educators, performers, and advocates. Can we try to have integrated bands? By race and gender?[47]

Stoll's comments, written in 2019 and 2020, could easily have been written at any point in the previous half-century or so. And indeed, the notion that jazz education was an endeavor dominated by White students and faculty had been accepted as a sort of conventional wisdom within the field. What makes Stoll's comments particularly important here is when we consider the nature of his "day job": he was (and remains at present) the vice president of Education for Jazz at Lincoln Center (JALC), an entity whose advocacy for jazz is fundamentally centered in the identity of jazz as an expression of Black American culture. Debates and discord concerning JALC's aesthetic and philosophical foundations have been discussed ad nauseam in other venues in full public view. What I am most interested in is how Stoll's comments represent a particular intersection between the discourses of jazz education and what has been labeled, for lack of a better term, the "neoclassicist" movement in jazz, which intentionally and assertively centers the role of Black identity.

Historically, jazz education as a discipline has remained somewhat distant from JALC and its central figure, Wynton Marsalis. To be sure, Marsalis has been invested in jazz education in some form since the earliest days of his career. Bringing jazz to younger audiences always seemed to be a central concern in his work. In 1986, Marsalis made an appearance on *Mister Rogers' Neighborhood*, where he talked about jazz and performed with the show's regular band (led by the criminally underappreciated pianist Johnny Costa). That same year, he appeared as a guest on another PBS program, *Sesame Street*, working directly with a group of children in a lesson; he would make a number of appearances on the program through the years. Outreach to children, it seemed, was a priority in his developing musical system. But connections to existing jazz education programs did not seem, at least at this point in time, to be a significant concern, save for the occasional masterclass or workshop at various institutions.[48]

In 2000, Marsalis was invited to give the keynote address for the annual convention of the International Association of Jazz Educators (IAJE) in New Orleans, his home city. IAJE keynotes often featured major figures in the jazz world, and given the location of that year's meeting, his invitation should not be terribly surprising.[49] Even so, one of the more remarkable things about Marsalis's remarks to the IAJE is how little he talked about jazz education, or to be more specific, jazz education as the field was constituted around the time (and certainly how it was reflected in the majority of IAJE's membership). Early in his address, he notes the efforts of NPR, the Smithsonian, and the Monk Institute[50] as well as JALC in bringing wider—and younger—audiences to the music. Most of his subsequent remarks focus on jazz's place in society or his own work at JALC and are in line with other public remarks he had given in other venues. There is nothing in his remarks that substantively addressed the numerous jazz education programs in colleges and universities or in high schools and middle schools, whose directors, comprising the bulk of IAJE's membership, were disproportionately White. This is how the term "jazz education" was—and still is—widely understood, yet Marsalis's speech steers clear of this, focusing instead on efforts from civic institutions like his own JALC. The only real exception is an anecdote about Marsalis's work with Ronald Carter (not to be confused with the bassist of the same name), who had worked as a jazz band director in the East St. Louis public schools.[51] Marsalis likened Carter's approach to that of his New Orleans mentor Danny Barker. Carter was, in this sense, a more traditional kind of teacher, which perhaps explains why he would eventually be pulled into Marsalis's orbit, becoming a core consultant to JALC. The *Jazz Educators' Journal* article that reprinted Marsalis's address also features a number of photos of student musicians from school jazz programs. When one considers the venue, this would make sense. But there is also a certain irony in their use. One photo in particular underscores this idea, featuring a group of students from West Hartford, Connecticut's Hall High School performing in the finals of the 2000 Essentially Ellington competition (Hall would ultimately capture first place that year). The students in the photo appear to be all White; all but one are male.

Why didn't Marsalis "call out" the IAJE, and by extension, the field of jazz education in general, the way that his colleague Todd Stoll would do later in his role as president of the IAJE's successor organization, JEN? Part of this, to be sure, is that Marsalis would seem to be acutely aware of his place as perhaps the most recognized figure in the jazz world of the time. It's likely that he was also aware of his own penchant for attracting criticism, some justified and some not, for his commentary and overall philosophy. Roughly one year after making these remarks, Marsalis would find himself at the center of a firestorm over his role in Ken Burns's mammoth PBS documentary *Jazz*, which would both solidify his place as America's most visible jazz personality and one of its most contentious figures.[52] That Marsalis's keynote happened at this particular IAJE conference was notable for several reasons. As previously noted, that year's conference was located in New Orleans, which, despite the city's place in the history of jazz, rarely hosted this conference, and in many ways, did not figure significantly in the contemporary discourses of jazz education (while a few institutions in New Orleans have very good jazz studies programs, by and large, they have not been considered to be among the elite programs in the field). As perhaps the city's best-known native son in the contemporary jazz world, Marsalis would seem a natural choice. Still, when given the chance to address the main professional organization in jazz education, he says virtually nothing about the systemic problems with respect to inclusion and equity facing the field itself. For all that Marsalis talks about the importance of learning about jazz, he says very little about the most contentious issues confronting the field of educators to whom he is speaking.

In the mid-1990s, the bands of Stan Kenton, Maynard Ferguson, and Buddy Rich were still the main historical models for most school jazz repertoires. There were, of course, exceptions. Thad Jones, for example, produced many of his most-recognized compositions in the preceding decades, which enjoyed wide adoption among school jazz groups. Similarly, Sammy Nestico's partnership with Count Basie provided a steady stream of charts for school groups, published by specialty companies like Kendor Music, which served to provide school musicians with works ranging from stock arrangements to those by major figures on the scene. (Nestico's work was exclusively distributed by Kendor, for example; the company also published much of Jones's work.) At the same time, younger writers, such as Gordon Goodwin, Bob Mintzer (an alum of Rich's band), Matt Harris (who had written a number of charts for Ferguson and Rich), John Fedchock (who wrote extensively for Woody Herman's last band in the 1980s), and Maria Schneider (a protégé of Bob Brookmeyer) produced numerous works that were published for school ensembles. The publication of charts geared specifically toward school jazz ensembles was, by this point, flourishing.

But there was one notable figure who was largely absent from the rehearsal folders of school jazz groups through the 1990s, and in a manner that perhaps could not be more ironic: the man widely regarded as jazz's greatest composer, whose work defined an entire era and whose death in 1974 seemed for many to mark the end of jazz's Golden Age, Edward Kennedy "Duke" Ellington. There are a number of reasons for the relative scarcity of Ellington's work in the student big band repertoire. For one, Ellington was not generally engaged in the practice of publishing his music for public performance. He kept his music close to the vest and, as a result, generally away from school jazz groups. But even those few charts that had somehow managed to make their way into students' hands were not often played, not having been written with the idea that they would eventually be marketed to school groups. When one considers the virtual absence of Ellington from jazz education through the 1990s, the idea can seem jarring; it would be as if student orchestras never played Mozart or Beethoven. The idea that a classical violin performance major could go through an entire degree program without ever having played a piece by one or both of these figures is nearly inconceivable. Yet, for jazz students, this is precisely the situation they faced with respect to the most highly regarded figure in jazz composition. To say this was a gap in the student jazz experience was an understatement, both musically and in the larger sense of what Ellington represented. But this would also provide a critical opportunity for Marsalis and JALC. During the 1995 to 1996 school year, JALC began distributing scores of Ellington's music to selected high school bands in and around New York City. This effort was part of a new JALC program that would, in the spring of 1996, bring a handful of bands to Lincoln Center for a weekend of performances and workshops. The name that was selected for this program reflects all too clearly the mission of the organization in establishing a jazz education canon that centered artists and music born of particular historical communities: Essentially Ellington.

Before proceeding with the discussion of this program, it might be useful to get a sense of JALC's place within the context of current jazz scholarship and criticism. Jazz at Lincoln Center has been at the nexus of a well-worn, three-and-a-half-decades-old debate that touches on musical style, historiography, race, gender, economics, national identity, and in a broad sense, who gets to define and speak for the music and whose vision of jazz will prevail. Some of the criticism has been caustic. Some of it has been justified. A thorough cataloging of these debates could itself fill multiple volumes, but I think a few observations are in order. Marsalis's role at JALC and his presence in Ken Burns's *Jazz* series were the most visible examples of jazz's public footprint at the millennium and arguably for a time afterward. Although there was no substantially direct relationship between Burns and JALC, his project cannot be easily untangled from the organization's mission. Some observers grew concerned that Marsalis et al. were acting as a kind of jazz monopoly, and numerous critical and scholarly works chastised JALC, Marsalis, Burns, and their associates. The centering of Wynton Marsalis in the film had the effect of making him America's de facto spokesperson for jazz, and this did not sit well with many observers. This was evident in the forceful reactions to the film. Critiques in the critical and scholarly press invariably dovetailed with critiques of Marsalis himself and with neoclassicism in general. As Farah Jasmine Griffin writes, the aesthetic decision made by Marsalis and JALC "informs Ken Burns's epic documentary *Jazz*."[53] Charles Hersch's review of the film expressed a commonly held perspective that while the film does a number of things well, it also "neglects the fundamentally collective nature of the jazz performance."[54] If allowed to go unchallenged, critics felt, this might become the prevailing narrative for jazz, crowding out other voices and perspectives. Many have suggested that this is precisely what happened.

More recent critical and scholarly work has sought to take a more nuanced view of JALC and its impact on the contemporary jazz world. One of the most thorough—and balanced—recent accounts of JALC comes from Kimberly Hannon Teal,[55] who examines the organization in her study of "jazz places." While acknowledging the critiques of JALC, Teal also acknowledges the unquestioned influence of the organization and not in an entirely negative sense. While the organization has been willing to exercise its considerable power, during the last decade or so, the rhetorical conflagration that consumed jazz critics and scholars has largely subsided, ushering in a period of relative détente between various constituencies. Nate Chinen speaks to this in his overview of jazz in the early twenty-first century, citing a collaboration that was, for the time, rather unexpected:

> John Zorn . . . seemed lathered up and agitated, alto saxophone hanging from a strap around his neck. This in itself wasn't unusual. But the circumstances were: Zorn and his band Masada were about to perform their half of a double bill with the redoubtable Cecil Taylor, under the auspices of Jazz at Lincoln Center . . . a first-time invitation for both . . . . "Let's hope this is the beginning of a trend of enlightening programming here!" he barked from the stage. "There are more young faces in the audience here than there have been since the inception of this place!" As Zorn made his proclamation, he was standing in the largest of three performance spaces in Frederick P. Rose Hall, Jazz at Lincoln Center's home on the fifth floor of the Time Warner Center at Columbus Circle . . . devotees of experimental music saw Rose Hall as loosely analogous

to the Imperial Death Star, while someone like Zorn—spontaneous, unruly, irrepressible—stood for the plucky rebellion."[56]

Pop culture analogies aside, Chinen points to a seeming thaw in the frosty relationships between the neoclassicists and the experimentalists, though to be sure, tensions persist. But as Chinen notes, the notion that JALC is (in the words of another writer) "sucking the life out of a beleaguered jazz community"[57] may represent something of an oversimplification, less of a "David and Goliath" scenario and more a function of "the complex ecosystem to which all parties can't help belonging."[58] The neoclassicist debates that roiled jazz communities two decades ago have not ceased, but today a "live and let live" attitude seems to have become more widespread. As Wynton Marsalis himself noted in a recent interview with Bill Maher, "Sometimes people get heated. When I was younger, I was very heated. As you get older, you start to learn how to not be that way."[59]

This shift is likely due to a number of factors, but there is one aspect of this that often goes unmentioned in jazz scholarship, and that is that JALC, from the perspective of its core mission, has been an unequivocal success by any objective measure. As Teal writes, "JALC racked up an impressive number of popular and financial successes in very short order, and has continued to increase its amount of programming each season from its very beginnings."[60] Among the most significant growth areas for JALC has been its educational and public outreach endeavors. In a January 2022 profile in *DownBeat*, Todd Stoll highlights programs like Essentially Ellington, Swing University (a lifelong learning program), and the Center's "Let Freedom Swing social justice school residencies" that the article notes "reached nearly a half million students topping 3,000 performances throughout a nine-year run."[61] There is little doubt that the easing of tensions over JALC's role in the jazz world has helped facilitate these kinds of public-facing initiatives. Jazz education programs, which initially were slow to engage with the Center, have recently begun to participate in and adopt JALC programs. Essentially Ellington is probably the best-known example of this, but other kinds of collaborations are becoming more common. One example is the Jack Rudin Jazz Championship, a college-level invitational jazz ensemble competition first held in 2020 and named for the late real estate mogul and former JALC board member. Envisioned as an annual event, the second competition (scheduled for 2021) was canceled, but the program restarted in 2022. Although less officially focused on Ellington or any particular aesthetic approach, the competition has nevertheless leaned heavily on the performance of works from the same canon that fuels JALC's other programming. At the same time, JALC's training and consultancy programs for jazz educators have grown significantly, filling a gap caused by the dissolution of the International Association for Jazz Education in 2008. Of course, all these experiences are still filtered through the lens of JALC's overarching aesthetic philosophy, but the critical pushback seems to be more limited than two decades ago. This is perhaps most evident in the Essentially Ellington program.

A significant aspect of JALC's larger Ellington project, of which Essentially Ellington is but one component, is the reconstitution of Ellington's work in the sphere of performance. In a sense, Essentially Ellington might be seen as an extension of the cultivation of the "repertory band" concept in which ensembles are devoted to the recreation of "important" works in the genre.[62] In an essay on the canonization of Mary Lou Williams, Kimberly Hannon Teal notes that such repertory performances, an integral component of JALC's programming in its formative years, help to make historical figures seem more "present":

> [I]n short, JALC is able to capitalize on the fact that the concerts it presents can never measure up to the ones we can now no longer attend, leaving audiences nostalgic for musicians they may have never heard. [The] priorities of both the living and the dead are negotiated in performances like the one celebrating Williams, and, after they are enlisted by JALC as musical and cultural representatives of "swinging" jazz and American democracy, historical artists emerge as never before.[63]

JALC's Ellington programming amplifies the processes that Teal describes. In a sense, without Ellington, there is no JALC; he was, and is, the ideal figure upon which to build a program that is centered on jazz, democratic principles, and a cultural memory emphasizing the experiences of Black musicians and their communities.

In establishing the Essentially Ellington program, JALC partnered with the Ellington estate as well as individuals such as David Berger, who played an indispensable role during JALC's early years, conducting the orchestra and penning transcriptions of Ellington and Strayhorn works that would constitute a good deal of the raw material utilized by JALC in building its Ellington-centric identity. Berger speaks to this in a *New York Times* profile shortly before the competition's debut, noting that the program "really is for everyone," adding, "I like being part of this effort to make sure this American art form is right at your fingertips."[64] In his autobiography, he speaks to the early conceptualization of what would become the Essentially Ellington program:

> Around 1989 or 1990 Wynton [Marsalis] was at my house one night. I remember this evening vividly. After eating, we retired to the living room, and he said that one of the reasons that young people are not drawn to jazz is that they are not exposed to it. Even when they play in their high school jazz bands, they are not playing the best music we have to offer. Then he said, "We need to offer them your Ellington transcriptions." To which I replied that I'd tried, but only a handful of schools had bought them. So he suggested that we could give them away. I said that the teachers wouldn't see the value in them, and would prefer to play music that sounds more like what is popular on the radio and TV. So he said that we could appeal to their football mentality and have a contest, awarding the winning band $10,000. And thus Essentially Ellington began.[65]

There are some important points to consider in this passage. First, Berger's account directly supports the idea that a primary motive for Essentially Ellington was exactly the kind of "reset" mentioned earlier, to give school jazz bands access to better quality music than they were currently performing. Second, Berger's comments about his unsuccessful attempts to market his music to school jazz programs speak to another consideration: as one of my colleagues once put it, in a discussion of the program, Ellington's music is "hard to play" for student groups, a point to which I can attest having played some of Berger's transcriptions in my days as a member of the Jazz Repertory Ensemble at UNT. A final point is Marsalis's comment about the nature of competition, invoking football in order to instill a competitive spirit that would, it was hoped, spur interest from students and teachers. Considering the somewhat skeptical attitude toward competitions expressed by many individuals in both the jazz world and in music education, his lean into the idea is notable. In retrospect, it must be acknowledged that Marsalis's instincts were absolutely correct. Regardless of any misgivings about musical competitions, the reality is that they are still very popular, a tangible way for institutions to demonstrate their success. Any drawbacks of competition are seen to be outweighed by the benefit of having Ellington's music more widely played by younger musicians.

In tying this new scholastic competition so directly to the personality of Ellington, JALC was making a clear challenge to jazz education in the United States in terms of practices, aesthetics, philosophies, and perhaps most critically, the nature of race within the field. As discussed in the previous section, contests and festivals around the country had long been dominated by primarily White bands that tended to hail from some of America's wealthiest urban and suburban communities, and by the mid-1990s, it was increasingly understood that this was a problem that the field needed to address. The establishment of Essentially Ellington in 1996, then, marked a significant development in the neoclassicists' engagement with jazz education. What had been somewhat tangential was suddenly characterized by a much more direct type of involvement. If jazz education faced a problem of racial representation, JALC had a ready-made solution, one which reflected its own particular perspectives and practices.

We should keep in mind that Essentially Ellington is, first and foremost, a contest. But Essentially Ellington is distinctive for several reasons. First, and perhaps most obviously, is the alliterative title, echoing another popular Lincoln Center program, Mostly Mozart. Established in 1966, Mostly Mozart is arguably the best-known concert series named for a particular artist in existence. In a similar manner, the program invites comparisons to other "named" competitions; among these, the best known are probably the International Tchaikovsky Competition, first held in Moscow in 1958, and the Van Cliburn International Piano Competition, founded in 1962, and named in honor of the original Tchaikovsky winner; similarly, the annual Thelonious Monk (now Herbie Hancock) competition in jazz can be said to occupy a similar role. But what is perhaps most important is the way in which the competition has offered a more conscious and focused intervention into contemporary jazz education, moving beyond the development of outreach programs that were designed to highlight a particular historical understanding of jazz and its place in American history and culture. Essentially Ellington marked a new front for this effort, directly taking on the world of high school jazz contests. In a larger sense, they were attempting, in their own way, to put the "jazz" back in jazz education, at least as it was understood by Marsalis and his collaborators at JALC. Such efforts were not lost on some observers, as Ben Ratliff implies in a review of the 1998 festival for the *New York Times*. Ratliff, evidently not a fan of what has emerged from high school jazz programs through the 1990s, positions Essentially Ellington as an important corrective:

> All the high-level performing, some of it on an unquestionably professional level, drove home one thing in particular: Americans in their 30's and 40's [sic] have good reason to remember their high school jazz bands as undistinguished. In the 1970's [sic], jazz stopped being dance music, and soon high school bands were basically playing light rock with horn sections. But it wasn't just an outbreak of bad taste. Music publishers were making a profit selling television and movie-theme

scores to high schools. There have always been plenty of secondhand, rearranged Ellington scores floating around, but they lack the colors and textures of the real thing. So it's easy to see why Jazz at Lincoln Center's project of disseminating free copies of Ellington's own arrangements to high schools—with scores transcribed accurately by an Ellington scholar, David Berger—is a simple and beautiful idea.[66]

Ratliff's praise is also revealing in another respect; intentionally or not, he points to the program's role as something of a gatekeeper of the Ellington legacy, an idea that correlates all too well with Wynton Marsalis's own reputation as a rather assertive public arbiter of "what jazz is—and isn't."[67]

If Essentially Ellington recenters Ellington in the jazz canon, by extension, it also repositions Blackness at the center of the discourse of jazz education. Ethan Iverson speaks to this point in a feature on Marsalis on his website, underscoring the importance of these efforts with respect to jazz education:

> When he started assembling an institution, Wynton was advocating for the primacy of the black aesthetic at a time when the white Stan Kenton-to-Gary Burton lineage dominated the academy. I like Kenton and Burton, but their institutional sway and undue influence in jazz education [are] part of this discussion. We needed less North Texas State and more Duke Ellington in the mix, and Wynton corrected our course.[68]

In a similar vein, jazz pianist and composer Horace Silver alludes to this idea in a 1997 interview:

> Duke Ellington is like Bach or Beethoven in the jazz field. He is on the same genius level as Bach, Beethoven and Mozart are in the classical realm, and our young people do not know anything about him. If you ask young people who Duke Ellington is, they do not know anything about him. So parents should see that their children get some kind of musical education or musical appreciation class, or they should teach their children who the following were: Ellington, Count Basie, Jimmie Lunceford, Coleman Hawkins, Lester Young and Art Tatum. All of these individuals were great people who passed but who left this great beautiful legacy of music, and these were Black people.[69]

It is this last point that I wish to dwell on for a moment. Silver's complaint is two-fold, that 1) young people don't have a clear sense of historical jazz figures such as Ellington, and 2) such a study must be grounded in their identities as Black artists. This idea, as articulated by Silver, overlaps perfectly with JALC's own mission, philosophies, and programming. Essentially Ellington, then, was yet another opportunity to operationalize these ideas, but this time in a direct engagement with the field of jazz education.

Placing Ellington at the center of this program accomplishes a number of goals. From a practical standpoint, it opens up a vast jazz ensemble literature, hundreds of arrangements, for student groups to perform. But it also allows Marsalis and JALC to further the institution's particular philosophies concerning race in American culture. On the surface level, placing a Black composer squarely within jazz education can only serve to reset the sense that the field is, for lack of a better way to put it, "too White." But of all artists to place in this position, Ellington brings much more to the table. As a "race man,"[70] Ellington's music is deeply imbued with Blackness. The program simply can't exist without engaging deeply with these ideas; "Essentially Ellington," by its very nature, *has* to be centered in Blackness.

For Dave Hammond, director of the jazz program at the Denver School of the Arts (a five-time finalist as of 2020, finishing as high as second place in 2017), Essentially Ellington's role is directly linked to JALC's project of centering Black music and culture, which he sees as filling a crucial gap in students' education, noting that "it's lost on many kids—what the African American experience has to offer all of us when we think about general oppression of a people, the loosening of that oppression and seeing a people rise. *That's what Duke Ellington's music is all about.*"[71] A similar sentiment was expressed in a 2018 congressional resolution honoring the Dillard High School band, which won that year's competition. Introduced by Florida representatives Alcee Hastings, Debbie Wasserman-Schultz, Frederica Wilson, Ted Deutch, and Lois Frankel, the resolution begins by emphasizing Dillard's own history in Black music and culture, linking this directly to JALC's underlying philosophy:

> Whereas Dillard High School was founded in the early 20th century, with funds from noted philanthropist and outspoken advocate for Black education James Hardy Dillard, as the first public school for people of African descent in Fort Lauderdale, Florida;
>
> Whereas the music program at Dillard High School, as part of the Dillard Center for the Arts, gained fame when the legendary jazz saxophonist Julian "Cannonball" Adderley served as an instructor of applied music in the 1940s;

>   Whereas jazz is an original American art form originating in African American communities from New Orleans in the late 19th and early 20th centuries and is considered to be America's classical music;
>   Whereas this is the third time the Dillard Center for the Arts Jazz Band won at the Essentially Ellington Competition, after having won in both 2011 and 2012:
>   Now, therefore, be it Resolved, That the House of Representatives
>   (1) congratulates the Dillard Center for the Arts Jazz Band for its first-place win at the Essentially Ellington; and
>   (2) commends the Dillard Center for the Arts for its contributions to the education and nurturing of outstanding jazz musicians.[72]

It should come as no surprise that the competition reflects the broader goals of JALC's programming and its emphasis on jazz's place and identity in American society. JALC's dual narrative of Black authorship and racial reconciliation are deeply embedded in the contest and are, in a sense, specifically enacted through its conduct. In a profile of the program in the journal *Philanthropy*, Eric Felton offers the following commentary:

>   Marsalis might add that we live in a time constantly trying to separate people of one race and ethnicity from another. The Essentially Ellington festival also shows young people how to close those gaps. Students of many backgrounds pour themselves into performing the music of an African American icon. There's no griping about "cultural appropriation." Instead there is shared celebration of the universality of great art, art that transcends fads and ideologies and backgrounds. "Regardless of race or gender," says [JALC's Vice President of Education Todd] Stoll, "art speaks across time."[73]

What Felton articulates here has been front and center in neoclassicist aesthetics from nearly the very beginning, that is to say, an emphasis on the Black experience as a gateway for racial healing and reconciliation. This is an enormously appealing strategy, that the program can be built on what is, in essence, a foundation of African American exceptionalism, an idea that is, to be fair, vigorously disputed. Such interpretations of JALC's work have been deployed as a means of criticizing the organization for sidelining White artists and perspectives; this can be seen, for example, as a core argument in Stuart Nicholson's polemic *Is Jazz Dead?* Nicholson devotes a chapter to what he terms "The Wynton Marsalis Phenomenon," followed by a chapter on "Jazz at Lincoln Center." To be clear, this is not a positive assessment of

Marsalis and JALC. Nicholson, in fact, tends to place just about all the blame for jazz's demise in the American market at the feet of Marsalis, his mentors Stanley Crouch and Albert Murray, and JALC's programming.[74] A core aspect of Nicholson's critique of Marsalis et al. is his contention that their continued adherence to an "African American exceptionalism" in jazz and its application to the contemporary jazz scene have prevented the music from progressing. For Nicholson, JALC is not preserving jazz; it is strangling it.

The other side of this, the notion that through an engagement with a Black-centered jazz narrative America can lift itself from its own history of racism and prejudice, serves as both a counterbalance to and a justification for precisely the kind of exceptionalism that Nicholson decries. Black centeredness does not exist here for its own sake; it is deployed very pointedly to create a multiracial space that will, it is hoped, provide a blueprint for a more just and democratic society, with jazz providing the soundtrack. It is this precise idea that constituted the fabric of Ken Burns's *Jazz* documentary series, in which Wynton Marsalis played an essential role.[75] All of this is very ambitious, and it is likely too much responsibility for one group or one jazz band contest to take on. But the program's centering of Ellington is about more than music. In expanding its reach into a nationwide contest, Essentially Ellington has also deftly constituted itself as a mechanism for engaging young people from across many different fault lines in America today: class, race, geography, gender. Essentially Ellington assembles a body of student participants that is, in this line of thinking, a true representation of what America is meant to be.

While the program's rhetoric emphasizes the nurturing of jazz among a broad cross section of American society, the actual results of the competition paint a different picture. Many of the Essentially Ellington finalists over the years have come from the ranks of performing arts magnet schools or from relatively affluent schools with long-established jazz programs. For example, the winner of the first Essentially Ellington in 1996 was from the LaGuardia High School of Music, Art, and Performing Arts, an NYPS magnet school in Manhattan, probably best known outside of arts education circles as the school that was the inspiration (before the merger with LaGuardia High School) for the film and television show *Fame*. LaGuardia has long been recognized as having an elite jazz program, frequently winning awards in other competitions (such as the annual *DownBeat* Student Music Awards). It is, in essence, a professional training program in music. The following year and the first year that the contest included bands from outside of the New York City area, the winner was from Foxborough High School in Massachusetts. A relatively small city situated between Boston and Providence (approximately twenty to thirty miles each way), Foxborough is probably best known as the location of Gillette Stadium, home of the New England Patriots and host to many large-scale concerts and events in the region. Compared to similarly situated communities in the region, Foxborough is a relatively affluent town, and the high school's student population is, in terms of race, out of alignment with the national average (about 80 percent White, 7 percent Black). Foxborough High School's prowess in jazz, like LaGuardia's, has been amply demonstrated by its fairly successful history in competitive festivals. The 1998 Essentially Ellington winner was Hall High School from West Hartford, Connecticut. Home to the University of Hartford and its Hartt School of Music, West Hartford is one of the wealthiest suburbs in the Hartford metropolitan region. A municipality that is about 80 percent White, 6 percent Black, West Hartford's median income far exceeds that of its larger urban center, Hartford. Hall's jazz program has long been recognized as one of the finest in the nation, regularly winning regional and national contests stretching back to the 1970s.

There certainly are exceptions to this idea, that the roster of Essentially Ellington winners are usually from affluent suburban schools or highly specialized performing arts schools. One school that has seen a good deal of success in Essentially Ellington in the last decade is Wisconsin's Beloit Memorial High School, whose demographic breakdown in terms of race looks to be much closer to the national average; the community's median household income of approximately $47,000 is approximately 80 percent of the national average and about half the average of its fellow comprehensive school finalists in the most recent competition. Compared to other comprehensive public high schools that have been successful in Essentially Ellington, Beloit is a clear exception. Fort Lauderdale's Dillard High School, referenced previously, is another interesting example. In terms of its student population, Dillard is, in many respects, a typical high school in America's urban landscape, with a student population that is 90 percent Black. In 2010, Dillard made its first appearance in the Essentially Ellington finals, placing second; the following year, they placed first, which they repeated the following year. With the exception of one year (2016), Dillard has been a finalist in every contest since 2010. These statistics aside, Dillard's identity as a performing arts magnet does make them somewhat unrepresentative of "typical" American high schools, even in an urban context.[76]

None of this is intended as a critique or slight against any of the schools mentioned here, nor against Essentially Ellington itself. These are all fine school music programs with exceptionally talented, dedicated students, outstanding, committed teachers, and networks of deeply supportive parents and community boosters. Their success is admirable. But it is not, ultimately, representative of American jazz education at large; they are, to borrow from the discussion in chapter two, outliers in the jazz education landscape. It might seem a bit obvious that schools with long-established, successful jazz programs would do well in a major national high school jazz competition, and indeed, Essentially Ellington is not the only example of where such schools have racked up awards and recognition. But regardless of the intent of Essentially Ellington as an expression of the "jazz democracy" espoused by JALC, the results point to continued disparities within arts education. None of this is the fault of Essentially Ellington or JALC nor (certainly) the students and teachers who participate (and I want to strenuously emphasize this point). But these results do, perhaps, reflect a reality that could be at odds with the professed goals of the institution and of this specific program. In the quarter century of the program's run (making exceptions for the first year as well as the impact of the COVID pandemic), there have been, in theory, somewhere in the neighborhood of more than three hundred potential finalist spots during Essentially Ellington's existence. Yet there have been approximately 120 finalist bands since the program's inception, with thirteen schools winning first-place titles across the program's history; four programs have captured first place at least three times (fourteen wins between them, representing more than half of the total). Around 10 percent are performing arts schools, community youth jazz programs, or regional ensembles (in other words, not "standard" high schools). This means, statistically speaking, that each year, somewhere between one-third and one-half of the finalists are bands that have already been in this position. In the most recent competition (2022), only three of the fifteen finalist bands had been in the finals fewer than three times. Orange County School of the Arts from Santa Ana, California (who placed third) and Bothell High School near Seattle were first-time finalists, while one (Indiana's Noblesville High School) was making its second finals appearance. On average, the 2022 finalists had made nearly eight appearances each in the finals in New York.[77] When one considers that thousands of schools have participated in the preliminary stages, to say nothing of the noncompetitive regional Essentially Ellington festivals, the roster of finalists reflects a relatively modest number. And to be fair, that probably should not be that much of a surprise; programs that reach the finals are, by and large, not "good" for a single year but sometimes have long records of excellence. Still, it must be acknowledged that Essentially Ellington, at least in terms of the selection of finalists for its marquee event, may not have had the discipline-altering impact that many assumed it would have. And a large factor in these disparities might be linked, at least in part, to something mentioned earlier, the fact that Ellington's music, compared to much of what is written for school jazz bands today, is simply difficult to play, often requiring advanced players with a good idiomatic grasp of jazz. Those schools that are able to meet this challenge will naturally have better outcomes.

This may be, admittedly, putting too many expectations on the shoulders of one organization and one competition. But JALC has, to its credit, begun to address the idea that only a limited number of schools have been successful at the higher levels of the competition. The "*Essentially Ellington* Equity and Inclusion Initiative" is intended to "develop and support systemically under-served and/or underrepresented jazz programs that show outstanding promise."[78] Among other criteria, participating schools must, according to the program's description on the JALC website, a) demonstrate Title I status (or have 40 percent of students who qualify for free/reduced lunch), and b) be comprised of "70% of students from diverse backgrounds as demonstrated by a variety of factors, including but not limited to: socioeconomic background, cultural heritage, race, ethnicity, and geographic origin."[79] As the COVID pandemic interrupted Essentially Ellington in 2020 and 2021, shifting the competition to a virtual format, the results of JALC's efforts will likely take years to properly assess. But the fact that the organization—really, any organization—has recognized the problem and taken specific actions to address it is itself a notable development in a field that has been largely resistant to such changes.

One thing we must consider is that no matter the efforts made by Marsalis and JALC, there are many factors outside of their control that will determine the success (or lack thereof) of any particular institution. Despite a more direct and focused effort to foster diversity and inclusion in the Essentially Ellington program, these efforts frequently run up against what are often deeply entrenched inequities in jazz education. Even the most successful Essentially Ellington participants themselves are not immune from these challenges. In a 2003 article in the *Seattle Times*, longtime jazz writer Paul de Barros highlighted the discrepancy between Seattle schools' demographics and the makeup of its public school jazz ensembles. De Barros focuses on the jazz programs at Garfield and Roosevelt High Schools, two schools that have arguably been the most successful in the history of the Essentially Ellington program, having won the competition four times each.[80] Several parents interviewed in de Barros's piece expressed shock at the wide gap between the racial makeup of the area's population and the students in the two schools' bands:

Angela Maxie, an African American, was perplexed. Her son, Clifton "Scooter" Maxie, goes to Garfield and plays music, but not in the jazz band. "How," she asked her son, "could Roosevelt beat you guys, when you've got all those black kids in the band?" "Mom," Maxie answered with a sigh, "there aren't any black kids in the band." Nor are there any black kids in the jazz band at Roosevelt. Or at Washington Middle School. Or at Chief Sealth High School.[81]

In searching for an explanation, de Barros lays the blame squarely on economic disparities at primary levels of the public school system, a viewpoint shared by the renowned director at Garfield, Clarence Acox:

Many black students have been priced out, or are opting out, of an art form that has its roots in African American culture. The majority of the district's black students are from low-income families who can't afford private music lessons. And music has become an expensive luxury at budget-strapped public schools forced to cut programs and staff .... Clarence Acox, black director of the Garfield jazz band, which made the Ellington finals again this year, says cuts in elementary-school music instruction mean low-income kids never get a chance to start.[82]

It is here, in the earliest levels of the music curriculum, that the kinds of economic disparities that lead to vastly different outcomes for Black and White students begin. And these gaps show up in very particular ways. De Barros contrasts the experiences of two Garfield students; first, a White student who is described as follows:

[The student] started on piano in second grade. At St. Joseph School and Lowell Elementary, he had general music; in fourth grade, an EIM [Elementary Instrumental Music] teacher started him on trombone. His mother immediately signed him up for private lessons .... No one subsidizes the private lessons Sam now takes from two different teachers, or the price of his excellent instrument.[83]

Meanwhile, the Black student referenced earlier took a very different path in a manner that resonates deeply with the discussion in the previous chapter:

Garfield sophomore Maxie, who is black, is a talented musician and athlete whom several kids in the jazz band describe as an "awesome" keyboard player. But when Maxie auditioned this year (one of only two African Americans out of 97 at Garfield who did), it turned out he couldn't read music.... Maxie went to Dunlap Elementary, where there was no general music teacher. At Hamilton Middle School, he played drums in jazz band but dropped out.... He says he would like to take lessons, but they are expensive, and now varsity football takes up most of his free time.[84]

Without focused, continued study and the economic resources required to sustain it, economically vulnerable students often cannot compete with their wealthier peers. Even a program like Essentially Ellington is not unaffected by such realities, despite its pronounced mission of fostering a more democratic experience for young jazz musicians. Within the framework of a jazz narrative that emphasizes its roots and development in Black American communities, the realities of racialized economic and social dynamics are seldom far away.

JAZZ PEOPLE AND PUBLIC PEDAGOGIES

DEFENDING JAZZ OR DEFENSIVENESS ABOUT JAZZ?

The year 2014 was a fairly rough one in the world of jazz. To be sure, there were many exceptionally good recordings released around the world; from the perspective of the music itself, jazz was as good as ever. At the same time, there was something else going on, something a bit darker. Much has been made of the declining state of the jazz audience in the US. The marginal state of modern jazz in the American music market is, of course, much dissected and well documented. Specific statistics are difficult to quantify, but one often-invoked figure emerging from an NEA report in the 1990s pegs the "jazz audience" at around 3 percent of the overall musical market. More recently, much has been made of the fact that jazz record sales had slipped even lower. Many articles proclaimed that by 2014, jazz was now neck and neck with classical music as America's "least favorite" musical style. Nielson's year-end statistics for the year bear this out. Both genres comprised approximately 1.4 percent of total musical consumption (i.e., sales); more concerning for those invested in both genres is that each accounted for only 0.3 percent of music streams, an ominous sign in any economic landscape.[1] This race to the bottom was, in early 2015, somewhat depressingly noted by a number of pieces lamenting jazz's new last-place status. This "alarming trend" was summarized by David La Rosa, who explains:

> Some have tried to explain away Jazz's continuing decline in the rankings by citing the fact that popular crossover albums, like Robert Glasper's *Black Radio* and *Black Radio 2*, are rarely classified as jazz. But the fact remains that new listeners are not engaging with jazz music as they once did and long-time jazz listeners often exhibit behaviors that result in them ignoring new releases, even by established artists . . . . This is indicative of an aging listenership that is slow to adapt to new

technologies. As more and more traditional record stores go out of business, it's becoming harder for these veteran stalwarts of the genre to access new releases, while the few digital natives that actively listen to jazz are clearly finding it difficult to carry the numbers.[2]

The question of why jazz has fallen to this point in the public eye has occupied jazz communities for some time. A 2010 essay by NPR jazz writer Patrick Jarenwattananon[3] notes the commonly held assumption that jazz is "too difficult" for the average listener. In the essay, he references a segment on the "jazz boyfriend" phenomenon, spotlighting comments from women who believed that they were in such a relationship. One respondent commented on her "jazz husband":

> My offenses include, but are not limited to . . . complaining about 28 min. songs and when asked how I like [Joe] Lovano's set at The Vanguard replying with, "I was too grossed out by the jazzgasms everyone was having to listen [to]" (you know—the head bobbing, facial contorting and moans that are required to listen to jazz) . . . . I'm too dumb to like jazz.[4]

Another respondent adds, "I'll have to admit that I am not smart enough for this type of music. I need someone to remind me of the melody at least every sixteen measures or so."[5] Jarenwattananon concedes that such complaints may have some merit:

> Jazz, as a whole, requires a bit of buy-in. Much of it is instrumental, and for people who listen to music for lyrics, that component often goes missing. Performance conventions can be uncommon: applauding in weird places, sitting down, being really quiet. Sometimes jazz composers also like to write complex harmonies, meters and forms not usually heard in pop music. But even before you get to "complex even for jazz" music, some of jazz's most treasured central precepts—swing, 12-bar blues, "rhythm changes" or AABA form, solo improvisation—are unfamiliar to many of today's music listeners in the first place. All things considered, the deck is stacked against jazz. That said, many jazz musicians manage to transcend these things nightly to convey some greater beauty or depth or joy.[6]

This is a formidable task, however, getting lay audiences to recognize the beauty within the complexity. The blame for this is often attributed to many factors, it seems; substandard music education, a recording industry that doesn't care about anything but sales, short attention spans, and often, stupidity. In the final analysis, it probably doesn't matter. The hard facts are what they are, and that is that jazz is not popular, and this does not look to be changing significantly any time in the immediate future. This has been a hard reality for many jazz people to accept and goes a long way to explaining the kinds of reactions we can observe in defense of the music.

The online angst over jazz's public position was skewered by a Twitter account that first appeared in 2013. "Jazz is The [*sic*] Worst" (hereafter JITW), as its name implies, was dedicated to the denigration and dismissal of jazz, often in comically brutal fashion. As more "serious" discussions of the current state of jazz simmered in newspapers, magazines, and blogs, JITW acted like something of a heckler in a comedy club, offering a running commentary on the music and its adherents. JITW became a focal point of discussion throughout 2014; in a sense, it was a microcosm of the larger existential debates within jazz communities about the place of the music in contemporary culture. JITW had a habit of posting tweets that were at once bitingly sarcastic takes on jazz life but that often contained kernels of truth that, for some, may have hit a bit too close to home. A frequent topic of JITW tweets concerned a perceived tendency among musicians to play solos that were too long. Take this tweet, for instance, posted on November 10, 2014, which reads in its entirety: "'Less is More': A phrase no Jazz Musician has ever said." Other posts highlighted problems in jazz education, such as this tweet from September 23, 2015: "Jazz School curriculums should be updated to include classes on Barista skills, SAT tutor training and borrowing money from your parents."[7] Advancing a pointed critique of both the economic challenges of the jazz world and the jazz education industrial complex, responses to this tweet indicated some acknowledgment that it might not be too far off-topic. One user named Charles Telerant replied that "I never knew I was majoring in 'Uber' the whole time I was at Berklee." A second user, Patrick Overturf, noted, "[A]dd pizza delivering and you're set." Another tweet, from October 21, 2014, references a recently announced collaboration between Berklee and pianist Kenny Werner related to musicians' wellness: "I assume this is some kind of counseling program to prep students for the fact that there are no gigs upon graduation."

For all that the JITW account roundly heckled jazz and jazz musicians, it's clear from many of the posts that the author was someone who had a great deal of knowledge of the community and its current debates. And this is why the JITW Twitter feed touched a nerve; there's just enough truth in what's being said to make it difficult to simply dismiss. We are left with the lingering sense that they might, after all, be right. In a tweet on December 4, 2014, JITW twists the knife a bit further, tweeting: "At this very difficult time, it's important to remember: Everyone hates jazz, regardless of race or background." Given the statistics that were about to drop from Nielson, this is not a sentiment that can be easily cast aside.

The apparent lack of interest in jazz from within the American listening public was a bitter pill to swallow, the latest indignity to confront jazz musicians, fans, and others in the industry. Jazz had become, for many, a subject of parody that had worked its way into other, more established forms of popular culture. Perhaps the best known of these is the character of Lisa on the long-running animated series *The Simpsons*. Among the many traits and quirks which define her persona are her intelligence, tendency toward know-it-all-ness, kindness, but most of all, her love for her baritone saxophone, which she dutifully plays as a member of the school band at Springfield Elementary. Inspired by her mentor, the late blues singer and saxophonist "Bleeding Gums" Murphy, Lisa's affinity for jazz is a frequent sonic presence in the show, often used as a device to establish that she is, in the context of the story, different from her peers; given her identity as a school-aged girl within a male-dominated school jazz world, the sense of difference is accentuated even further. Lisa's seriousness about jazz is one of the numerous qualities that make her, in the eyes of her classmates, somewhat strange. We can see a similar dynamic at work in a scene from the NBC comedy series *Parks and Recreation*. The main character, Leslie Knope (Amy Poehler), reads a lead-in for the local public radio station's jazz-themed program called "Jazz Plus Jazz Equals Jazz," which features different jazz recordings played simultaneously (in this case, "a recording of Benny Goodman, played over a separate recording of Miles Davis") with predictably chaotic results. Leslie's reaction to this mashup is a look of pained confusion, while her host insists (via Dan Castellaneta's dead-on impersonation of a local public radio personality) that "research shows that our listeners . . . *love jazz*."[8]

Sometimes, the intertwined threads of parody and reality can be more difficult to sort out. One particularly striking example of this idea can be seen in a controversy that erupted in late 2014 following the publication in the *New Yorker* of a piece by comedy writer Django Gold. Written in the form of an "as told to" memoir from Sonny Rollins, the piece presents a narrative of the saxophonist as a figure who regrets his choice of career and who, it turns out, does not really like jazz. The fictitious Rollins's observations range from "[t]he saxophone sounds horrible. Like a scared pig" to "[j]azz might be the stupidest thing anyone ever came up with" to a final reflection on his career: "I hate music. I wasted my life."[9]

Who exactly was this piece intended for? Probably not Rollins himself, whom Gold has acknowledged he admired before he wrote the piece. And it is unlikely that Gold is aiming for a broad non-jazz audience who likely knows very little about Rollins and thus would probably not get the joke. One possible target for Gold's satire might be people who take jazz—and themselves as jazz people—far too seriously, a condition which he notes is "ripe for satire."[10] The aforementioned "jazz boyfriend" comes to mind. And indeed, there is a certain amount of humor to be had in a parody of perhaps jazz's most sacralized living figure, simply in contemplating the very fact that jazz lovers might be indignant or even angered by a simple piece of parody. For better or worse, Gold got what he was looking for, and far more.

For many readers who were deeply invested in jazz, the *New Yorker* piece was simply too much to take. Reactions to the piece came quickly, and the authors did not pull their punches. Marc Myers attributes the article to the prevalence of "jackass culture," a reference to an MTV program.[11] For Myers, channeling the sentiments of legions of angry Sonny Rollins fans, Gold's piece was a direct attack on jazz itself:

> In the case of the Sonny Rollins spoof, there's a disturbing subtext. Boiled down, the fun at Sonny's expense seems to be saying something more—that jazz is a joke and a futile endeavor, that Sonny is a fool and a laughing stock [sic] who has been wasting his time with that saxophone of his, that jazz's struggle to remain relevant in an age of nihilistic pop is side-splitting funny—like videos of an injured giraffe repeatedly struggling to get to its feet.[12]

One of the highest-profile—and most impassioned—responses to the *New Yorker* piece came in the form of an essay on the Arts Journal website written by Howard Mandel, one of jazz's best-known and most widely read critical figures. For Mandel, Gold's essay was not simply the case of a joke that didn't land. It was a deep, insulting, and callous affront to both jazz and Rollins himself. Mandel writes:

> I'm aghast at *The New Yorker*'s rip-off of Sonny Rollins' good name and great heart to slag jazz in the guise of "humor." A *Daily Shouts* piece bylined "Django Gold" (surely a pseudonym) purports to be "Sonny Rollins: In His Own Words" and controverts the very essence of the art form this grand hero has embodied for more than half a century —without raising a chuckle (at least from me) .... Shame on *The New Yorker*. What would [Whitney] Balliett, Robert Gottlieb

(*TNY* editor 1987–82, editor of *Reading Jazz*), or such immortal *TNY* humorists as Robert Benchley, James Thurber, S. J. Perelman or Donald Barthelme, author of a genuinely silly New Yorker-published spoof, "The King of Jazz" say? For shame, for shame. Not that jazz is sacrosanct, but "funny" must be *funny*.[13]

It would have been easy enough for Mandel and other writers to simply state that they didn't find the piece particularly funny, a position which, I would note, I share with them. I am in complete agreement with Sean O'Connell's assessment, appearing in the *Village Voice* shortly after the original essay, that Gold's jokes "fell flat."[14] I recognized that it was satire, although I would add not particularly well executed. I did not see the piece as an "insult" against Rollins's music or his character; it was the equivalent of a standup comic telling a joke, only to hear no applause coming back from the crowd.

But given the response to the piece, it does not appear that my reaction was typical. Such negative assessments led Will Layman, writing in the online journal *PopMatters*, to suggest that jazz has an "image problem."[15] In commenting further on this controversy, Layman hits upon a particularly resonant note in asking, near the beginning of the essay, "What happens when an *art form* wears khakis—or seems like it does?"[16] He writes that "this 'incident' provides a case study. How do you defend and promote a still evolving, still 'cool' thing that is taught in academies and seems as up to date as a bow tie? How do you laugh off a joke about it without helping to bury it along the way?"[17] Layman's juxtaposition of coolness and the role of "academies" certainly seems to echo the sentiments of many observers over the years, noting the inherent tension between institutional validation and the music's identity as a countervailing force to the classical canon. Layman is asking a good question here: Can jazz people take a joke?

For some, the answer seemed to be an emphatic "no," and the likely reason wasn't that Gold had created a complete fiction; rather, it was that certain moments in the essay *felt like they could be real*. Gold certainly understood his audience as well as what buttons to push to get a rise out of them. And he knew this because he knew how such articles often played out in the pages of *DownBeat* or *JazzTimes*. Layman continues, commenting on a jam session with Bud Powell and Charlie Parker (which the fictionalized Rollins calls "the worst day of my life"):

> That's funny because, if you're a jazz fan, you've read countless interviews with musicians that read exactly like this, with a legend like Bird or Bud showing up and then they're playing till morning. It's

funny to imagine that this was *not* a great impromptu jam session for a guy who just finished playing his own loooong night of music for (I'm imagining) little pay. So never mind that a jazz great came into your life—having to jam with him all night could be such a drag. It's funny because it's surprising, because it disrupts a well-known trope of music writing, and because it injects a dose of real life into what is usually presented as a kind of late-night fairy tale.[18]

To say that Gold's piece touched a raw nerve is an understatement, to put it mildly. But why? What was it about this that spurred on this intense, furious reaction? Not being able to take a joke only gets us so far, I think. There is something else going on here.

And that something else is deeply connected to a sense of defensiveness that has, over the past two decades or so, taken hold within jazz communities. Jazz is not simply something to be appreciated; it must be *defended* against criticism and attack. A parody based on Rollins was particularly galling. Sonny Rollins is very likely jazz's senior elder statesman, and more importantly, arguably the last major living link to jazz's immediate postwar period. Like Armstrong or Ellington, Rollins is a figure for whom jazz people widely express a sense of reverence, and like those other artists, there is a tendency toward "hero worship" and a protectiveness with respect to his legacy. Attacks on him are nothing less than attacks on the very soul of the music, and any such attacks must be forcefully countered.

That being said, other examples of public engagement with jazz have, perhaps, led to a sense that the ire felt by many jazz defenders might well be justified. Pouring a robust heap of salt directly into the wound that was opened by Gold's *New Yorker* essay, Justin Moyer took to the pages of the *Washington Post* about a week later to explain to his readers how Gold's piece was "funny because it was true."[19] Moyer deploys a number of familiar tropes in what amounts to a full frontal assault on the music; it is boring, inaccessible, stagnant . . . it has "retreated from the nightclub to the academy." For whatever reason, there seems to be a not-insignificant cadre of people who hate jazz, and Moyer is here to give them voice.

Hate is one thing. But most public reactions to jazz seem to have more to do with indifference, or to return to a theme we examined earlier, lack of knowledge. As jazz's profile declines in the public sphere, such discussions are seen to be increasingly important by the music's advocates. Howard Mandel writes that the joke "is nothing to laugh at," which "turns on the seed of punkish resentment sophisticates presumably harbor against the music."[20] It is precisely the fact that jazz has such a modest public profile that heightens Mandel's concern. People whose knowledge of Rollins is limited have no frame of reference within which to understand Gold's essay. Without knowing anything about Rollins, it is certainly conceivable that someone could read Gold's essay and believe that it was real. But . . . why should this matter? What is the actual harm to Rollins, or to jazz in general, that was caused by Gold's essay? Will fewer people listen to jazz after reading it? Will fewer people buy Rollins's recordings? Is not Sonny Rollins, one of jazz's truly titanic figures, established enough not to be bothered by some mediocre satire in the *New Yorker*?

As it happens, we don't have to speculate. A few days after the publication of the essay, Rollins sat down with "Jazz Video Guy" Bret Primack for a wide-ranging interview. Rollins addressed the controversy head-on, comparing Gold's essay to the irreverent humor of *Mad* magazine, stating that while he appreciates satire and ironic humor, the piece "seems to be ridiculing jazz music a little too much."[21] But at another point in the interview, Rollins seems to make a more pointed critique, saying that "these people, young guys practicing, thought that I said something as stupid as that. I mean, that hurt me . . . I got very upset about it . . . . They were saying some very insulting, very derogatory things about jazz . . . . I can't even repeat it and read the article now. I can't take it."[22] These two sentiments would seem to be at odds. On the one hand, Rollins seems to be dismissive, or even forgiving, of Gold's essay, likening it to a classic American satirical outlet. But later, the sense of forgiveness is replaced by an expression of being hurt and insulted. What's notable in this context about Rollins's comments is not simply the idea that he was "attacked." It is that jazz itself was the subject of the insult, and this simply takes things too far. But can a style of music really be insulted? Does jazz have feelings that are hurt by such comments? Per Rollins's comments and similar comments from other defenders (Mandel is an obvious example), the answer would seem to be yes.

One wonders if Gold ultimately achieved his seeming objective here, to "troll" the jazz purist crowd. Judging from the reaction, one could certainly make this case; if he believed that jazz people are too serious, they stepped up to prove the point. For his part, Gold addressed the situation in follow-up interviews. His comments to *Newsweek* indicate that he sees much of this as an overreaction: "I was not trying to kill jazz," he replied, "and I doubt I would have had much success if that was my intent. The idea that 500 words of text could have any impact on an entire genre of music—or the legacy of someone who has enjoyed a 60-year career at the top of the mountain—is pretty unrealistic."[23] He makes a similar point to *JazzTimes*, saying, "I'm dubious that

I succeeded in having any impact on Sonny's legacy, Google Search results be damned."[24] There is a point that Gold makes here that I think is worth considering, the idea he expresses that his "500 words of text" would have the power to kill jazz. While it's probably a stretch to say that all of Gold's critics believed that he could,[25] there is a sense that they felt that things like his essay might be hastening the death of jazz. There is a palpable sense of this fear, that the fragility of jazz in the public sphere is an existential threat to the music and its culture.

Lackluster sales, bad parodies, hecklers on Twitter . . . jazz in 2014 couldn't seem to catch a break. As if all this were not enough, later in the year, there was one more event that would send ripples of discontent through the jazz world. On October 10, Sony put into wide release Damien Chazelle's new film *Whiplash*, which had received rave reviews from the Sundance Film Festival earlier in the year. *Whiplash* tells the tale of a young jazz drummer and his relationship with his obsessive, abusive teacher. While *Whiplash* got a very warm reception among film critics (in large part due to the performance of J. K. Simmons as teacher Terrence Fletcher, a role for which he would win a well-deserved Academy Award for Best Supporting Actor), for many jazz people the reception of the film was, shall we say, not quite as positive. Richard Brody, writing in the *New Yorker*, referred to the film's portrayal of jazz as a "grotesque and ludicrous caricature."[26] I would be remiss if I did not note that Brody's review came only a few weeks after the publication of the infamous Django Gold piece and in the same publication.

In a year-end retrospective on jazz later in 2014, Nate Chinen, writing in the *New York Times*, positions the film's premiere in January at Sundance as a catalyst for what he terms "Jazz's Year of Complaint." A major factor in all this was that in 2014, jazz seems to have been caught up in the surge of social media-fueled "outrage," which Chinen calls the "lingua franca of our social media age."[27] Chinen writes:

> Jazz in 2014—or more accurately, the discourse around jazz in 2014—often resembled a crescendo of gibes and gripes, with each new affront calling forth a fresh wave of umbrage. In the end it wasn't any single skirmish that led to my air of weary resignation, but rather a brisk accumulation of them, quickening into a blur. And what surprised me was the exasperation I felt not only with jazz's cynical assailants, but also with its gallant defenders, some of whom could seem as starchy and reflexively scandalized as Margaret Dumont in a Marx Brothers flick.[28]

I'd like to follow Chinen's example here and invoke a little historical anachronism of my own. In discussing the changing media landscape in jazz over the last two decades, I often joke to my students about my belief that if Miles Davis were still living today, 1) he would almost certainly have a Twitter account, and 2) it would be incredibly entertaining to read.

What is to be done about all this? What can jazz people do to ensure that their music continues to survive and becomes, once again, a vital, visible, and viable presence in American culture? The remainder of this chapter attempts to shed light on how jazz people have attempted to grapple with these questions. In the first of these discussions, I examine the concept of "public pedagogy," efforts aimed at education for nonspecialists within the context of the public sphere. Although such efforts would seem to represent a "noninstitutional" approach to jazz education, I posit that particular institutional forces are still present and exert a powerful influence on the nature of such discourses. Following this, I examine issues involved with the use of jazz as a metaphor, in which particular ideas about jazz are applied to other concepts; jazz's relative unfamiliarity among the general public presents particular difficulties for the effectiveness of these kinds of ideas, complicating efforts directed toward public pedagogy. I conclude with an examination of the production of and reaction to Damien Chazelle's two best-known films, *Whiplash* and *La La Land*. In particular, I am interested in how these films reflect Chazelle's own experiences as someone for whom jazz performance was a formative experience; now, as a "jazz civilian," Chazelle's channeling of his own jazz experiences through his films has caused a considerable reaction in the jazz world. Chazelle's films provide a fascinating opportunity to see such processes playing out, particularly as they 1) originate in a root experience in jazz education, 2) engage with similar kinds of public pedagogies as are seen in other contexts, and 3) invite similar kinds of reactions from jazz people.

"PEOPLE NEED TO BE EDUCATED": THE IMPERATIVE OF JAZZ'S PUBLIC PEDAGOGY

If many jazz commenters are to be believed, the public must be *educated* about this music, and doing so is imperative to the music's survival. Indeed, the notion that the general public "needs to be educated" is a frequent theme in discussions of jazz. Consider the following example. In January 2018, *JazzTimes* and Jazz at Lincoln Center jointly sponsored an event in New York. Dubbed the "Jazz Congress," the event, according to publicity materials published on the JALC website:

... [w]ill serve the musicians, professionals, and advocates of the community as a place to network, learn, and be inspired to continue their vital work on behalf of the music. With reverence for our tradition and history, the Jazz Congress will also be forward looking, offering a chance to consider how the community and our work can evolve and embrace developments in technology, shifting audience trends, and music consumption habits.[29]

The keynote address for this event was given by Kareem Abdul-Jabbar, former UCLA Bruin and LA Laker, Basketball Hall of Fame inductee, kung fu enthusiast, and ardent jazz supporter. In his remarks, Abdul-Jabbar noted that those who were committed to the music had a particular responsibility:

We need to educate the next generation that the joys of jazz are greater than those of K-pop and other music trends. Most courses teach students how to make a living; art and music teaches them how to enjoy life. [We need] more outreach programs in schools—especially since Trump recently proposed severe budget cuts that could eliminate many music and art programs.[30]

Digs at Donald Trump and K-pop notwithstanding, Abdul-Jabbar referenced an idea that is very often articulated by jazz people, the notion that the public needs to be "educated" about the music, that public outreach and engagement with potential audiences, especially younger audiences, is key to the music's success. Given jazz's tenuous place in the public culture market, Abdul-Jabbar's comments are certainly not out of place. Educating potential audience members can, among other things, help to shore up a genre that is facing steep economic challenges due to a consistently declining audience over the last several decades. As audiences age, the cultivation and development of new listeners and concertgoers will be essential for the continued viability of the music.

What I would suggest is that what Abdul-Jabbar is really talking about here is "public pedagogy," a concept that has come into increased usage in recent years. As the term implies, public pedagogy is outward facing to the public. It is, admittedly, a somewhat nebulous construct, undertheorized and inconsistently applied. But there are some basic ideas that we can highlight. Sandlin, Schultz, and Burdick refer to public pedagogy as "spaces, sites, and languages of education and learning that exist outside of the walls of the institution of schools. As this collection illustrates, however, they are just as crucial—if not more so—to our understanding of the developments of identities and social formations as the teaching that goes on within the classroom."[31] Efforts to promote jazz among the general public would seem to fall squarely within this understanding of the term. Most studies of public pedagogy emphasize how expressive forms such as music, art, literature, and the like can serve as conduits for public pedagogies; William Pinar suggests that public pedagogy can be facilitated "through music" and other forms of media.[32] I draw attention to the phrasing *through music*. Music in this context is the means through which this pedagogy can be accomplished. While a public pedagogy of jazz might well use the music to teach other concepts (and indeed, we will explore this later in the chapter), if the music is relatively unfamiliar, much of the pedagogical energy must, by necessity, be directed toward learning about jazz. And it is this idea that interests me here: the ways in which public pedagogies are enacted to promote an understanding of jazz itself, not simply in the service of another idea, but for its own purpose. Sentiments like Abdul-Jabbar's, emphasizing the need "to educate the next generation [about] the joys of jazz," are in line with these ideas. Much of jazz's public pedagogy is characterized by efforts and initiatives that are intended to secure and solidify the place of jazz in the public marketplace of ideas by making the public more aware of jazz. One can be "aware" of jazz in many different ways, however; one could love it, but one could also hate it. Both of these stances would theoretically require an awareness of the genre to make such a judgment (whether or not this is true in practice is another question).

Public pedagogy is by no means a recent development in jazz. Consider Paul Whiteman's "Experiment in Modern Music" event in 1924, known today mainly for its premiere of Gershwin's *Rhapsody in Blue*. Whiteman's intent with the concert was explicitly pedagogical, as Whiteman's manager Hugh Ernst noted in the original program notes. "The experiment," Ernst wrote, "is to be purely educational. Mr. Whiteman intends to point out, with the assistance of his orchestra and associates, the tremendous strides which have been made in popular music from the day of the discordant jazz."[33] The concert also included the Whiteman orchestra playing Elgar's *Pomp and Circumstance*, signifying—perhaps a bit too literally—jazz's graduation into the realms of elite culture. Other jazz artists have taken the music to non-jazz audiences in a more direct manner. Kelsey Klotz has examined Dave Brubeck's role as a "'jazz evangelist' who opened jazz to a new audience" as a "respectable" artist who appealed to an audience comprised largely of middle-class White women.[34] Another pianist, Billy Taylor, was a crucial figure behind the establishment of the "Jazzmobile" program in partnership with local arts patron Daphne Arnstein. Founded in Harlem in 1964, Jazzmobile's mission has been to bring jazz artists directly to the local community, and in so doing, serves as a model for civic jazz programs around the US and the world. One of jazz's most enduring and endearing public pedagogues was Fred Rogers, the creator and host of the long-running PBS program *Mister Rogers' Neighborhood*. Filmed in Pittsburgh, each program opened with music provided by a trio of musicians led by pianist and local jazz legend Johnny Costa. Another regular on the program was Joe Negri, who portrayed a music store owner and, in "make believe sequences," the local handyman; off-screen, Negri is himself a highly regarded jazz guitarist, occasionally performing on the show.[35] Rogers would often feature other jazz musicians on the show to introduce a generation of young children to the music that he held in such high regard. Efforts such as these have continued over the last several decades, as evidenced by the plethora of outreach programs, community jazz arts programs, and the like that are aimed at educating the public about jazz.

The imperative that people "need to be educated" about jazz is an idea that frequently appears in these kinds of public discourses. A typical example of this comes from Travis Kemp, a West Texas radio host who had this to say in a feature on International Jazz Day, of which he is an organizer: "I'm celebrating International Jazz Day because people need to be educated about jazz music [and] its impact on music in America, as well as all over the world.... People need to understand how [and] why jazz is so important to popular music today. They have to know about jazz's past, in order for it to have a future."[36] Far to the north, the Calgary Jazz Orchestra lists as one of the organization's goals "to educate the audience, adults and children alike on the complexity, beauty and importance of jazz music."[37] Even on the other side of the globe, educating audiences persists as a core concern, as Chinese pianist Yiling Lin notes: "[I]t takes time and effort to cultivate and educate the audience. It is definitely not an easy job, but the potential is there."[38] Lin's statement could easily be made in New York, New Orleans, or any other place where jazz people circulate.

Education of the non-jazz public also occurs as a more "official" endeavor. The Smithsonian describes the intent of Jazz Appreciation Month as being:

> ... to draw greater public attention to the extraordinary heritage and history of jazz and its importance as an American cultural heritage. In addition, JAM is intended to stimulate the current jazz scene and encourage people of all ages to participate in jazz—to study the music, attend concerts, listen to jazz on radio and recordings, read books about jazz, and support institutional jazz programs.... Many people do not fully appreciate the joys, power, and glories of jazz. JAM is an effort by those who are passionate about jazz to share it with those

who are not as familiar with it. JAM will encourage people to take jazz more seriously as a vital part of America's cultural patrimony and as a great gift to the world, as well as to have fun with it.[39]

I would spotlight one particular passage here, that JAM is "an effort by those who are passionate about jazz to share it with those who are not as familiar with it." This passage might well describe nearly every interaction between jazz people and the non-jazz public, an opportunity to correct this presumed lack of knowledge. In some cases, such interactions are meant to be inviting. In other cases, the nature of these interactions may not be as positive. Fervent advocacy can easily turn to annoyance. Worse, one can be determined to be a "jazz snob," a description common enough to appear in the Urban Dictionary, the web's best-known resource for contemporary slang, which defines the phrase as a reference to "[a]n annoying or stubborn person whom [sic] denies any, or most, kinds of music other than Jazz. Has a self-indulgent illusion of sophistication about himself and, in particular, his tastes."[40] Educating the audience, then, can be a delicate balancing act; on the one hand, jazz people often want to share their enthusiasm, while on the other, too much enthusiasm risks turning off potential audiences.

Jazz knowledge (or the lack thereof) is sometimes cited as a prerequisite for a full appreciation and enjoyment of the music. A notable example that received a good deal of coverage was the highly contentious juxtaposition of Cecil Taylor and Branford Marsalis in Ken Burns's *Jazz* series. Near the end of a segment on the pianist, in which he was described as the symbol of "everything people loved, and everything people hated about the avant-garde," Taylor was reported as saying that "since he prepared for his concerts, the audience should prepare too."[41] No sooner had narrator Keith David finished this statement than the scene switched to Branford Marsalis, who did not hold back in his assessment: "That's total self-indulgent bullshit, as far as I'm concerned. I love baseball, but I mean, I'm not going to go catch 100 grounders before the game."[42] Marsalis's comments (and especially their intentional placement in the film) only served to fan the flames of the inferno that Burns's film had ignited in the jazz world. A number of observers have suggested that Branford Marsalis's comments were taken out of context and that he was not directly addressing Taylor. But given other comments the saxophonist has made, his statement might not be that much of a surprise.

What's at issue here is not simply a dispute (real or imagined) between two musicians; it reflects a fundamental disagreement over how to engage the non-jazz public. For Taylor, knowledge of his music represents a responsibility on the part of the audience, while for Marsalis, such expectations are "self-indulgent." A similar sentiment was expressed in the film *The Commitments*, which centers on a group of Dublin musicians who form a soul band. The group's trumpeter, a supposed veteran of American soul groups in the 1960s and 1970s, explains to the saxophonist, after playing a somewhat Charlie Parker-like solo, that jazz is "musical wanking." This comment likely felt like a deep insult to many jazz people. But one senses that, implicitly, they know that this is a common perception, even if expressed less colorfully.

There are certainly dissenting voices with respect to jazz's public educational imperative. Again, I turn to Branford Marsalis who, in a sprawling interview with Bill Milkowski for *JazzTimes*, casts doubt on such efforts. In an exchange concerning the relatively low popularity of jazz, he states:

> I never really bought into the whole idea of education as an answer. First of all, this music is not easy to listen to. Most of my regular friends, when they would talk about music, they would recite the lyrics. So they're not even listening to the music. So how are you going to get a person like that to make a leap from that into pure instrumental music? How are you going to get people to make a leap from pop [music], which is an interactive music, to what jazz has become, which is kind of a passive listening experience? That's too much of a leap for these people.[43]

Later in this section, he draws a clear distinction between pop and "art music" performance cultures:

> Like, if you go to a pop concert.... And then the song comes on: "Oh, that's my jam!" So what do they do? They sing along with it. Now, you know, I like opera. When I go to the Met, what would happen to me if I started singing along with the tenor? They'd throw me the fuck out the building. So in opera you have the situation where we pay large sums of money to hear some of the best people in the world sing, as opposed to the pop world, where most of my friends pay large sums of money to sing along with the people who are the best at what they do. The idea that you're going to get these people through education to stop being the way that they're going to be is ridiculous. It's absolutely absurd.[44]

Similar (if more succinct) sentiments were expressed in a tweet from Jazz is The Worst on July 3, 2013: "Jazz musicians talk a lot about 'educating' the audience. No one needs to be educated into enjoying an ice cream sundae."[45]

_____ IS JUST LIKE JAZZ: THE "JAZZ METAPHOR" AND PUBLIC PEDAGOGY

Every encounter, whether through a jazz outreach program or a jazz fan trying to convince a friend of the value of the music, represents a chance to make a case for jazz, an opportunity for the enactment of public pedagogy. One strategy that has become increasingly common over the last two decades is the connection of jazz to various aspects of people's lives, be it through economics, careers, politics, sports, and so forth. The list of ways in which jazz can be inserted into the public imagination through linkages to non-jazz ideas is extensive. The most widespread of these ideas can be seen in what has come to be known as the "jazz metaphor," in which jazz serves as a model for particular ways of thinking and behaving.[46] In this context, jazz is positioned as an alternative to traditional practices and assumptions, offering a paradigm in which freedom and an improvisational approach are emphasized. This kind of application of the metaphor is not unlike the ways in which jazz has been pressed into the service of US diplomacy and geopolitics. The best known of these efforts were the early tours in the late 1950s featuring the elite of the current jazz scene, including Louis Armstrong, Benny Goodman, Dave Brubeck, Duke Ellington, and Dizzy Gillespie, among others. For the State Department, which organized these tours, jazz represented, officially at least, the core democratic principles that made the US both successful and unique. A "musical enactment of American democracy,"[47] the State Department's Jazz Ambassador program sought to tip the balance of cultural power toward the US and away from the Soviet Union. The tours were generally well received by local audiences and by the Foreign Service staff and embassy officials who coordinated their visits. Noting the reaction to the original Gillespie tour, Penny Von Eschen writes, "Observing the popular success of Gillespie's band in Yugoslavia, the US ambassador wired Washington that 'Gillespie's band has made our job much easier.'" The *New York Times* reported from Beirut that the reception of the band was "beyond expectations" and that US diplomats there "hope the noise stays in the walls for a long time to come."[48] These tours were, and remain today, a fascinating narrative in jazz history. What underpins such efforts is the use of jazz as a metaphor for freedom, an explicit idea that the State Department wished to promote through the Jazz Ambassadors program. In a similar manner (and with similar intent), Willis Conover, the longtime host of "Jazz Hour" on the Voice of America radio network (similarly a US government program), put it this way in the introduction to an episode of his show: "The music of jazz parallels the freedom that we have in America, something that not every country has."⁴⁹ Von Eschen quotes Conover speaking about this in a bit more depth:

> Jazz is a cross between total discipline and total anarchy. The musicians agree on tempo, key and chord structure but beyond this everyone is free to express himself. This is jazz. And this is America. That's what gives this music validity. It's a musical reflection of the way things happen in America. We're not apt to recognize this over here, but people in other countries can feel this element of freedom. They love jazz because they love freedom.⁵⁰

For someone hearing Conover for the first time and presuming they understand English, would they necessarily be able to hear the parallel of which he speaks? Would they hear the freedom? This is a particular challenge for the use of jazz as a metaphor. If one does not understand what jazz is, can the metaphor truly be effective?

What theoretically makes this metaphor viable is that it is simple—the *idea* of jazz is really doing the metaphorical work here rather than specific musical characteristics or performance practices. This is especially advantageous when dealing with potential audiences whose familiarity with jazz might be relatively limited (a point I shall return to later in the chapter). The level of jazz-related knowledge required to teach or disseminate the metaphor would be presumed to be at least above that of the average person. As an example, an entry on the Publishing Perspectives website written by Anna von Veh outlines ways that online publishers should take a more improvisation-based approach to their work. She opens the discussion with a personal anecdote:

> One evening I was listening to jazz (Duke Ellington's "Take the A Train") and it suddenly all came to me: jazz was the perfect vehicle to integrate our different approaches and to make sense of everything I wanted to say about agility in the digital age . . . . Jazz—structure, separation, integration and improvisation—provides an analogy for discussing context, the content itself, technology and creativity, the organisation, as well as relationships with authors and readers. It shows us how to be ready to act seemingly spontaneously to whatever may come.⁵¹

Religion, and in particular Christian ministry in the United States, is another area where the jazz metaphor has gained traction in recent years. Dwight Zscheile emphasizes the fluidity and agility of jazz in his aptly named 2014 book *The Agile Church*, writing that "[t]he metaphor of jazz is instructive as an alternative imaginative space for churches to inhabit in ministry. When we identify the inherited practices and stories that shape our identity as people of the Way of Jesus, we are free to improvise on them in new ways."[52] Zscheile elaborates on this metaphor, writing that "[c]ontrol simply doesn't work in jazz. Jazz is about acting and paying attention to what unfolds, while being willing to 'court disaster' by surrendering to the music and its possibilities, even as this takes the players to places that disrupt expectations."[53] The following year, David Buschart and Kent Elders make a similar point, likening adherence to tradition to "a classical music performance that follows a highly annotated score" as opposed to "a jazz lead sheet that guides an improvisation but leaves a wide berth for development."[54] The authors propose that "the metaphor of jazz improvisation reminds us to train our attention on the work of the Spirit while reminding us to receive what has been given through past performances."[55] A few years later, Columbia Theological Seminary hosted a workshop on using the jazz metaphor in ministry; the promotional site for the program would "explore how jazz as an art form can influence the practice of ministry. Improvisation, which is central to jazz, will be highlighted as a way to encourage creative responses in this time of intense and rapid change." Attendees would also "have a chance to visit a local jazz club to hear and see the jazz improv in its secular context as well."[56]

"The greatest thing by far is to have a command of metaphor." So says Aristotle, by way of I. A. Richards's influential text *The Philosophy of Rhetoric*.[57] Whether Aristotle's claim is or is not correct, I cannot say. But he and Richards are certainly onto something in emphasizing the metaphor's fundamental importance to human consciousness, an "omnipresent principle of language . . . . We cannot get through three sentences of ordinary discourse without it."[58] In commenting on the nature and structure of metaphors, Richards developed a framework for conceptualizing a distinctive relationship between what he terms "tenor" and "vehicle." This formulation has become a common feature in rhetoric and communications, and I want to spend a bit of time on its application to jazz metaphors.

"Tenor" refers to the object or concept that is to be understood or characterized through the use of the metaphor; the "vehicle" is the idea from which such understanding will be drawn. In the case of the jazz metaphor, publishing, business management, ministry, or democracy is the tenor, that which is (ideally) to be understood; we want to know what democracy is, how it works, etc. Jazz, on the other hand, is the vehicle; we draw certain ideas from jazz that we believe will facilitate this process of understanding. A third idea is also necessary for the metaphor to be effective, what is referred to as "ground." Simply put, ground refers to the aspects of the tenor and the vehicle that are relatable to each other. As Ray Malewitz puts it, "[T]he ground is what enables the metaphor to work—to make sense."[59] Let us consider an example to illustrate this using a song that I recently heard on the radio, Tom Cochrane's 1991 hit song "Life Is a Highway." Here, life is the tenor, the highway is the vehicle, and the ground is what they share; for example, both life and highways can often involve long journeys. Or we could use the oft-cited "life is like a box of chocolates," popularized by the film *Forrest Gump*. In this case, the ground is the uncertainty ("you never know what you're going to get") that is shared between the uncertainty of life and the similar uncertainty of what you are going to bite into from a box of Whitman's. In both of these cases, the ground is easy to conceptualize. On the other hand, if we were to say, "Life is like a lampshade," the ground might be a bit more difficult to conceptualize. Or if we used "life is like string theory," this might be similarly difficult, particularly if one doesn't know what string theory is.

If it appears that I am spending a lot of time explaining what seems like a fairly simple concept, I would suggest that at least with applications of the jazz metaphor, it can be a bit more complicated. Let us examine the jazz-and-democracy metaphor in a bit more depth. In this metaphorical construction, democracy is often explained in terms of freedom through improvisation, a sense of collaborative decision-making, and a space where each individual can have their voice heard. All of these are commonly understood as core guiding principles of American democracy (if perhaps in an idealized way). As Ken Burns states in an interview for PBS:

> Jazz is open and free. And yet, jazz itself adheres to some pretty important rules. In some ways, people are playing within that, which is much like democracy. We're given freedom, but we know that freedom has to occur within certain bounds and constraints, not just of the law, but of other people's freedoms, and their desires to express it. So jazz becomes a mirror that way.[60]

A relatively literal reading of this would highlight a discrepancy between the opening claim that jazz is "open and free" and the later reference to "bounds and constraints." Shortcomings of the metaphor are often recast as reflecting a continual work in progress, ultimately leading to something better, not to a perfect union, which is likely an unattainable goal, but a *more* perfect union, allowing for an overriding sense of idealism that can remain intact. Still, some have pointed to contradictions in the jazz-as-democracy metaphor. In *Knowing Jazz*, I pointed to a somewhat natural conflation between "neoclassic" and "neoconservative," particularly in reference to the zeal with which many adherents of either paradigm pursued their goals. Dale Chapman takes this idea in a somewhat different direction in his book *The Jazz Bubble*, pointing to a similar resonance between neoclassicism and neoliberalism. Chapman sees JALC's physical presence as a critical aspect of this relationship, situating it squarely within the debates over neoliberal economics, the real estate market, and corporate philanthropy. He writes that:

> ... the corporate ecology inhabited by Jazz at Lincoln Center in Midtown Manhattan, its occupancy of a "highly bourgeois, corporatized space" alongside the luxury condominiums and upmarket boutiques of the Time Warner Center, embodies something of the ideological contradiction at the core of JALC's identity. Even as it projects an almost populist encomium to the democratic potentiality of "swing," this term is ultimately stripped of its experimental or insurgent possibilities: the tacitly conservative orientation of JALC's preoccupation with "swing" is the aesthetic correlate of the center's business model, which relies upon an affluent donor class and exclusionary ticket prices.[61]

Mark Laver has also noted this relationship in an article examining JALC's efforts to open a satellite center in Doha, Qatar, noting how JALC's efforts echoed both neoconservative and neoliberal perspectives, "promoting democracy and capitalist economics."[62] Kimberly Hannon Teal points more directly to the dissonance between JALC's jazz-as-democracy rhetoric and the realities of the Center's structure, writing that "[e]ven as Marsalis makes the case for democracy and shared power in music and life, he did so from what was for many years a position of unparalleled power and influence in the field, a position many jazz commenters have accused him of abusing."[63] For Teal, JALC's role in contemporary jazz cannot be separated from its presence in the middle of the most exclusive (and expensive) of prime Manhattan real estate, pointing to "the grandeur of the venue" as a significant factor in its work.[64] Benjamin Givan also touches on these ideas in a recent essay, noting that "most professional jazz groups don't truly aspire to egalitarianism or inclusivity at all.... [T]he music is far from democratic in any ideal sense of the term."[65] Even the strongest advocates of this metaphor admit some of these discrepancies; Givan quotes Wynton Marsalis as suggesting that "swing has a hierarchy, like a government."[66] His essay provides a very thorough and much-needed critique of an idea that has taken hold in many jazz institutions during the last few decades, yet is—as he amply demonstrates—rife with contradictions and misassumptions. This confluence of jazz, democratic ideals, late capitalism, political economies, and competing nationalisms results in a complex matrix that complicates easily made and easily marketed assumptions about jazz's place in public discourse.

And yet such assumptions are still widely made and marketed; there is no shortage of works linking jazz to democracy aimed at the general public. This perspective seems to forcefully resonate with jazz peoples' concern for public perception and a larger project of public pedagogy and advocacy. Here, jazz is positioned as something that is, like democracy, a public good, that is worthwhile, that has clear social and aesthetic benefits. The best face must always be put forward, even if sometimes it's in the form of a mask. An illustrative example of how the metaphor is tailored can be seen in JALC's "Let Freedom Swing" initiative, which involves no small measure of teaching jazz to "lay" audiences. This is by no means unique; when jazz metaphors are used in the context of the non-jazz-knowledgeable, the music must be explained and applied in relatively specific ways. People who patronize these programs need to be taught about jazz, but *what* they are taught is not entirely clear. Is jazz being used to teach democracy? Or is it the other way around, with the objective being the teaching of jazz as a means of engaging and nurturing potential audiences? After all, if one's knowledge of jazz is limited, as is the case with most of the public, then how can jazz be, as Wynton Marsalis suggests, "the perfect metaphor for democracy"?[67] This has significant ramifications for the use of jazz metaphors; jazz might as well be particle physics or a plate of pancakes or a lawnmower if the target audience is unfamiliar with it. Metaphors can only work when the tenor and vehicle align; in order for this to happen, the vehicle must be something with which an audience is familiar. If it is not, either a) these concepts must be conveyed to the audience in some way, which necessitates a form of pedagogy, or b) the metaphor may fail.

Many jazz metaphor-based programs, lectures, and discussions are supplemented with professional jazz performances to illustrate these ideas. This has been particularly evident in presentations relating to business and organizational management. A significant development in this literature came in the form of a special issue of *Organization Science* in 1998, in which numerous authors explored the application of jazz principles directly to business management settings.[68] More recently, the jazz metaphor has become common on the lecture circuit. Let me point to one example that illustrates how such ideas play out in this context. In a 2015 TEDx talk, Jim Kalbach presents jazz as a model for "radical collaboration." An author and consultant on business organization and strategy, Kalbach is like many advocates for the jazz metaphor, a fan and sometime musician, noting that he "play[s] jazz bass and dabble[s] in jam sessions and local jazz festivals in Jersey City."[69] In a video posted to the TEDx YouTube channel, Kalbach uses a well-known example to ease the audience into the particulars of jazz:

> In 1959, Miles Davis entered the studio with his band to record what became the best-selling, most influential jazz album of all times. Entitled *Kind of Blue*, it is in all respects the perfect jazz recording. But there were no rehearsals for this date. In fact, Miles gave the musicians the music as they entered the studio. And except for one song, each first complete take was the complete only take which got pressed on the album. So we ask ourselves how this is possible, how can a group of musicians come together and so spontaneously create great music?[70]

As he continues to speak, a band stands behind him on the stage. The bass noticeably rests on a stand in the back, presumably at the ready for when Kalbach finishes talking. Jazz is, according to him, grounded in three principles: empathy, uncertainty, and patterns, which form the basis of what he refers to as "radical collaboration." I use the term "grounded" here intentionally, as a reference to metaphorical construction. Empathy, uncertainty, and patterns are broad concepts that could certainly be applied in many contexts and would likely be understood by a nonspecialist population. What they might not understand is how these concepts are embedded in jazz improvisation in specific ways.

At this point, Kalbach and his group proceed to demonstrate these ideas more directly. His descriptions of jazz practice are, for the most part, fairly straightforward for those who are familiar with the music, emphasizing the interplay between choice and structure, flexibility and role-playing, individual expression and group collaboration. His discussion of form provides a useful example of how public pedagogy can distill esoteric concepts into easily digestible ideas. Kalbach uses a graphic with four lines of rectangular figures, each representing one phrase of the thirty-two-bar AABA form (the third line, representing the bridge, is a different color than the other three); he then explains how this form serves as the "glue" that holds everything together. This would appear to be an effective, clear way to get nonspecialists to understand the concept, that is, unless someone does not know what a "bar" is, other than a place to get a drink. Kalbach's description leads into a performance of "There Is No Greater Love," followed by a debrief and then by some further linkages between the jazz concepts the audience just heard and non-jazz organizations; as an example, he likens jazz performance to

Spotify's use of "empowered teams" noting that "this does not look like a corporate org chart." Neither, one would presume, does a jazz group.

Still other metaphor-based programs take the use of performance a step further. This can be seen in the work of the Jazz Leadership Project, headed by the husband-and-wife team of Greg Thomas and Jewel Kinch-Thomas. The JLP is "designed to optimize leadership capacity and accelerate team development for heightened workplace engagement and achievement. Engagement and interaction are core aspects of the workshop flow. No music knowledge is needed to gain an understanding of how jazz principles and practices can promote creativity, strengthen leadership capacity, and elevate inclusive team synergy."[71] Per their biographies on the JLP website, Kinch-Thomas is "an executive leader of several arts institutions," who has "over 20 years of experience in organizational operations, budget management, and program development." Her husband and partner, meanwhile, is described as follows:

> Greg has been instrumental in developing humanities programs for top cultural organizations such as Jazz at Lincoln Center. As a journalist and scholar, he has conducted in-depth research and conducted hundreds of interviews over the course of his career. Greg has given presentations on jazz, culture, race, and democratic life and values for a range of online platforms and institutions such Columbia, Hamilton, and Harvard.[72]

In an introductory video clip, the couple explains: "[JKT] We wanted to make this video today, because we hear time and time again how very hard it is to adapt to the massive changes in the world of business. [GT] One thing we all can agree on is that companies need innovative solutions now more than ever." As this dialogue is spoken, jazz piano music is heard in the background. Shortly after Greg Thomas begins speaking, there is a scene shift to a JLP workshop in which the two become facilitators for a group of attendees who are engaged with playing along to the music using toy percussion instruments. This is an interesting extension of the metaphor in that the participants are engaging in a more direct way with experiencing the music. As Greg Thomas refers to "collaborative excellence and team synergy," we see a shot of the JLP Trio; little information is given about this group (including the identities of the musicians themselves, but as all three are wearing face masks, it stands to reason that the clip was made in 2020 or 2021).[73] Other areas of the website give more specific information on their programs, including a page of testimonials from various organizations such as the Human Capital Institute, JP Morgan Chase, the New York Police

Department, and Verizon, whose VP and Deputy General Counsel David Hubbard writes, "At the JLP workshop, the metaphor of Jazz was an effective vehicle for demonstrating how everyone has shared ownership of a project as well as individual ownership of projects. For example, we considered: How does antagonistic cooperation help us make each other better?"[74] The philosophy of JLP is probably best summarized by an entry on the website's blog that states that "[j]azz is creative. Jazz generates a sense of structure, freedom and collaborative possibility via shared purpose, trust, and innovation."[75]

I draw attention to something that was mentioned in Greg Thomas's brief bio on the site, specifically his work as a consultant for Jazz at Lincoln Center. In particular, I refer here to the program titled, in true JALC style, Syncopated Leadership, described as "[a] team building workshop using lessons from jazz improvisation."[76] Further down the main page, we are introduced to the "United We Swing: Business Workshops," which are described as follows:

> Like a business team, the jazz ensemble must deliver a quality product in high-pressure environments while still leaving room for each team member's voice to be heard and valued.
> United We Swing engages and nurtures these team skills. Through interactive activities, team exercises, and business discussions, participants leave with an appreciation of the jazz skills that cross over from music to business.[77]

Also included on the main page is a video introduction to the program. For the most part, the video parallels those made for organizations like JLP. We even see participants in the United We Swing workshop playing along to the music with toy rhythm instruments. A bit of internet sleuthing reveals that this is not a coincidence; Thomas's page on the LinkedIn platform lists, among other things, an entry as "Consultant and Syncopated Leadership Facilitator" for JALC. Clearly, then, Thomas's work for JALC overlaps significantly with his own (and his wife's) efforts with JLP. Perhaps more to the point, the program is, in Venn diagram terms, a nearly perfect circle in relation to JALC's other outreach efforts, particularly with respect to situating jazz as a metaphor for democracy.

I want to return for a moment to the use of toy instruments in teaching the principles of jazz to an adult audience. These instruments are, at first glance, not dissimilar from what would be seen in an Orff-centered children's music classroom. I do not believe it is too far of a stretch to speculate that the use of such instruments and methods is but another extension of jazz and public pedagogy. While most examples of public pedagogy in jazz revolve around discourse and verbal communication (either in spoken or written form), here the pedagogy is based on musical performance, albeit at a level that nonspecialists can engage with. As this is very likely a group whose participants have very little formal musical training or experience, they are, in essence, at least with respect to their knowledge of jazz, at an elementary level. As such, the use of classroom-type instruments such as these would make sense. These programs once again underscore the central role of pedagogy in applying the jazz metaphor. Participants need to be taught about jazz; sometimes, this is done through an article or a lecture or even a lecture demonstration. In other instances, the interaction and exchange of information are more visceral and direct. Regardless of the particular context, jazz is almost always presented in a circumscribed, simplified, and easy-to-digest way. In these examples and numerous others, we see the metaphor in action, brought to the lay audience and explained to them in clear, simple terms. Reaction shots of the audiences show people who seem to be engaged, attentive, and, it seems, interested in the message of the presenters. But what, specifically, are they reacting to? Is it the idea of an improvisational work environment? Do they like or understand the music that is being performed? Or does the attractiveness of the metaphor operate on more of a visceral, emotional level, relying on a feeling? The point here is not to take issue with particular interpretations or perspectives; in fact, I tend to agree that there are meaningful resonances to be found between jazz improvisation and other non-jazz concepts. Where the metaphor runs into some difficulties, however, is in the characterization of the common ground, speaking in rhetorical terms. Refer back to the previous example of the song "Life is a Highway." I would wager that relatively few people do not know what a highway is. But there are many people who don't know the particulars of jazz, and so the metaphor will often include an element of public pedagogy in an effort to familiarize the audience with jazz so that it can be effectively used as a metaphor, as its effectiveness is ultimately predicated on a sense of familiarity.

There is one thing that seems to be missing from the literature of jazz metaphors: do they work? In asking this question, I am not referring to the metaphorical constructions themselves; these will largely remain subjective determinations. Rather, do these efforts demonstrably lead to tangible, measurable, and meaningful results? What happens when a business, for example, adopts a "jazz-like" mindset in practice? While connections and parallels are common in the literature, real-world manifestations are less frequently cited. The metaphor provides a compelling model, but whether that model is ultimately effective is less apparent. Mike Ford's recent doctoral dissertation from Columbia University stands as something of an exception to this trend. Ford, who himself has experience with a startup as well as being a musicologist, makes more direct connections between his own experiences in business with the jazz metaphor.[78] But such detailed accounts are relatively unusual. In general, advocates of the metaphor are more inclined to emphasize its possibilities and potential.

Taking this into account, one wonders if these efforts really have less to do with the "jazz of business" than with the "business of jazz," utilizing public pedagogy to cultivate new audiences and new markets for a music facing an uncertain future. As cynical as that might sound, given the economic challenges of the contemporary jazz scene, it is most certainly a worthwhile exercise; if programs like these lead to attendees becoming "jazz people," so much the better. There is a sense of irony that is rather deeply embedded in these types of efforts, however. A lack of knowledge about jazz might seem to be a formidable barrier to those who seek to position it as a model for more open and improvisatory ways of thinking. And indeed it is, as the extensive efforts toward public pedagogy will illustrate. But might this lack of knowledge work in the metaphor's favor? Put another way, explanations of the metaphor can define jazz in whatever manner they see fit, tailoring their rhetoric in order to draw out particular ideas that might resonate more forcefully with particular audiences. The fact that audiences know so little might make the work of selling the jazz metaphor easier than it would if the audience were more knowledgeable about, say, alternative views of jazz based in less canonical, circumscribed approaches. It is unlikely that a corporate seminar on a jazz-based organization is going to draw heavily upon an artist like Albert Ayler or Cecil Taylor. Once again, the question of institutional knowledge comes into focus. Who gets to speak for jazz and whose viewpoints will be heard will once again exert a powerful influence on the conversation.

GETTING JAZZ "WRONG": DAMIEN CHAZELLE AND JAZZ'S PUBLIC DISCOURSE[79]

One of the most talked about films of the 2014 independent film circuit was Damien Chazelle's *Whiplash*, which won both the Audience and Grand Jury prizes at the Sundance Film Festival. Named for a Don Ellis big band chart composed by Hank Levy (discussed in chapter three), *Whiplash* tells the story of aspiring collegiate jazz drummer Andrew Neiman (played by Miles Teller) in his studies at the fictional Schaffer Conservatory in New York. Neiman's idol is jazz drummer Buddy Rich, a point driven home during one scene in which he practices obsessively while looking at a photo of Rich taped to the wall of his practice studio. Looming over the jazz students at Schaffer is Terrence Fletcher, a dominating, abusive conductor whose main goal in life seems to be the achievement of a technically perfect performance by any means necessary. *Whiplash* began its life in 2013 as an eighteen-minute-long film about a jazz drummer with J. K. Simmons as Fletcher (which he would reprise in the feature version) and Johnny Simmons (no relation) playing Andrew. The narrative of the short basically follows the same course as the longer version in which Andrew first plays with the school jazz ensemble. Intended as a "proof-of-concept" for the feature-length version, the short film received wide acclaim and won top honors at the Sundance Film Festival (which its feature-length successor repeated the following year).

The feature film entered wide release in October 2014, and the reaction among jazz people was swift and fierce. Despite its overwhelming critical (and modest commercial) success, *Whiplash* was met with harsh criticism from many jazz musicians, writers, and fans, who argued that the portrayal of such an abusive relationship is not true to the spirit of jazz. It is not difficult to understand why *Whiplash* has elicited such strong reactions. It is, in many ways, a caricature of the teacher-student relationship. In a pivotal (and much-discussed) scene from the film, Neiman plays for the first time with the conservatory's top jazz ensemble, which is under Fletcher's leadership. After an extended sequence in which Fletcher tries to get Neiman to play at a particular tempo as he struggles to find precisely the right groove, Fletcher casually picks up a folded chair and hurls it directly at the drummer. Numerous critics of the film have pointed to scenes such as this as providing a distorted view of jazz. Indeed, narrative film has never exactly been a site where accuracy has really mattered. *Whiplash* presents a distorted view of jazz in the same way that, say, Indiana Jones presents a distorted view of archaeologists or *Braveheart* a distorted view of Scottish history.

But the reaction to *Whiplash* seems to go beyond these kinds of common complaints about inaccuracies, reflecting a discomfort on a much more visceral level. As J. R. Jones writes in the *Chicago Reader*, jazz fans might actually be *offended* by the film. Referring to the film as having "nothing to do with jazz," Jones writes that "[t]he jazz musicians I know may be incredibly exacting like Fletcher, but the good ones also understand that generosity and camaraderie are integral to a great ensemble, and that the easiest way to ruin a number is to let it turn into an ego competition, with every player disinterestedly marking time until the spotlight comes to him."[80] Other reviews of the film have drawn on a somewhat idealized view of jazz that echoes many advocacy-based efforts to enhance jazz's public profile. In an essay on the backlash to the film in the *Independent* in early 2015, drummer Mark Fletcher notes that, unlike its portrayal in the film, "[j]azz isn't just a 'genre,' it's a lifestyle. Nay, a life form."[81] Similarly, Philip Conklin, writing in the online magazine *The Periphery*, comments at length about these ideas:

> Maybe it sounds sentimental, but, contrary to the [individualist] philosophy presented by *Whiplash*, jazz is, by its nature, a communal, collaborative art form. What distinguishes jazz from other genres apart from stylistic differences is the importance of collective improvisation. For this to happen successfully, all players must be constantly listening and responding to each other, must be sensitive to the smallest variations of form and style, must, in short, be constantly in communication. Jazz doesn't entail competition, but reliance on other musicians. Jazz is performed in groups, and the best jazz musicians play with others as often as they can . . . . In a group of jazz musicians, there will necessarily be a *community* of players who practice together, who call one another for gigs, and who learn from one another.[82]

Conklin's emphasis on community (the italics are in the original) speaks to another aspect of jazz's perceived nature, that of a shared space where musicians improvise together to form new relationships. Fletcher's approach is diametrically opposed to this idea, focusing instead on the cultivation of individual skill. What many of these reviewers have in common is a view of jazz as a space where artists are free to collaborate, communicate, and cooperate in a different type of social world. The jazz world of *Whiplash*, by contrast, reinforces traditional teacher-student hierarchies, institutionalized pedagogical practices and repertories, and an overriding emphasis on technical skill.

Jazz people took the film very personally, it seems. As Nate Chinen points out, the reception of *Whiplash* can't be detached from "jazz's year of complaint." Like other works that were seen to denigrate jazz around this time and that generated fierce backlash, *Whiplash* was said to present an inaccurate, distorted view of the music, one which must be resisted and countered. In his *New Yorker* review, Richard Brody focuses on one particular scene in the film in which Fletcher, trying to explain to his student why he uses the methods that he does, invokes a legendary incident involving Charlie Parker and Papa Jo Jones. As Brody writes that "[i]n Fletcher's telling, Parker played so badly that Jones threw a cymbal at his head, nearly decapitating him.

After that humiliation and intimidation, Parker went home and practiced so long and so hard that he came back a year later and made history."[83] Brody contrasts this interpretation of the event with an account from bassist Gene Ramey (via Stanley Crouch), who characterizes Jones's actions as "musical snark" intended to teach the young Parker a lesson rather than an attempt at outright humiliation. Note well the use of Brody's phrasing in referring to Ramey, "who was *there*," as if to place a rhetorical trump card on the table. What is notable here is the way in which Brody constructs two opposed narratives, those of abuse and of a humorous moment within the context of a community of like-minded jazz lovers.

Later in his review of the film, Brody contrasts this experience with those whom he regards as being more *real* jazz musicians, again referencing Charlie Parker in the aftermath of the Jones incident. As he writes, "Here's what Parker didn't do in the intervening year: sit alone in his room and work on making his fingers go faster. He played *music*, thought *music*, lived *music*. In *Whiplash*, the young musicians don't play much *music*."[84] I stress the word *music* in Brody's account to emphasize the special privilege granted to this idea. What is played in the film is not understood as *music* in this sense: "The movie has no music in its soul," Brody writes.[85] Whatever one might think about Don Ellis, Hank Levy, college jazz big bands, or jazz education in general, to suggest that this is not music is to cross a certain kind of rhetorical Rubicon, to erect a boundary between jazz and all the rest that is deemed not to be jazz, wherever that boundary may reside. This mindset is neatly summed up at the conclusion of his review: "[I]t's a work of petty didacticism that shows off petty mastery, and it feeds the sort of minor celebrity that Andrew aspires to. Buddy Rich. Buddy fucking Rich."[86]

The invocation of "Buddy fucking Rich" is, given Fletcher's penchant for lobbing verbal abuse at his students, somewhat on the nose. Rich serves in the film as Neiman's idealized version of the jazz drummer. In the "real world," Rich was known not only as a dazzling technician but as a bandleader who, like Fletcher, was not above the occasional foray into abusive behavior. This is perhaps best documented in the infamous "Buddy Rich tapes," a secretly made series of recordings of the drummer chastising his band. These tapes are today the stuff of jazz legend, and to be sure, they are not for the fainthearted.[87] It's difficult to imagine a more intimidating experience in jazz than to be a young musician sitting on a tour bus after long days on the road, enduring such a tirade, and indeed, this might be exactly the point. A figure such as Buddy Rich is thus positioned as decidedly unrepresentative of the jazz world, an arrogant, abusive bandleader whose approach to "jazz" was as much about the showcasing of his own technique as it was *not* about community, transcendence, or improvisation as a means to achieving a more just social space. It is easy to exclude a figure like Buddy Rich (or Terrence Fletcher) if our view of *what jazz is* rests on particular narratives about the music that emphasize its positive qualities.

I would also note that arrangements from Rich's big band are still today a staple in college-level jazz ensembles in many jazz education programs, and there is one thing that I suggest might be missing from discussions of the film; in the final analysis, *Whiplash* may be less a film *about jazz* than a film *about jazz education*. Writing in *Salon*, Patrick Berkery alludes to this idea in his review of the film, noting that "Chazelle's aim seems to be showing how cutthroat jazz is in a scholastic setting, where it's all about the competition—amongst the players in your own ensemble, and against rival programs. He succeeds in showing how much work goes into being not just good but great, and much of it joyless."[88] Such criticism resonates forcefully with a great deal of writing about jazz education itself; Berkery is certainly not the first to make such a claim about institutionalized jazz, as many jazz writers have, over the years, argued that jazz education has had a stultifying effect on the music. Bruce Klauber writes in a blog post on the website Broad Street Review that the fictional Schaffer Conservatory is "based not on Juilliard School of Music's jazz school, but the ultra-competitive jazz school at North Texas State University."[89] This, in fact, is not correct: the band depicted in the film is based on Chazelle's experiences as a student drummer at Princeton High School in New Jersey, which was a regular (and very successful) participant on the jazz ensemble competition circuit when he was a student. That Klauber makes such an error, however, says much about the reputation of that particular collegiate program and about jazz education in general.

Because of this, some jazz educators themselves seem to understand that criticism of jazz education and criticisms of *Whiplash* might in fact be treading on some of the same rhetorical ground. Shelly Berg, a jazz pianist and educator who currently serves as the dean of the Frost School of Music at the University of Miami, was "disgusted" by the film, the premise of which "turned his stomach."[90] Most notably, such attitudes were forcefully expressed by the late John Murphy, an ethnomusicologist, jazz saxophonist, and professor in the jazz studies division at the University of North Texas. Murphy goes so far as to suggest that the film needs a "trigger warning," a play on a current trend in American academic circles to warn students of potentially upsetting or offensive material. For Murphy, the film presents "a catalog of what not to do." Like many other critics, he explicitly invokes a more utopian view of jazz, albeit this time within the context of institutional study:

As a representation of music-making in university jazz programs, it fails to show the centrality of improvisation and collaboration . . . . While it's a good thing when students win recognition as individuals or as part of ensembles, winning competitions is not the goal. The goal is positive development as a musician and as a person. Everything about the performances in the film, especially the rehearsal techniques, struck me as unmusical . . . . [P]ositive mentoring relationships, such as the one between Thelonious Monk and John Coltrane, are much more common, and are given much more respect in the jazz community.[91]

For Murphy, there is no distinction to be made between jazz and jazz education, and *Whiplash* is insulting to both. In closing, Murphy makes his thoughts abundantly clear: "I strongly disliked this film."[92]

Having gone through the same jazz studies program as Murphy, who was a student there in the 1980s, I can sympathize with his position (especially given the potential comparisons to his own program). The film is obviously an exaggeration, even a caricature of the interactions among jazz musicians and among teachers and students. This is not to imply in any way that abusive teacher-student relationships do not exist, even in jazz education. But what is portrayed in the film does not seem to be "normal." And yet, it would be folly to suggest that the scenarios depicted in *Whiplash* are completely without some grounding in experience. I must confess that when I watched the film for the first time, there were some moments that felt, for lack of a better term, a bit familiar, not with reference to any specific incident (I never had a chair thrown at me, for example), but on a more visceral level. This is reflected in a recent discussion on Reddit titled "Watching the movie *Whiplash* brings back some memories. Jazz education is a crazy world."[93] While the majority of user comments were critical of the film and defended jazz education, some comments, like the original post, linked *Whiplash* to their own experiences. Another commenter explains at length with respect to the school they attended:

> That school also had a giant test after second year that covered all the tunes and material of the previous two years. You'd go in front of a panel of all faculty members with your rhythm section and they'd grill you. The exam was pass or fail. Pass and you continue fail [sic] and you are out of the jazz program. Only about 25% of students passed and there was no chance to redo. Many folks were traumatized by this experience and they eventually stopped doing it.[94]

The commenter adds, however, that "[f]or me it was a life changing experience and taught me how to practice for things waay [sic] in advance which is an invaluable tool for a professional musician." Another user's response is more succinct: "I legit can't bring myself to watch it,"[95] although the reason for this act of avoidance is not specified. Might there, then, be a grain in truth in *Whiplash* after all? It likely depends on one's particular perspective and particular experience and, it would seem, on how exactly one defines jazz.

I doubt that it was Damien Chazelle's intent to set the jazz internet aflame in making *Whiplash*. As a filmmaker, his primary responsibility is not to jazz advocacy but to tell a story as he sees it. Yes, that story may be flawed in some ways. But jazz's "year of complaint" reveals something deeper, I believe, than dislike for a particular film. It signals a latent but profound insecurity about the music's place in public discourse that has suddenly been brought to the surface. Nate Chinen cautions us from succumbing to the "culture of outrage" that seems to be a significant feature of the contemporary online world, and in doing so, he helpfully provides a bit of perspective:

> Missing from some of the grumbling [about the film] was that *Whiplash* is a student-teacher psychodrama, no more a movie about jazz than *Titanic* was a movie about iceberg avoidance. At issue was a problem of representation—and the tendency, on the part of many jazz fans, to regard every turn in the spotlight as a chance for outreach.[96]

Chinen thus makes an explicit link between *Whiplash*, "jazz complaint," and the proclivity for "public pedagogy" that preoccupies so many in jazz today. What is at issue here is that the public has to be made to understand the nature of the music. *Whiplash* made this task more difficult; Chazelle's follow-up film would only amplify this problem.

Talking Over the Band

As previously noted, Chazelle's characterization of Neiman in *Whiplash* was primarily inspired by his own experience as a high school drummer. In his public statements, Chazelle has himself engaged in a fair bit of public advocacy for jazz. I am particularly struck by Chazelle's comments on his linking of jazz and film in an interview with *Vulture* in December 2016; he states, "There's the personal reason and then the intellectual reason. On a personal level, jazz is important, has always been important, and will always be important to me. I grew up playing it and having it in the household. So the allusions are there for that reason, because the music matters to me."[97] If

Neiman's goal was to play like Buddy Rich, the character of Sebastian (Seb) in Chazelle's *La La Land* had as his purpose nothing less than saving the music. *La La Land* has, of course, been the subject of many reviews, articles, blogs, and other forms of commentary. The critical reception of the film was largely positive on its release in 2016, culminating in its win at the Golden Globes and seeming win at the Oscars before it was revealed that the incorrect winner had been announced (the actual winner was the film *Moonlight*). Despite this very public snatching-of-defeat-from-the-jaws-of-victory, *La La Land* has been, by any objective measure, an enormous commercial and critical success, particularly for a musical in contemporary Hollywood (notwithstanding the conveyor belt of Disney features).

Like its predecessor, *La La Land* precipitated an avalanche of opinion pieces from the jazz commentariat. And like *Whiplash*, much of the commentary focused on how the film advanced a distorted view of jazz that, in the hands of a less-than-jazz-educated public, could be damaging to the music. The film was certainly (and perhaps justifiably) greeted with skepticism, given Chazelle's previous film. In *La La Land*, Chazelle's characterization of Seb, a jazz pianist who struggles not only with making a living as a musician but also in about every other aspect of his life, has been a particular focus of criticism from within jazz circles. Seb may well represent an extreme example of jazz's educational imperative, constantly weighing in on why jazz is important, why it should be appreciated. A number of observers saw this as precisely the problem, with Seb inhabiting the worst, most off-putting stereotypes of the jazz purist. Like J. K. Simmons's abusive jazz ensemble director Terrence Fletcher in *Whiplash*, Seb is a walking caricature of the "jazz obsessive" whose love of jazz is exceeded only by his desire to convince you to love it, too. He is what might be termed a "jazzsplainer," enlightening everyone he can with his thoughts on why jazz mattered and how he was going to rescue it from oblivion. This is amply demonstrated in one particular scene that has been the topic of frequent discussion, especially within the context of online media. In a key conversation early in their relationship, Mia (Emma Stone, who won the Best Actress Oscar for her performance) explains to Seb that she "hate[s] jazz." As Seb exhibits a look of astonished disbelief, the scene abruptly switches to a local jazz club; as a band plays onstage, they engage in a (largely one-sided) discussion about jazz and its importance. I quote the dialogue from this scene at length:

> SEB: I just think people, when they say they *hate jazz* [subdued voice], they don't have a context, they don't know where it comes from. Jazz was born in a little flophouse in New Orleans, and because people were

crammed in there, they spoke five different languages, they couldn't talk to each other. The only way they had to communicate [gestures to the band] was with jazz.

MIA: Yeah, well what about Kenny G ? [Seb's head sinks in response]

SEB: What?

MIA: What about Kenny G, I mean, what about elevator music, you know, *jazz* music that I know . . . I find it relaxing.

SEB: It's not . . . Sidney Bechet shot somebody because they told him he played a wrong note.

MIA: Where I grew up there was this station called KJAZ 103,[98] and people would put it on when they had a cocktail party. And everyone would just talk over it [as the band continues playing onstage].

SEB: You have to *see* it; you have to *see* what's at stake [Seb gestures enthusiastically toward the band and becomes more animated] . . . . It's conflict, and it's compromise, and it's just new every time; it's brand new every night. It's very, very exciting.

The continued talking over the music was a point that did not go unnoticed by some observers, and given Mia's comment about people talking over the jazz radio station at parties, it seems to be a bit of an ironic wink from Chazelle. At the same time, is also directly at odds with Chazelle's stated desire to "film jazz in an exciting way," unless you define "exciting" as peering at the band from between the backs of Ryan Gosling and Emma Stone's heads. Writing about the film for the online magazine *The Cut*, Anna Silman underscores this scene, referring to Seb as "a self-serious bore" given to "musical mansplaining," whose love for jazz forms the core of the story: "[R]est assured that there is one form of true love that the movie valorizes, one love that no heartbreak can tear asunder. And that is the love between a man and jazz."[99]

There is also the persistent question of race. It is nearly impossible not to see Seb as embodying the role of the "White savior" within the film, a White musician who will, it seems, save jazz from obscurity. In the scene referenced above, there is a starkly defined racial dynamic at work. Seb and Mia, two White twentysomethings, seem to think nothing of talking over the all-Black band on the stage. Bjorn Heile calls attention to this in a 2018 essay on jazz in contemporary film. Addressing *Whiplash* and *La La Land* in tandem, Heile notes that the racial dynamic of the two films plays out somewhat differently: "the 'Whitewashing' of jazz in *Whiplash* . . . could be seen as an implicit criticism of conservatoire culture, the reduction of African American music to some kind of authenticating 'blackdrop' for the white and straight romance between musician and jazz aficionado Sebastian (Ryan Gosling) and actress Mia (Emma Stone) in *La La Land* . . . is harder to explain."[100] Krin Gabbard seems to take the opposite tack, aiming his critique more squarely at *Whiplash*:

> Significantly, there are no important black characters in *Whiplash*, while Andrew aspires to play like the white showoff Buddy Rich. The driving, intense arrangements programed [*sic*] by Fletcher recall the music that big bands led by white musicians such as Rich and Maynard Ferguson performed in the 1970s and 1980s. In *La La Land*, however, Seb wants to play a much less macho music than Andrew and is devoted to great African American jazz artists such as Thelonious Monk, whose solo on his 1967 recording of "Japanese Folk Song" Seb is resolutely trying to master in the opening moments of the film. There is nothing in *Whiplash* like this scene early in *La La Land* in which the white hero honors the black jazz artists who have inspired him.[101]

Despite his more positive comments on *La La Land*, Gabbard is careful to note other aspects of the film, in particular the positioning of Seb in the "White savior" position.[102]

Weighing in on the film for the *Hollywood Reporter*, Kareem Abdul-Jabbar has a similar line of critique of the problematic framing of race in the film, noting the way in which the character of Keith, Seb's friend and pop superstar (played by John Legend) is cast as something of an antagonist whose success is sharply contrasted with Seb's penchant for aesthetic purity, and who turns his back on the jazz tradition:

> I'm also disturbed to see the one major black character, Keith (John Legend), portrayed as the music sellout who, as Sebastian sees it, has corrupted jazz into a diluted pop pablum. Wait just a minute! The white guy wants to preserve the black roots of jazz while the black guy is the sellout? This could be a deliberate ironic twist, but if it is, it's a distasteful one for African Americans.[103]

Echoing complaints about Chazelle's previous film, Abdul-Jabbar would seem to think that *La La Land* might not be, shall we say, the best vehicle to "educate" the public about jazz. This idea was echoed by Seve Chambers in a piece for *Vulture*:

> [I]f you know anything about music, the movie stops dead in its tracks when Sebastian, played by Ryan Gosling, starts to profess his love for jazz. It's not just Emma Stone's Mia who finds his jazz pedantry annoying. Nearly every jazz musician under 40 would be peeved, too, and with good reason: Sebastian would hate what they're doing. What should be a homage to jazz turns out to have narrow vision of the genre, aiming to draw hard boundaries around what it should and shouldn't be—a stance that's out of step with what the jazz scene actually looks like today.[104]

Chambers's comments, which he expands upon at length in his essay, proceed from the idea that Chazelle's interpretation of jazz, at least as it comes to us through the character of Seb, is completely out of step with much of the contemporary jazz world. What Chambers implied—and to be clear, it may go well beyond implication—is that Chazelle is simply not knowledgeable enough about the contemporary jazz world to serve as an effective messenger and advocate for the music. Chazelle (in Chambers's telling) approaches jazz with a stilted view, favoring an interpretation of the style that would seem to be fairly narrowly defined. Such an attribute can also be seen in the characterization of Chazelle's previous jazz protagonist Andrew Neiman, whose singular obsession with Buddy Rich has seemed to blind him to other possibilities. Pianist-blogger Ethan Iverson wrote at length about *Whiplash* and its centering of Buddy Rich over other pioneering drummers such as Art Blakey, Tony Williams, and Elvin Jones. The Rich aesthetic, which is seemingly on full display in *Whiplash*, is heavy on precision and perfection, attributes that Terrence Fletcher values as well. Late in his piece, Iverson gets to the point: "In light of the Whiplash phenomenon, I have no problem saying that if you think Buddy Rich is the greatest jazz drummer, you are racist."[105] This is a bold statement that seems to be aimed not only at Chazelle and his film but at a particular kind of musician, that to idolize Buddy Rich as the "greatest drummer" in jazz is a racist act. When we see a photo of Rich hanging from the wall in Neiman's practice room, how are we to understand this? Is Iverson calling Neiman a racist? And what about Chazelle himself, who largely modeled the character on his own experience and who has often acknowledged Rich's influence on his own musical worldview? Iverson does not say so specifically, but the implication remains.

A "Little Knowledge" Is a Dangerous Thing

There is a single question that remains at the heart of all this: what does Damien Chazelle actually know about jazz? This is not a rhetorical question; it is, I think, important to understanding the portrayal of jazz in his films. In numerous interviews and profiles, Chazelle has spoken about the importance of jazz in his own development. In particular, he cites his experiences as a student musician at Princeton High School in New Jersey. The school is home to a very highly regarded, much-lauded jazz program that centers on its premier "Studio Jazz Band." Under the leadership of the late Anthony Biancosino (until his death in 2003), the band won numerous awards at festivals and competitions around the country. As a member of the band, Chazelle would learn first-hand about the pressures of performing in advanced-level student ensembles, experiences that would eventually provide the inspiration for *Whiplash*. As Rebecca Ford notes in a 2014 profile of Chazelle:

> It certainly doesn't hurt *Whiplash*'s audience appeal that the film happens to be largely autobiographical. Growing up in Princeton, N.J. (his mom and dad are college professors), Chazelle himself was a music prodigy, a jazz drummer in the hypercompetitive Princeton High School Band. And, like the protagonist in the film, he too suffered under an abusive instructor. He remembers sitting behind his drum kit, head down, cowering from the bullying, growing so frustrated he'd later punch his fist through his drum. "You're rushing, you're dragging, not my tempo!" Chazelle remembers his teacher's constant, insulting shouting. "Those are the words I heard most often throughout all of high school."[106]

They are also words that are heard throughout *Whiplash*. Chazelle was blunt about his student experience in a *Los Angeles Times* feature in late 2014:

> I was a jazz drummer, and it was my life for a while, what I lived and breathed every day.... It started out, as these things often do, as kind of a hobby and fun and enjoyable and self-expression—all that artistic stuff. And then it became like boot camp. It became like going every day up for execution, and wondering if you were going to get a stay of execution.[107]

He expressed similar sentiments in an essay he wrote for *Moviemaker* in 2015:

My experience as a jazz drummer had felt that way to me. I had a conductor who scared the living daylights out of me. I had anxiety nightmares about missing beats, losing the tempo, coming in early or late. I'd skip meals, lose sleep, practice 'til my hands bled and my drum-heads broke. It was an all-or-nothing, no-holds-barred immersion into music at its most physical, its most psychologically and emotionally demanding.... I wanted to capture what those years felt like to me. You see that perspective in war movies, in sports movies, in gangster movies, in any movie where physical violence is hovering just around the corner. *Guy and Madeline* was about the joy of making music. *Whiplash* needed to be about the terror and the pain.[108]

At other times, Chazelle has seemed somewhat conflicted about his high school experience and its influence on the film. Krin Gabbard notes this in his essay on Chazelle, writing that "[w]hen talking with Terry Gross about *Whiplash*, Chazelle was careful to add that his own teacher, on whom the character of Fletcher (J. K. Simmons) is based, was not at all as sadistic and violent as the character in *Whiplash*."[109] In a profile appearing in the Princeton High School student newspaper shortly after the film's release, Chazelle was careful to draw a distinction between the teachers in his real life and Fletcher's behavior in the film: "We all loved Dr. B. I'm very careful to stress that . . . the character of the teacher in my movie is not Dr. Biancosino," said Chazelle. "He wasn't throwing chairs."[110] Still, Biancosino's demanding style seems to have made an impression on the young drummer-turned-filmmaker:

Although the fear caused by the band director in *Whiplash* could be viewed as a negative influence, the fear that Chazelle experienced was ultimately the driving force behind his personal successes in music. "I always felt this massive nervousness, [because the drummer is] supporting the whole band. There's this responsibility that, if you drop the ball, the entire band crumbles, and it's your fault," said Chazelle. "Being in Studio Band was the first time in my life that I'd ever been motivated creatively by fear.... A lot of movies about the arts don't focus on how fear can be a motivator, so I wanted to make a movie that captured that fear."[111]

The profile continues, noting the connections between Chazelle's experiences and the film:

The emotional effects that Biancosino had on Chazelle are highlighted in *Whiplash*, but the film also illustrates how the experience was ultimately for the better. "I was terrified of him, as a lot of students were. Rehearsals were super nerve-wracking and really intense, and he would yell and scream and all that stuff," he said. "But at the same time, he was also ultimately a really loving teacher and really inspired everyone in the band. It wound up being this very positive experience."[112]

While seen as a gross distortion of the jazz experience by many observers, for Chazelle, *Whiplash* reflected the reality of his own experience in jazz. Criticisms of Chazelle for allegedly distorting jazz may be largely beside the point. On the surface, it may seem simple enough to dismiss performance experiences in jazz that did not last beyond high school. What does he know, critics may ask? The answer, of course, is that Chazelle knows precisely what he knows, and this is what informs his film. As Nicholas Pillai succinctly puts it, "*Whiplash*, and films like it, do not exist to provide comfort to the musician."[113] To dismiss a figure such as Chazelle as distorting the portrayal of jazz, of saying that his films do not truly represent the jazz world, is to say that his jazz experience is not a real jazz experience. Are such experiences common? Perhaps not. But everyone's experience in jazz is not the utopian ideal that so often characterizes jazz rhetoric. For some, jazz may represent freedom; for others, a sense of community and connection; and for still others, it is a deeply spiritual experience. But for others, their experience might be more about terror and pain.[114]

What we see here, once again, is a debate over who does, and who should, speak for the music. For many jazz people forced to endure the insults of Django Gold et al. earlier in the year, *Whiplash*, with its allegedly grotesque take on jazz, was yet another slap in the face; their angst would be seemingly confirmed two years later with the appearance of *La La Land*, with complaints rising from the crowd that, once again, Damien Chazelle's perceived lack of real knowledge about jazz has been channeled into a Hollywood blockbuster at the expense of an accurate portrayal of their music. Chazelle has, it seems, made jazz people's jobs harder; the public might be learning about jazz, but it was not learning the *right* things about jazz. But I do wonder if, at some level, what really bothers many jazz people about these two films is not that they are distortions of jazz, but that, like the Jazz is The Worst Twitter feed, they might hit a bit too close to home. Chazelle's experiences as a high school drummer are just as real as anyone else's experiences in jazz. Why should they not take their place in the story of the music, and what might we learn from them?

CODA

What's in a Domain Name?

Before the end of 2014, jazz's *annus horribilis* would provide one more seeming cause for complaint. Late in the summer, Jazz at Lincoln Center began using the "jazz.org" internet domain to direct web traffic to its website in place of the previous "jalc.org." What seems like a simple matter of internet commerce that largely flew under the radar when it first happened would soon become yet another skirmish in the disputes over JALC's outsized place in the jazz world. Jazz.org gave the organization an online identity as the singular jazz site on the internet. The implications of this were not lost on critics; sending nascent jazz web surfers to JALC could send the message that JALC's version of jazz "intentionally conflat[ed] its brand with the genre it serves to drive greater revenues for itself."[1] When informed about this by students in my jazz history class shortly before the end of the fall semester, my reaction was twofold. First, it made sense, given the course of JALC's public engagement and position. Second, I sensed that some intrepid scholar was going to write about this someday. *Q.E.D.*

There is scant information on the jazz.org domain prior to its adoption by JALC. In 2001, it seemed to belong to a company called Thruport, which advertised a product called "Thruport Jazz," advertised as "an e-mail message and productivity suite." A snapshot capture hosted on the Internet Archive website brings up a username and password prompt along with a brief description: "This is the place where you can get a free Jazz E-mail account that you can use anywhere in the world! In addition to a very cool E-mail address, get 10MB of storage, an online calendar, an address book, and a to-do list. All for free."[2] Holding the cursor over the "Register" button brings up a URL with a "jazz.org" domain. This would have been active before the .org domain was placed under the control of the Public Interest Registry, an organization charged with the oversight of .org websites. The effect of this change was to largely limit .org sites to nonprofit entities, making such domains highly desirable for organizations doing work in public outreach, education, or advocacy. As a result, jazz.org was arguably the most valuable piece of real estate on the jazz internet, a fact that presumably was not lost on the powers that be at Lincoln Center.

Nate Chinen reported on the jazz.org dustup a bit later in a piece for *JazzTimes*, recounting the efforts of former JALC executive Andre Guess, who launched an online petition to reverse the switch.[3] Guess writes in the petition's description that "the organization has intentionally or unintentionally branded and positioned itself as the very art form that it was founded to uphold and support."[4] The petition ends with a statement that channels many of the criticisms of JALC over the previous two decades:

> I petition that Jazz at Lincoln Center cease from using the domain name jazz.org and further I petition that they donate jazz.org to be used as an independent third-party website that would be curated and administered by a collection of sister organizations and individuals from the broader jazz community. This new site would be democratic, inclusive and would allow for the uninitiated Google searcher to have a much broader view of this beautiful art form called jazz.[5]

Alas, Guess's efforts were to no avail. Chinen notes that at the time of his article, the petition was "a dozen shy of the 100 supporters he'd set as a modest goal."[6] As I write this seven years later, the petition (which is now closed) stood at ninety-nine. JALC's acquisition of jazz.org stands as a good representation of what is at stake for the music in an increasingly online world. In a web-centered information system, the idea that "jazz.org" would send the online masses straight to Wynton Marsalis and associates had real-world implications, which did not sit well with his critics.

When I finished my first book, I ended the final chapter, which was concerned with jazz communities on the internet, with a brief reference to a relatively new, emerging social media platform called "Twitter." Revisiting this chapter now feels like time travel; so much of what I examined has become, at best, outdated, and at worst, utterly obsolete (who uses message boards anymore?!?). The Wikipedia article on jazz, which I examined as a site of debate and contention, has now mostly settled into a comfortable middle age. The intervening years have witnessed massive changes in both the infrastructure and culture of online life. This point was driven home for me recently. I was teaching a class in which the topic was music and media, and I was referring to different types of listening experiences over the course of my life. In a segment on listening to cassette tapes, I made a reference to a tape being "eaten." Looking out over the class and noticing their blank expressions, it dawned on me that not a single student understood what I meant by this (this was confirmed in a follow-up discussion). Another milepost on the journey into elderly life has been passed.

But there are some things that have not changed. The idea of "what is jazz" is still hotly contested, even if those who are contesting it have themselves grown weary of the debate. Jazz is even less popular than it was, having reached new lows in terms of record sales and market share. Much as jazz advocates would like to ignore such dismal statistics, they do, in fact, matter, pointing to the increasingly difficult path for jazz artists and others in the music's "art world." More recently, jazz has been deeply impacted by events outside of the realm of music. In particular, the rise of the #metoo initiatives and the police killing of George Floyd seem to have led to a heightened sense of urgency; jazz students, in particular, have taken it upon themselves to demand change in their institutions and programs. Challenges to the canon, long the purview of scholars and critics, are increasingly the domain of younger, more change-minded actors. Calls to reconsider the ways in which jazz is taught and learned are not yet finished reverberating through the hallways, classrooms, and studios of jazz academia. And this is a good thing.

Throughout this book, I've spent a great deal of time on the idea that jazz learning, broadly defined, has served as a site where different understandings of the music's essential character are continually reworked. I would suggest that the same is true here, in full public view, in debates such as those surrounding Damien Chazelle and his films. This raises important questions: whose vision of jazz will win out, and whose voice will carry the most weight and have the greatest impact on the creation and maintenance of jazz's public image? How this will play out is anyone's guess, but digital media is sure to play a significant role. A decade ago, Twitter had yet to achieve the level of ubiquity it enjoys today. A decade before that, Facebook was but a twinkle in Mark Zuckerberg's eye; step back another decade, and no one had heard of a thing called a blog. Few individuals along the way could have imagined how these and other developments would reshape public discourse in such profound ways, and the jazz world is no exception. In the days when jazz commentary was limited to what came from a printing press, a film like *Whiplash* might have generated controversy, but it's unlikely that this would play out as publicly as it does now. Looking ten years into the future, it is similarly difficult to see how such matters will play out. But one thing is certain—as long as there are people who are passionate about this music, there will almost certainly be an effort to educate, to engage in new forms of public pedagogy and advocacy. And whatever form this takes, whenever and wherever it happens, we can rest assured that, as has always been the case with this music, it will be the subject of a robust and spirited conversation.

NOTES

INTRODUCTION

1. Wynton Marsalis, "In the Countdown to Friday's Inauguration," *Wynton's Blog*, January 18, 2017, https://wyntonmarsalis.org/blog/entry/in-the-countdown-to-fridays-inauguration.
2. "Wynton Marsalis Speaks Out on Trump's Proposed Arts Funding Cuts," *CBS This Morning*, April 3, 2017, https://www.cbsnews.com/news/wynton-marsalis-jon-batiste-jazz-traditions-trump-proposed-cuts-arts-funding/.
3. "Jazz in the Age of Trump," *JAZZIZ* (Special Issue) (2018), 3.
4. Ibid., 5.
5. Ibid., 9.
6. David van Drehle, "Trump's Jazz Combo of National Distraction Gets Some New Members," *Washington Post*, September 10, 2019, https://www.washingtonpost.com/opinions/trumps-jazz-combo-of-national-distraction-gets-some-new-members/2019/09/10/e8133b08-d3ed-11e9-9343-40db57cf6abd_story.html.
7. David Graham, "Trump's Dangerous Love of Improvisation," *The Atlantic*, August 9, 2017, https://www.theatlantic.com/politics/archive/2017/08/get-on-board-the-trump-trane/536379/.
8. Ken Prouty, *Knowing Jazz: Community, Pedagogy, and Canon in the Information Age* (Jackson: University Press of Mississippi, 2012). See chapter 1.
9. "Quarantine Big Band Helsinki—Some Skunk Funk," YouTube, June 19, 2020, https://www.youtube.com/watch?v=QC28BgOvF70&ab_channel=AnttiKujanp%C3%A4%C3%A4.
10. See Ben Sisario and Giovanni Russonello, "Jazz Lives in Clubs. The Pandemic Is Threatening Its Future," *New York Times*, September 8, 2020, https://www.nytimes.com/2020/09/08/arts/music/jazz-clubs-coronavirus.html.

CHAPTER 1: TO JAZZ, OR NOT TO JAZZ

1. This chapter engages in discussions of early twentieth-century popular music, a good deal of which involved deeply racist references and stereotypes. In a few instances, the sources in question employ language that, by today's standards at least, is regarded as highly offensive.

In the interest of engaging in a full and open discussion, I have, in these cases, used such terms and phrases as they were originally published.

2. No recording was made of the original Aeolian Hall performance, but Whiteman's orchestra would record a version later in June 1924, also with Gorman on clarinet; this recording is the source for the timing cited above. This recording can be heard online at https://www.youtube.com/watch?v=VGvuUOtHGkk.

3. David Schiff and Julian Rushton, *Gershwin: Rhapsody in Blue* (Cambridge and New York: Cambridge University Press, 1997), 102.

4. Norman Lebrecht, *Genius & Anxiety: How Jews Changed the World, 1847–1947* (New York: Scribner, 2019), 208. Lebrecht notes that Gorman was not Jewish, seemingly crediting Gershwin with the potential nod to klezmer. That said, a clarinetist of Gorman's skill and experience would almost certainly have also been very familiar with klezmer, and at any rate, the overlap between klezmer and other popular forms at the time, including jazz, was fairly significant.

5. This program was probably the most overt manifestation of Whiteman's desire, invoking an oft-cited but never explicitly documented passage, to "make a lady out of jazz." Other sources have referred to Whiteman as making an "honest woman out of jazz"; Mario Dunkel cites Edward Abbe Niles as attributing that statement to German conductor and New York music impresario Walter Damrosch. See Mario Dunkel, "The Stories of Jazz: Narrating a Musical Tradition," *Jazzforschung/Jazz Research* 48 (2016): 126.

6. The section is an adaptation of a paper I delivered at the annual meeting of the American Musicological Society in 2015.

7. The terminology used in this discussion might seem somewhat confusing. "Smear" and "jazz" (in this context) are both vernacular terms for a glissando. The term "smear" is often used to refer to both the actual musical figure (i.e., a glissando) and to compositions in which that figure was a defining characteristic (such as many of Fillmore's works for band). For purposes of clarity, I am reserving the use of the term "smear" for the latter, except where the term is quoted in a different context. With respect to the specific musical device, I use the terms "gliss" or "glissando," except when discussing particular aspects of these pedagogical works in which the term "jazz" is used in this manner.

8. This figure was taken from a blog post by Douglas Yeo, a widely recognized trombonist who occupied the bass trombone position with the Boston Symphony for nearly three decades. Yeo's post directly addresses the racialized, even racist nature of Fillmore's "trombone family," culminating with a call for trombonists to cease performing these works (especially "Lassus Trombone," a piece that has been a staple of American wind band performance until relatively recently). Yeo cites another contemporary advertisement which refers to the collection as "7 Niggah Smears," with a somewhat caricatured description of each piece. See Douglas Yeo, "A Path Forward from Henry Fillmore's 'Lassus Trombone.'" *The Last Trombone* (blog), July 6, 2020, https://thelasttrombone.com/2020/07/06/a-path-forward-from-henry-fillmores-lassus-trombone/.

9. Trevor Herbert, *The Trombone* (New Haven: Yale University Press, 2006), 38.

10. Charles Marie Widor, *The Technique of the Modern Orchestra: A Manual of Practical Instrumentation* (New York: J. Williams, 1906), trans. E. F. E. Suddard, 86.

11. Carl Weber, *Premier Method for B♭ Tenor Slide Trombone* (Philadelphia: J. W. Pepper, 1897), 31. Italics added.

12. R. N. Davis, *Imperial Method for Slide Trombone* (Philadelphia: J. Church, 1898), 86.

13. Ibid., 87.

14. Ibid., 87. Emphasis added.

15. Thomas King, *Daily Exercises: Scales and Lip Drills for the Slide Trombone* (Cleveland: H. N. White, 1908), 56.

16. J. H. Reginald Dixon, "The Misuse of the Trombone," (letter), *Musical Times* 66, no. 989 (July 1925): 635.

17. Harold E. Watts, "The Misuse of the Trombone," (letter), *Musical Times* 66, no. 991 (September 1925): 833.

18. See for example Alan Merriam and Fradley Garner, "Jazz—the Word," *Ethnomusicology* 12, no. 3 (1968).

19. Henry Fillmore, *Henry Fillmore's Jazz Trombonist: A Unique Treatise Showing How to Play Practical Jazzes and How and Where to Insert Them into Plain Trombone Parts* (Cincinnati: Fillmore Music House, 1919), 4.

20. Quoted in Trevor Herbert, "Trombone Glissando: A Case Study in Continuity and Change in Brass Instrument Performance Idioms," *Historic Brass Society Journal* 22 (2010): 1.

21. Douglas Yeo, *An Illustrated History for the Modern Trombone, Tuba, and Euphonium Player* (Lanham, MD: Rowman and Littlefield, 2021), 65.

22. Mayhew Lake, *Great Guys: Laughs and Gripes of Fifty Years of Show-Music Business* (Grosse Pointe Woods, MI: Bovaco Press, 1983). This book was published posthumously, as Lake died in 1955.

23. M. L. (Mayhew) Lake, *The Wizard Trombone Jazzer* (New York: Carl Fischer, 1919), 3.

24. Ibid., 3.

25. Ibid., 13.

26. I was able to find a declaration form for Sordillo dated October 10, 1960, in Boston.

27. Douglas Yeo noted in a discussion on "The Trombone Forum" that Sordillo had been fired from the Boston Symphony during the musicians' strike of 1920, which resulted in a significant turnover of personnel. Also associated with the orchestra during this period were Carl Hempe and Johannes Rochut, who (as Yeo notes) also produced important method books; the Rochut *Melodious Etudes for Trombone* remains a cornerstone of trombone pedagogy to this day. See Douglas Yeo, "Fortunato Sordillo: 'The Art of Jazzing for the Trombone,'" *The Trombone Forum*, February 4, 2011, accessed March 12, 2013, http://tromboneforum.org/index.php?topic=55155.0.

28. "Sordillo School advertisement," *Jacobs' Band Monthly* 6, no. 1 (May 1921): 82. *Jacobs' Band Monthly* was a periodical published in Boston by Walter Jacobs between 1910 and 1941.

29. An entry in the Library of Congress's copyright registry shows that Sordillo registered his "Scientific Method of Playing Brass Instruments" as a distinct work in 1917.

30. "Sordillo School Advertisement," 82. See also Michael D. Martin, "Band Schools of the United Stated: A Historical Overview," *Journal of Historical Research in Music Education* 21, no. 1 (1999): 57.

31. Martin "Band Schools," 57.

32. "Highlights from 1930 to Today," *Boston Gas History 1822–1972* (Boston: Boston Gas, 1972), 8. This publication was produced by Boston Gas as part of the company's 150th anniversary.

33. The patent number for this mute is 1,338,108. The application was filed on November 14, 1919, and the patent was granted on April 27, 1920. Sordillo also held patents for a separable mouthpiece that could be used interchangeably with different brass instruments (patent number 1,327,970, registered on January 13, 1920) and for improvements to the folding music stand (patent number 1,480,788, registered in 1924).

34. Fortunato Sordillo, *The Art of Jazzing for the Trombone* (Boston: Ditson & Co., 1920), 2.

35. Ibid., 4.

36. "The Jazz Problem," *Keeping Time: Readings in Jazz History*, ed. Robert Walser (Oxford and New York: Oxford University Press, 1998), 50. Reprinted from *The Etude*, August 1924.

37. Tim Gracyk, *Popular American Recording Pioneers: 1895–1925* (London and New York: Routledge, 2012), 80–81.

38. A much-expanded version of this discussion can be found in my article "Smears, Laughs, and Barnyard Hokum: Early Jazz Trombone and the Problem of Novelty," *American Music* 40, no. 3 (2022): 388–413.

39. Charles Hiroshi Garrett, "The Humor of Jazz" in *Jazz/Not Jazz: The Music and its Boundaries*, eds. David Ake, Daniel Goldmark, and Charles Hiroshi Garrett (Berkeley: University of California Press, 2012), 58.

40. Samuel Charters, *A Trumpet Around the Corner: The Story of New Orleans Jazz* (Jackson: University Press of Mississippi, 2008), 135.

41. Lawrence Gushee. Liner notes to *Steppin' on the Gas: Rags to Jazz 1913-1927*. New World Records NW 269, 1977. LP record.

42. This section is adapted from a paper given at the 2021 meeting of the American Musicological Society.

43. Merriam and Garner, "Jazz—the Word," 391–92.

44. Ibid., 391.

45. Lawrence Gushee, "Improvisation and Related Terms in Middle Period Jazz," in *Musical Improvisation: Art, Education, and Society*, eds. Gabriel Solis and Bruno Nettl (Urbana: University of Illinois Press, 2009), 263–80.

46. Ibid., 272. The quoted passages are from Miff Mole, *"Original Breaks" and "Hot Choruses" for Trombone and Alto Saxophone* (self-published, 1925).

47. Miff Mole, *100 Jazz Breaks for Trombone* (New York: Alfred, 1926), 3.

48. This resonates with later texts based on the learning of specific lines and phrases. A book such as Jerry Coker's widely used *Patterns for Jazz* is an obvious example.

49. Mole did later record this song with his "Nicksieland" band in 1944, likely taking advantage of the renewed interest in older forms of jazz that would become known as the "Dixieland Revival." He does not take a solo chorus on that recording.

50. Brian Rust and Malcolm Shaw, *Jazz and Ragtime Records, 1897–1942, Volume 1* (Mainspring Press, 1971), 21–22.

51. See "Original Memphis Five," *Red Hot Jazz Archive* (archived), accessed November 13, 2021, https://syncopatedtimes.com/original-memphis-five/.

52. This group should not be confused with the group called McKinney's Cotton Pickers, another ad hoc group that was under the umbrella of Detroit-based pianist and manager Jean Goldkette.

53. Scott Yanow, *Classic Jazz: The Musicians & Recordings That Shaped Jazz, 1895–1933* (San Francisco: Backbeat Press, 2001), 9.

54. Henderson's main trombonist at the time was Charlie Green, who was probably the main rival to Mole on the New York scene at the time.

55. Gushee, "Improvisation and Related Terms," 272.

56. Miff Mole, *100 Jazz Breaks for Trombone* (New York: Alfred, 1926), 3. Emphasis added.

57. Ibid., 3.

58. George Crozier, *50 Jazz Breaks in Loose Leaf Form* (New York: Alfred and Company, 1926), 1–2. Italics added.

59. Ibid., 1.

60. The relationship between music publishing and "real-world" jazz performance has been the subject of a number of studies. The most expansive of these is certainly David Chevan's 1997 doctoral thesis on the role of written scores in early jazz, which considers in depth the place of published "stock" arrangements in the jazz scene of the 1920s. Chevan's fifth chapter tackles this topic directly, providing a thorough cataloging of recordings that employed stocks prior to 1930. Jeffrey Magee, meanwhile, has examined a particular example in the context of his detailed examination of Fletcher Henderson's 1924 recording of the popular song "Copenhagen." Magee makes a convincing case that Henderson's landmark recording was heavily influenced by a published stock arrangement, which he argues "was based on an earlier recording" (44). Such relationships are outside the scope of this study, but the relationships between stocks and recordings is certainly an area that is ripe for additional scholarly attention. See David Chevan, "Written Music in Early Jazz," (PhD dissertation, City University of New York—Graduate Center), 1997; Jeffrey Magee, "Fletcher Henderson's 'Copenhagen' Revisited," *Journal of the American Musicological Society* 48, no. 1 (1995): 42–66.

61. Glenn Miller, *Glenn Miller's 125 Jazz Breaks for Trombone* (Chicago: Melrose Bros., 1927), 3.

62. Ibid., 3.

63. Tommy Dorsey, *100 Hot Breaks for the Trombone* (New York: Robbins-Engel, 1927).

64. Mayhew Lake, *The American Band Arranger: A Complete and Reliable Self-instructor for Mastering the Essential Principles of Practical and Artistic Arranging for Military Band* (New York: Carl Fischer, 1920), 14.

65. Frank Cipolla and Donald Hunsberger, *Wind Band Activity in and Around New York ca. 1830–1950* (Van Nuys: Alfred, 2006), 98.

66. Jack Kopstein, "Mayhew Lake, Altissimo! Recordings" (website), February 24, 2014, https://militarymusic.com/blogs/military-music/13516481-mayhew-l-lake.

67. The term "dirt chorus" is not well known today, and its origins are somewhat obscure, although, as Lawrence Gushee notes in his essay on the early jazz lexicon, the term "was common during the late 1920s and early 1930s" (275).

68. Lester Brockton, *Trix Tromobinx* (Boston: Carl Fischer, 1927), front cover.

69. Ibid., 1.

70. Ibid., 1.

71. Ibid., 7.

72. Ibid., 8.

73. Louis Armstrong, *125 Jazz Breaks for Hot Trumpet* (Chicago: Melrose, 1927), i.

74. James Lincoln Collier, *Louis Armstrong: An American Genius* (Oxford and New York: Oxford University Press, 1985), 178.

75. Elmer Schoebel and Herman Openneer (interview), "The Elmer Schoebel Story," *Doctor Jazz* no. 32 (October 1968): 6–7.

76. It seems certain that these two books were published separately despite the fact that a later reprint combined them into a single volume. A library recording from the Louis Armstrong House for *50 Hot Choruses* notes that the (presumably back) cover of the book mentions *125 Jazz Breaks*. See "Online Catalog," *Louis Armstrong House Museum*, accessed November 10, 2021, https://louisarmstrong.pastperfectonline.com/library/ABFF8ECD-AED5-4C21-8F77-382422176346.

CHAPTER 2: WE DON'T KNOW WHAT WE DON'T KNOW

1. Sherrie Tucker, *Swing Shift: All-Girl Bands of the 1940s* (Raleigh, NC: Duke University Press, 2000).

2. This introduction was given the all-too-accurate title "It Don't Mean a Thing If It Ain't in the History Books."

3. Tucker, *Swing Shift*, 4.

4. Ibid., 4.

5. Scott DeVeaux, "Constructing the Jazz Tradition: Jazz Historiography," *Black American Literature Forum* 25, no. 3 (1991): 525.

6. Richard Sudhalter, *Lost Chords: White Musicians and Their Contribution to Jazz, 1915–1945* (Oxford and New York: Oxford University Press, 1999).

7. Ibid., xvi.

8. Christi Jay Wells, "The Ace of His Race: Paul Whiteman's Early Critical Reception in the Black Press," *Jazz and Culture* 1 (2018): 81.

9. David Johnson and David Baker (interview), "The Basics of David Baker, pt. 2," *Night Lights*, Indiana Public Media, August 29, 2007, https://indianapublicmedia.org/nightlights/the-basics-of-baker-part-2-our-conversation-with-jazz-educator-david-baker.php.

10. See Bernard Gendron, "Moldy Figs and Modernists: Jazz at War (1942–1946)," *Discourse* 15, no. 3 (1993): 130–57.

11. Frederic Ramsey Jr. and Charles Edward Smith, ed., *Jazzmen* (New York: Harcourt Brace, 1939).

12. Hal Smith, "Bunk Johnson," *The San Francisco Traditional Jazz Foundation Collection*, Stanford University, accessed November 30, 2021, https://exhibits.stanford.edu/sftjf/feature/bunk-johnson.

13. Ibid.

14. David Sager, "Richard Sudhalter. *Lost Chords . . .*" (review), *Current Musicology*, nos. 71–73 (2001/2002): 510.

15. Ibid., 517.

16. Schaap died on September 7, 2021, from cancer. See Martin Johnson, "Phil Schaap, Iconic Jazz DJ and NEA Jazz Master, Dies at 70," NPR.org (website), National Public Radio, September 8, 2021, https://www.npr.org/2021/09/08/1035132383/phil-schaap-nea-jazz-master-radio-dj-dies.

17. Corey Kilgannon, "In a Life of Jazz, a Jarring Note," *New York Times*, May 27, 2001, section 14, page 1.

18. Ibid., 1.

19. Lewis Porter, "Some Problems in Jazz Research," *Black Music Research Journal* 8, no. 2 (1988): 195.

20. A parallel concept in ethnography (and ethnomusicology) is that of the "ideal informant," an individual who provides a primary point of entry into a particular culture; such individuals are often selected due to their seemingly greater ability as culture brokers, community leaders, or musical performers, distinct from others in the communities. See Bruno Nettl, *The Study of Ethnomusicology: 31 Issues and Concepts* (Urbana: University of Illinois Press, 2005), chapter 10. Originally published in 1983.

21. Research for this discussion was conducted at the Center for Black Music Research, Columbia College, Chicago. I am grateful to the staff, past and present, for their assistance. Portions of this section were the subject of a paper at the 2017 meeting of the American Musicological Society.

22. John Gennari, *Blowing Hot and Cool: Jazz and its Critics* (Chicago: University of Chicago Press, 2010), 95. Gennari cites Miller as "Paul Edward Miller," a common misspelling in such references.

23. "Jazz Critic Paul Miller Dies at 64," *San Francisco Examiner*, December 10, 1972, 47.

24. Ronald G. Welburn, "American Jazz Criticism, 1914–1940" (PhD dissertation, New York University, 1983), 161.

25. Ibid., 98.

26. Wil Haygood, *Sweet Thunder: The Life and Times of Sugar Ray Robinson* (Chicago: Chicago Review Press, 2011), 106.

27. Paul Eduard Miller, "Jazz—Not for Morons Only," *DownBeat*, February 1, 1939, 20.

28. Paul Eduard Miller, "Roots of Hot White Jazz are Negroid," *DownBeat*, April 1937, 5.

29. This source is often listed as *Down Beat* and *DownBeat* in different written sources. I have chosen to consistently use the spelling and format *DownBeat* in keeping with the magazine's own references to its title.

30. Ron Welburn, "Jazz Magazines of the 1930s: An Overview of Their Provocative Journalism," *American Music* 5, no. 3 (1987): 267.

31. Paul Eduard Miller, *Miller's Yearbook of Popular Music*, (Chicago: PEM Publications, 1943), vii.

32. Ibid., viii. Emphases added.

33. I had the good fortune to review these manuscripts as a research fellow at the Center for Black Music Research, Columbia College Chicago in 2012, which I was able to review again in a subsequent follow-up visit. I wish to express my deep appreciation to the staff at CCC/CBMR as well as to Bonnie Miller Barnes (Paul Eduard Miller's daughter) for her perspectives and consent to include these unpublished materials in this chapter.

34. Columbia College Chicago, "The Paul Eduard Miller Collection,1934–1950," *Center for Black Music Research Collection*, accessed May 26, 2021, https://digitalcommons.colum.edu/cgi/viewcontent.cgi?article=1027&context=cmbr_guides.

35. Paul Eduard Miller, *Testimonial to Jazz* (unpublished manuscript), The Paul Eduard Miller Collection, Center for Black Music Research Collection, Columbia College Chicago, Chicago, IL, 25. Strikethroughs are in the original manuscript.

36. This term refers to "an abrupt transition from a lofty style or grand topic to a common or vulgar one." It is drawn from an eighteenth-century essay by Alexander Pope to refer to "an amusingly failed attempt at presenting artistic greatness." See "Bathos," *Wikipedia*, accessed March 20, 2023, https://en.wikipedia.org/wiki/Bathos.

37. Ibid., 86. Note that the page number of these manuscript drafts is, in some cases, incomplete and inconsistent.

38. Ibid., 43.

39. Gennari, *Blowin'*, 152.

40. Paul Eduard Miller, "Blind Critics Add Confusion to Jazz: Symphonic Sweet and Hot Jazz Need Real Standards of Comparison," *DownBeat*, September 1936, 2.

41. Ibid., 2.

42. Ibid., 2.

43. Paul Eduard Miller, *The Best Jazz* (unpublished manuscript), The Paul Eduard Miller Collection, Center for Black Music Research Collection, Columbia College Chicago, Chicago, IL, 4. As with Miller's other unpublished manuscript, pagination in this example is somewhat inconsistent.

44. Ibid., 4.

45. Paul Lopes, *The Rise of a Jazz Art World* (Cambridge, UK: Cambridge University Press, 2002), 176.

46. Lawrence Levine, *Highbrow/Lowbrow: The Emergence of Cultural Hierarchy in America* (Cambridge, MA: Harvard University Press, 1988).

47. John Sullivan Dwight, *Dwight's Journal of Music* (editorial preface), January 1, 1881, iii.

48. Miller, *Testimonial*, 63–64.

49. Lopes, "Rise of a Jazz Art World," 161.

50. Portions of this section were adapted from an article published in *Popular Music and Society*. See Ken Prouty, "Searching for Charles Johnson: The Outlier and the Ordinary in Jazz," *Popular Music in Society* 37, no. 5 (2014): 595–617. This material is used by permission of Taylor & Francis. https://www.tandfonline.com/.

51. There is some disagreement as to where the film was shot. A large majority of sources lists the location as Copenhagen, but Krin Gabbard writes that the location was "a studio in Sweden." See Krin Gabbard, "Another Other History of Jazz in the Movies" in *The Cambridge Companion to Film Studies*, ed. Mervyn Cooke and Fiona Ford (Cambridge: Cambridge University Press, 2016), 188.

52. Ben Ratliff, "Louis Armstrong in 2 Minutes, 53 Seconds," *New York Times*, Nov 23, 2009, https://artsbeat.blogs.nytimes.com/2009/11/23/louis-armstrong-in-2-minutes-53-seconds/.

53. Burns included this film clip in his 2001 PBS documentary.

54. Charlie Rose, "Jazz," Charlie Rose (website), January 8, 2001, https://charlierose.com/videos/17595.

55. Mike Springer, "Watch the Earliest Known Footage of Louis Armstrong Performing Live in Concert (Copenhagen, 1933)," *Open Culture*, June 18, 2013, https://www.openculture.com/2013/06/earliest_known_footage_of_louis_armstrong_performing_live_in_concert

.html. Despite Springer's assertion to the contrary, the performance was not, in fact, "live." As Krin Gabbard notes, the film was "re-edited to give the impression that a live audience was present." See Gabbard, "Another Other History," 188.

56. This film was, as noted before, made on a soundstage. The shots of the audience were spliced in later.

57. Crouch himself was, in fact, a recipient of the MacArthur Foundation's "genius grant" in 1993.

58. Stanley Crouch, *Considering Genius* (New York: Basic Civitas, 2006), 65. Italics added.

59. Ibid., 167. Italics added.

60. In a recent essay hosted by the online version of *Psychology Today*, Andrew Robinson suggests that when we are "pressed to be more precise, we find it remarkably hard to define genius, especially among individuals of our own time." See Andrew Robinson, "Can We Define Genius?" *Psychology Today*, November 30, 2010, https://www.psychologytoday.com/us/blog/sudden-genius/201011/can-we-define-genius.

61. This is despite the fact that Collier includes a closing chapter titled "The Nature of Genius," which in reality is a meditation on Armstrong's career rather than an argument for the nature of Armstrong's genius.

62. Bob Yurochko, *A Short History of Jazz* (Lanham, MD: Rowman & Littlefield, 1993), 288.

63. Crouch, *Considering Genius*, 294.

64. James Lincoln Collier, *Duke Ellington* (Oxford and New York: Oxford University Press, 1987).

65. Richard Williams notes Collier's "negative if not downright dismissive" attitude and a "fundamental lack of respect" toward Ellington. Paul Machlin suggests the book "serves to . . . further its author's limited and idiosyncratic interpretation of Ellington's character and his contributions to music." Even works that do not directly review Collier's book take issue with his arguments; Scott DeVeaux, in an essay on Ellington's tone poem *Black, Brown, and Beige*, criticizes Collier's "patronizing" and "insulting" statements about the composer. See Richard Williams, *The Blue Moment: Miles Davis's* Kind of Blue *and the Remaking of Modern Music* (New York: Norton, 2010), 339–40; Paul Machlin, "Review." *College Music Symposium* 28 (1988): 143; Scott DeVeaux, "*Black, Brown and Beige* and the Critics," *Black Music Research Journal* 13, no. 2 (1993): 141–42.

66. Krin Gabbard, "The Reception of Jazz in America: A New View" (review), *American Music* 7, no. 3 (1989): 345–46.

67. Ibid., 360.

68. The use of the term "hero" in the literature of jazz is, like that related to "genius," relatively frequent and equally unsystematic. Jazz figures are referred to as "heroes" or "heroic" figures in many different contexts. An example is John Fordham's 1998 book *Jazz Heroes* (London: Collins and Brown, 1998), in which this term serves little more purpose than including it in the title. One notable exception to this is Tony Whyton's *Jazz Icons: Heroes, Myths, and the Jazz Tradition* (Cambridge: Cambridge University Press, 2010). Whyton engages in a deep examination of the trope of "heroic" jazz figures, in particular emphasizing the role of such ideas as connected to the neoclassicist discourse of Wynton Marsalis, Stanley Crouch, and especially Albert Murray. *Jazz Icons* is a welcome intervention into the literature in terms of its careful critique of such concepts. Still, the idea persists;

David Ake alludes to this in *Jazz Cultures* (Berkeley: University of California Press, 2002). In a discussion of the use (or misuse) of Coltrane's "Giant Steps" in jazz education, Ake notes that this perpetuates a "narrative [that] supports both a discourse of complexity and the legend of the jazz musician as a solitary hero" (133).

69. This term is most commonly employed in statistics, defined by Frank Grubbs as "[a]n outlying observation . . . that appears to deviate markedly from other members of the sample in which it occurs." See Frank Grubbs, "Procedures for Detecting Outlying Observations in Samples," *Technometrics* 11, no. 1 (1969): 1–21.

70. Malcolm Gladwell, *Outliers: The Story of Success* (New York: Little, Brown & Co., 2008), 17.

71. Bob Reisner, "Bird: A Biography in Interviews," *Jazz Review* 3, no. 9 (1960): 8.

72. Isidore Granoff was a Russian-born music teacher who ran an independent music school in Philadelphia starting in the late 1940s.

73. Lewis Porter, *John Coltrane: His Life and Music* (Ann Arbor: University of Michigan Press, 2000), 52.

74. K. A. Ericsson, R.T. Krampe, and C. Tesch-Römer, "The Role of Deliberate Practice in the Acquisition of Expert Performance," *Psychological Review* 100, no. 3 (1993): 363–406.

75. Brooke N. Macnamara and Megha Maitra, "The Role of Deliberate Practice in Expert Performance: Revisiting Ericsson, Krampe & Tesch-Römer," *Royal Society Open Science* 6, no. 8 (2019), https://royalsocietypublishing.org/doi/10.1098/rsos.190327.

76. Brian Resnick, "The '10,000-Hour Rule' Was Debunked Again. That's a Relief," *Vox* (website), August 23, 2019, https://www.vox.com/science-and-health/2019/8/23/20828597/the-10000-hour-rule-debunked.

77. David Burkus, "The Truth About The 10,000-Hour Rule with Anders Ericsson," *Radio Free Leader* (podcast), May 25, 2016, https://davidburkus.com/2016/05/0721-the-truth-about-the-10000-hour-rule-with-anders-ericsson/.

78. Eric Levinson, "Malcolm Gladwell Defends Disputed '10,000-Hour' Rule," *The Atlantic*, August 23, 2013, https://www.theatlantic.com/culture/archive/2013/08/malcolm-gladwell-defends-disputed-10000-hours-rule/311884/.

79. Malcolm Gladwell, "Complexity and the Ten-Thousand-Hour Rule," *The New Yorker*, August 21, 2013, https://www.newyorker.com/sports/sporting-scene/complexity-and-the-ten-thousand-hour-rule.

80. In saying this, I by no means wish this to sound in any way like a mitigation for the often-egregious segregation—legal and otherwise—that led to the demographic formation of school such as Attucks or Westinghouse, both of which served predominantly Black communities.

81. Gabriel Solis, *Monk's Music: Thelonious Monk and Jazz History in the Making* (Berkeley: University of California Press, 2007), 60.

82. Preston Love, *A Thousand Honey Creeks Later: My Life in Music from Basie to Motown—and Beyond* (Middletown, CT: Wesleyan University Press, 1997), 248.

83. Scott Yanow, *Bebop* (Milwaukee: Backbeat/Hal Leonard, 2000), 96.

84. Whitney Balliet, *Collected Works: A Journal of Jazz 1954–2001* (New York: St. Martin's Griffin, 2002), 293.

85. Johnson, for example, rose to prominence through his work with Charlie Parker. Tyner and Morgan are best known for their work with John Coltrane and Art Blakey, respectively.

86. The online version of the Lord discography was used for this study. This can be accessed at https://www.lordisco.com/ but a subscription is required to retrieve discographic information.

87. The Lord discography also cites another "Charlie Johnson" as having played with Armstrong in Europe the following month. This is certainly the same person. Unfortunately, Lord lists a number of sessions for this particular "Charlie Johnson" that show him to have played on alto sax, piano, and clarinet. It is possible that this is simply a placeholder "Charlie Johnson" for miscellaneous recordings.

88. Eugene Chadbourne, "Charlie Johnson," *All Music Guide*, accessed December 3, 2021, https://www.allmusic.com/artist/charlie-johnson-mn0002001526/biography.

89. Ibid. The Lord discography cites him as having done one recording session with Ellington, the 1926 date that produced "Animal Crackers" and "Li'l Farina." He is listed in the same "placeholder" Charlie Johnson entry as cited previously. As if this were not confusing enough, Timmer's *Ellingtonia* lists the Charles Johnson who played with Ellington in 1926 as "Charles Wright Johnson," which is the same name as the famed bandleader Charlie Johnson. It is, of course, possible that the two shared a middle name. See W. E. Timmer, *Ellingtonia: The Recorded Music of Duke Ellington and His Sidemen*, 5th ed. (Lanham, MD: Scarecrow, 2007).

90. Recordings of these performances can be heard at http://dippermouth.blogspot.com/2008/10/75-years-of-louis-armstrong-and-his-hot.html.

91. Quoted in Gordon Jack, *Fifties Jazz Talk: An Oral Retrospective* (Lanham, MD: Scarecrow, 2004), 90.

92. Grego Applegate Edwards, "Dave Schildkraut, Last Date, August 12, 1979." *Gapplegate Music Review*, November 30, 2011, http://gapplegatemusicreview.blogspot.com/2011/11/.

93. Thomas Greenland, "Pilgrims in the Big Apple: Improvisation, Interaction & Inspiration in the Jazz Village" (PhD thesis, University of California, Santa Barbara, 2007), xii.

94. For further discussion, see Ake, *Jazz Cultures*, 112–45.

95. Ben Ratliff, *Coltrane: The Story of a Sound* (New York: Picador, 2008), 33.

96. Carl Woideck, *The John Coltrane Companion: Five Decades of Commentary* (New York: Schirmer, 1998), 78.

97. Bill Crow, *Jazz Anecdotes* (Oxford and New York: Oxford University Press, 1990), 18.

CHAPTER 3: SIGHT-READING, VIRTUOSITY, AND IDENTITY

1. In my case, when I was a student at UNT, the improvisation audition consisted of going to the studio of one of the jazz studies faculty members and playing along with a couple of Aebersold tracks. The entire process took five to ten minutes.

2. "Jazz, the Medium, and the Message: Introducing the One O'Clock Lab Band," *UNT University Union*, September 12, 2018, https://untunion.com/2018/09/12/jazz-the-medium-and-the-message-introducing-the-one-oclock-lab-band/.

3. I was a student in the UNT program in the mid-1990s and a member of the One O'Clock Lab Band during the 1996 to 1997 school year.

4. Kenton Hall has been the main rehearsal and recital space for the North Texas jazz program for many years. In June 2020, the *North Texas Daily* reported that an effort was underway to rename the space in light of Kenton's questionable record on race as well as an allegation of sexual misconduct leveled in a memoir written by his daughter, Leslie Kenton. John Richmond, dean of UNT's College of Music, noted that the topic of renaming the space was "under serious review by the university." I would call attention to the fact that as of early 2023, the College of Music's web page highlighting performance spaces refers to the room as "Lab West" with no reference to Kenton. See Samuel Gomez, "College of Music Considering Renaming Kenton Hall After Racism, Sexual Abuse Allegations Against Its Namesake," *North Texas Daily*, July 9, 2020, https://www.ntdaily.com/college-of-music-considering-renaming-kenton-hall-after-racism-sexual-abuse-allegations-against-its-namesake/; "Facilities," *UNT College of Music*, accessed March 17, 2023, https://music.unt.edu/facilities.

5. Michael Spencer, "Jazz Education at the Westlake College of Music, 1945–61," *Journal of Historical Research in Music Education* 35, no. 1 (2013): 56.

6. Michael Sparke, *Stan Kenton: This is an Orchestra!* (Denton, TX: UNT Press, 2010), 3.

7. Harvey Kubernik, *Hollywood Shack Job: Rock Music in Film and on Your Screen* (Albuquerque: UNM Press, 2006), 349.

8. Frank Hayde, *Stan Levy: Jazz Heavyweight* (Solana Beach, CA: Santa Monica Press, 2016), 143.

9. Joshua Barrett and Louis Bourgois III, *The Musical World of J. J. Johnson* (Lanham, MD: Scarecrow, 2002), 155.

10. Dick Weissman and Frank Jermance, *Navigating the Music Industry: Current Issues & Business Models* (Milwaukee: Hal Leonard, 2003), 50.

11. Alexander Stewart, *Making the Scene: Contemporary New York City Big Band Jazz* (Berkeley: University of California Press, 2007), 51.

12. Leon Breeden (introduction), "Clams, Anyone?" *Lab 67* (North Texas State University), NTSU Lab Jazz 100, 1967, LP.

13. Leon Breeden, *From the Cowbarn to the Concert Hall with Music!* (Denton, TX: Harold Gore Publishing, 2001), 168.

14. Leon Breeden, "A Few Thoughts on the Future of Jazz Education," *Music America*, February 5, 1977, 1, 5.

15. A photo of the band visiting the White House can be seen at https://blogs.library.unt.edu/unt125/1967labband-breeden-1stlady/. Lady Bird Johnson can be seen in the red dress at the center of the photo. To her right is Lou Marini, while Breeden is third from the right.

16. Scotty Barnhart, *The World of Jazz Trumpet: A Comprehensive History & Practical Philosophy* (Milwaukee: Hal Leonard, 2005), 178.

17. Ibid., 178.

18. Julia Eklund Koza, "Listening for Whiteness: Hearing Racial Politics in Undergraduate School Music," *Philosophy of Music Education Review* 16, no. 2 (2008): 148.

19. Ibid., 148–49.

20. Clovis Seems, *The Regal Theater and Black Culture* (New York: Palgrave MacMillan, 2006), 37.

21. Ibid., 30.

22. David Chevan, "Musical Literacy and Jazz Musicians in the 1910s and 1920s," *Current Musicology* nos. 71–73 (2001–2002): 200–231.

23. Ibid., 226.

24. Ibid., 226.

25. See Gendron, "Moldy Figs and Modernists," 130–57.

26. Ibid., 149.

27. Joseph Kuhn Carey, *Big Noise from Notre Dame: A History of the Collegiate Jazz Festival* (Notre Dame, IN: University of Notre Dame Press, 1986), 18–19.

28. Ibid., 26.

29. Breeden, *From the Cowbarn*, 154–55.

30. "The One O'Clock Lab Band with Stan Kenton on ABC, 1966," *UNT Digital Library*, University of North Texas Music Library, accessed May 17, 2021, https://digital.library.unt.edu/ark:/67531/metadc849911/m1/.

31. Morris Eugene Hall, "The Development of a Curriculum for the Teaching of Dance Music at a College Level" (master's thesis, North Texas State Teachers College, 1944), 18.

32. Sparke, *Stan Kenton*, 140.

33. Quoted in Leonard Feather, *The Jazz Years: Earwitness to an Era* (New York: Da Capo, 1987), 122.

34. Ibid., 123–24.

35. Steven B. Elworth, "Jazz in Crisis, 1948–1958: Ideology and Representation," in *Jazz Among the Discourses*, ed. Krin Gabbard (Raleigh: Duke University Press, 1995), 70. Elworth does not note who the "few" musicians are.

36. At issue was the admission of three Black students to Alabama on the orders of a federal district judge. Wallace, perhaps only symbolically, "blocked" the entrance to the university's auditorium.

37. Gerald Early, "White Noise and White Knights: Some Thoughts on Race, Jazz, and the White Jazz Musician," in *Jazz: A History of America's Music*, ed. Geoffrey Ward and Ken Burns (New York: Knopf, 2000), 327.

38. Ibid., 325.

39. Ibid., 326. As absurd as it might seem, this anecdote is supported by Carol Easton in her 1973 biography of Kenton; Easton also cites the bandleader's support of Wallace, whom he was said to have referred to as "profound—a great human being." See Carol Easton, *Straight Ahead: The Story of Stan Kenton* (New York: Morrow, 1973), 228, 240.

40. Dan T. Carter, *From George Wallace to Newt Gingrich: Race in the Conservative Counterrevolution* (Baton Rouge: LSU Press, 1996), 48.

41. While Early does acknowledge this point, he also argues that the overall "*character* of the band was always overwhelmingly white." See Early, "White Noise," 326. Italics in original.

42. Simon Renter, "Stan Kenton at 100: Artistry in Rhythm," *A Blog Supreme*, National Public Radio, February 17, 2012, https://www.npr.org/sections/ablogsupreme/2012/02/17/147040413/stan-kenton-at-100-artistry-in-rhythm.

43. Specifically, Lindsay cites marijuana use as a significant problem, noting that "NAJE is working on the answers." See Bryan Lindsay, "Stage Band or Jazz Ensemble," *NAJE Educator* 2, no. 5 (June/July 1970), 5.

44. Ibid., 5. Emphasis added.

45. Ibid., 5.

46. North Texas was officially desegregated in 1956, though they did admit a Black PhD student two years earlier.

47. For full disclosure, I was the editor of *Jazz Perspectives* when this article was published.

48. Fritz Schenker, "Jazz Freedoms: Balkan Music, Race, and World Music," *Jazz Perspectives* 9, no. 3 (2016): 13.

49. Stan Kenton, Introduction to "Chiapas," *Live at Redlands University*, Creative World ST-1015, 1970, LP.

50. Portions of this section were adapted from papers delivered at the 2021 meeting of the International Association for the Study of Popular Music—US Section, as well as the 2022 annual meeting of the Society for Ethnomusicology.

51. "Maynard Ferguson" was one of several "named" features written for the band by Rogers and by Kenton himself. Also included among these dates were "Art Pepper" (Rogers), "June Christy" (Kenton), and "Shelly Manne" (Kenton).

52. Timothy Leary, *Flashbacks: A Personal and Cultural History of an Era* (New York: Putnam, 1983), 117.

53. Lisa Ferguson, "Interview with Lisa Ferguson—Millbrook Kid and Director of 'Children of the Revolution,'" *Timothy Leary Archives*, accessed May 18, 2021, http://timothylearyarchives.org/interview-with-lisa-ferguson-millbrook-kid-and-director-of-children-of-the-revolution/. Lisa Ferguson notes that the family's move was delayed by several days due to the Kennedy assassination on November 22, 1963.

54. Tom Moulton, "Disco Mix," *Billboard*, January 22, 1977, 78.

55. Columbia Records (advertisement), "Maynard Ferguson's 'Conquistador.' His Victory is Your Reward," *Music America Magazine*, May 1, 1977, 3.

56. "Maynard Ferguson: Conquistador," *Ontario Library Review*, 1978

57. Larry Birnbaum, "Conquistador" (review), *DownBeat* July 14, 1977, 42.

58. Ken Emerson, "Maynard Ferguson Antics," *New York Times*, June 29, 1979, C20.

59. David Sterritt, "Maynard Ferguson—Jazz's Style Blender," *Christian Science Monitor*, December 20, 1976, 22.

60. Ernie Santosuosso, "If You Think Big Bands Are Big, Think Again," *Boston Globe*, January 22, 1984. I would note that this description tracks very closely with my own experience when Ferguson played at my high school in 1989. As far as food was concerned, the band was quite impressed that our small town in Maine had recently seen the opening of a Popeye's chicken restaurant (the only one in New England at that point), where we and the band went for dinner before the show. As Ferguson was currently traveling with a small group, this was both economically and logistically feasible for a group of high school students.

61. Leonard Feather, "The 'Mystic Art' of Maynard Ferguson," *Los Angeles Times*, September 25, 1977, U82. Emphasis added.

62. Ferguson recorded Mike Abene's arrangement of the Sonny Rollins composition on his 1977 album *New Vintage*.

63. I'd suggest that this reference was made in error and that the pitch referred to here is in fact a "double C" or a C_7 in standard pitch notation (which would be the "concert" pitch of $B\flat_6$). While Ferguson did play up to the "triple C" (C_8 or $B\flat_7$ in concert pitch) on occasion, it was relatively uncommon; one commenter on the "Trumpet Herald" message board notes

that while Ferguson could reach the pitch, the sound was "more of a 'whistle' than a note." It is unlikely that even a trumpeter of Ferguson's startling ability in the upper range would play a perfect fifth above this point.

64. John Seery, *America Goes to College: Political Theory for the Liberal Arts* (Albany: SUNY Press, 2002), 80.

65. Christine Hoppe, Melanie von Goldbeck, and Maiko Kawabata, eds., *Exploring Virtuosities: Heinrich Wilhelm Ernst, Nineteenth-Century Musical Practices and Beyond* (Hildesheim, Zurich, and New York: Georg Olms Verlag, 2018), 12.

66. Dana Gooley, *The Virtuoso Liszt* (Cambridge, UK: Cambridge University Press, 2004), 203–4, 214.

67. Ivan Raykoff. *Dreams of Love: Playing the Romantic Pianist* (New York: Oxford University Press), 200, 200.

68. Clare Hall, *Masculinity, Class, and Music Education: Boys Performing Middle-Class Masculinities through Music* (London: Palgrave, 2018), 152.

69. Steritt, "Maynard Ferguson," 22.

70. "Maynard Ferguson 1977 Clinic," *YouTube*, June 3, 2012, https://www.youtube.com/watch?v=uuK_WWPqNVQ.

71. David VanderHamm, "The Social Construction of Virtuosity: Musical Labor and the Valuation of Skill in the Age of Electronic Media" (PhD dissertation, University of North Carolina Chapel Hill, 2017), 13–14.

72. "Maynard Ferguson 1977 clinic."

73. VanderHamm, "The Social Construction of Virtuosity," 15.

74. Ibid., 16.

75. A similar case might be made for Dizzy Gillespie, who famously played throughout his career with puffed cheeks, an anathema to good brass technique, and was regarded as something of a medical curiosity. One scientist coined the term "Gillespie's Pouches," but this condition, in which muscles in the cheeks are gradually stretched over time, has often been referred to in the medical community as a manifestation of "Glassblowers' Disease" in reference to the trade that can produce similar physiological effects. See Kyle Hill, "Why Did Dizzy Gillespie's Cheeks Balloon Like a Bullfrog?" *Nerdist*, June 3, 2016, https://nerdist.com/article/why-did-dizzy-gillespies-cheeks-balloon-like-a-bullfrog/.

76. Billy Taylor, "Current Show: Maynard Ferguson," *Billy Taylor's Jazz at the Kennedy Center*, National Public Radio, accessed August 1, 2019, https://www.npr.org/programs/btaylor/pastprograms/mferguson.html.

77. This performance can be seen at https://www.youtube.com/watch?v=2Df3KFdGeRc.

78. J. N. Burk, "The Fetish of Virtuosity," *Musical Quarterly* 4, no. 2 (1918): 282.

79. Ibid., 282.

80. Ibid., 282–83.

81. Supid Bose, "Music: On Virtuosity: A Mastery of Technique Ought to Be Exalted, Not Disdained," *The American Scholar* 74, no. 3 (2005): 116.

82. David Von Drehle, "Maynard Ferguson's Horn Screamed with Vulgar Passion," *Washington Post*, August 26, 2006, http://www.washingtonpost.com/wp-dyn/content/article/2006/08/25/AR2006082501440.html.

83. Krin Gabbard, "Signifyin(g) the Phallus: *Mo' Better Blues* and Representations of the Trumpet" in *Representing Jazz*, ed. Krin Gabbard (Durham: Duke University Press, 1995), 109–10. I would note that within the context of my own high school experience, the term "jazz jock" was a not-uncommon descriptor for students who were deeply involved with the jazz program.

84. Krin Gabbard, *Black Magic: White Hollywood and African American Culture* (New Brunswick, NJ: Rutgers University Press, 2004), 213. As Gabbard notes, in a later scene in the film, when the teacher listens to Bix Beiderbecke's "Jazz Me Blues" in his classroom, his students commence to smashing his collection of records.

CHAPTER 4: UNDERSTANDING JAZZ EDUCATION'S "RACE PROBLEM"

1. Frank Alkyer, "Jazz on Campus: UNT Jazz Celebrates 75th," *DownBeat*, February 2022, 69.
2. Tracy McMullen, "Chords & Discords: When Black Lives Matter" (letter), May 2022, 10.
3. Ibid., 10.
4. Ed Soph, "Chords & Discords: In Defense of UNT History" (letter), *DownBeat*, July 2022, 10.
5. Ibid, 10.
6. "Datawheel," *Wikipedia*, accessed November 4, 2021, https://en.wikipedia.org/wiki/Data_USA.
7. The entire text of the declaration can be found at https://www.blackpast.org/african-american-history/gary-declaration-national-black-political-convention-1972/.
8. Baker recounts this effort in an oral history for the Smithsonian Jazz Oral History Program conducted by his wife, Lida, in conjunction with Baker's receipt of the NEA Jazz Masters award in 2000. A transcript of the interview can be found at https://americanhistory.si.edu/sites/default/files/file-uploader/David%20N.%20Baker%20SI-NEA%20oral%20history%20%282%29.pdf.
9. Charles Suber, "Boom in School Stage Bands," *Music Journal*, September 1, 1962, 58.
10. John S. Wilson, "Campuses Bubbling With Jazz," *New York Times*, April 26, 1964, 15X.
11. Leonard Feather and Ira Gitler, *The Encyclopedia of Jazz in the Seventies* (New York: Horizon, 1976), 369.
12. See R. M. Longyear, "The 'Banda Sul Palco': Wind Bands in Nineteenth-Century Opera," *Journal of Band Research* 13, no. 2 (1978): 25–40; Linda Tyler, "Striking up the Banda: Verdi's Use of the Stage Band in His Middle-Period Operas," *The Opera Journal* 20, no. 1 (1990): 2–22.
13. David Herfort, "A History of the National Association of Jazz Educators and a Description of its Role in American Music Education, 1968–1978" (DEd dissertation, University of Houston, 1979), 23–24. The men in question were Matthew (Matt) Betton (director of the Stan Kenton clinics), Clement DeRosa (Cold Spring Harbor Schools), Morris E. "Gene" Hall (Stephen F. Austin University, who had earlier founded the North Texas jazz program), Donald Joseph (Drury College), Stan Kenton, Bill Lee (University of Miami), John Roberts (Denver Public Schools), and Jack Wheaton (Cerritos College).
14. Herfort, "A History of the National Association of Jazz Educators," 20.
15. Ibid., 85.

16. Ibid., 129.

17. Ibid., 177.

18. John S. Wilson, "Kennedy Center is 'Home' to College Jazz Festival," *New York Times*, May 30, 1972, 42.

19. Joseph Kuhn Carey, *Big Noise from Notre Dame: A History of the Collegiate Jazz Festival* (Notre Dame, Indiana: University of Notre Dame Press, 1986), 102–3.

20. Ibid., 104.

21. Ibid., 104.

22. Recordings of the band from the 1972 Notre Dame Festival can be found at https://www.youtube.com/watch?v=x8M1AkgMK1g ("Music for Gong Gong") and https://www.youtube.com/watch?v=X2cYXEy4b_s (an arrangement of Deep Purple's "Hush").

23. George Lewis, *A Power Stronger than Itself: The AACM and American Experimental Music* (Chicago: University of Chicago Press, 2008), 309, 390.

24. Walton's collected papers are housed in the archives of the Chicago Public Library. See https://mts.lib.uchicago.edu/collections/findingaids/index.php?eadid=MTS.walton.

25. Dr. Charles Hurst, "Introduction," *Afro-American Jazz Ensemble* (Malcolm X College), 1972, LP.

26. The album can be found here: https://www.youtube.com/watch?v=uLshIttwZSI.

27. "About Us," *African American Jazz Caucus* (website), accessed August 20, 2022, https://aajc.us/about-us.

28. Charles (Chuck) Suber, quoted in David Baker, *Jazz Pedagogy: A Comprehensive Method of Jazz Education for Teacher and Student* (Van Nuys, CA: Alfred Music Publishing, 1989), vi. Originally published by Maher in 1979.

29. Suber, in Baker, *Jazz Pedagogy*, vi.

30. Ibid., vi.

31. Charles (Chuck) Suber, "Diary of a Stage Band," *Music Journal* 21, no. 4 (April 1963): 70.

32. "Mobile High School Jazz Band Contest," *Billboard*, May 27, 2972, 4.

33. "Mobile Jazz June 6 to 9," *Billboard*, June 2, 1973, 30.

34. Lehman, Chris, "Kashmere Stage Band," *Handbook of Texas*, Texas State Historical Association, June 10, 2013, https://www.tshaonline.org/handbook/entries/kashmere-stage-band.

35. *Thunder Soul*, directed by Mark Landsman (2010; Los Angeles: Snoot Entertainment), DVD and streaming.

36. Mark Olsen, "Revisiting the 'Soul' of a Remarkable High School Jazz Band," *Los Angeles Times*, June 20, 2010, https://www.latimes.com/archives/la-xpm-2010-jun-20-la-ca-indie-focus-20100620-story.html.

37. *Thunder Soul*, 11:39–12:23.

38. Ibid., 35:08–35:37.

39. Several commenters have made direct connections between Conrad's work at Kashmere and Cab Calloway. See "Capturing the Heart and Thunder Soul of Kashmere High School," *Houston Chronicle*, September 22, 2011, 35; David Hinckley, "'Thunder Soul' Follows Rise of Kashmere Rhythm and Blues High School Band with Jamie Foxx at Helm," *New York Daily News*, September 19, 2011, https://www.nydailynews.com/entertainment/tv-movies/thunder-soul-rise-kashmere-rhythm-blues-high-school-band-jamie-foxx-helm-article-1.953820.

40. *Thunder Soul*, 36:22–36:32.

41. Ibid., 35:38–36:03.

42. Ibid., 40:16–40:30.

43. Ibid., 40:33–41:12.

44. Christopher Kelly, "Putting the Band Back Together," *Texas Monthly*, October 2011, https://www.texasmonthly.com/articles/putting-the-band-back-together/.

45. Todd Stoll, "It's Deeper than the Notes," *Jazz Education Network*, June 12, 2020, https://jazzednet.org/its-deeper-than-the-notes/. Boldface and italics in original.

46. Ibid.

47. Todd Stoll, "Diversity," *Jazz Education Network*, July 18, 2019, https://jazzednet.org/diversity/. Boldface in original.

48. I attended one such workshop in the late 1980s at the University of Maine in Orono, which preceded his group's performance at the Maine Center for the Arts.

49. The address was published as "Jazz Education in the New Millennium," *Jazz Educators Journal* 33, no. 2 (2000): 46–48, 51–52. All references to Marsalis's address in this discussion are drawn from this article.

50. Of all these organizations, the Monk Institute was probably the closest to an institutional jazz education program. Established in 1986, the Institute was founded in honor of the legendary pianist and composer. The best-known component of the Institute's programming has been the Thelonious Monk International Jazz Competition, which began in 1987. In 1995, the Institute began sponsoring a graduate-level jazz program, hosted first by the New England Conservatory until 1999, when it moved to the University of Southern California. In 2007, the program moved again, this time relocating to Loyola University in New Orleans, where it would remain until 2011. The Institute then moved once more, forging a partnership with the University of California, Los Angeles, where it remains today. In 2018, the Institute and the Monk family ended their relationship, and it was renamed the Herbie Hancock Institute of Jazz in honor of the renowned pianist, who also happened to be the chairman of the Institute's board of directors at the time.

51. Carter would later direct the jazz studies program at Northern Illinois University.

52. Perhaps not coincidentally, Burns was also a speaker at the 2000 IAJE convention, where he previewed segments of his upcoming film.

53. Farah Jasmine Griffin, *If You Can't be Free, Be a Mystery: In Search of Billie Holiday* (New York: Random House, 2002), 125.

54. Charles Hersch, "America Without Dissonance: Ken Burns's *Jazz*," *Polity* 34, no.1 (2001), 108.

55. Kimberly Hannon Teal, *Jazz Places: How Performance Spaces Shape Jazz History* (Berkeley: University of California Press, 2021).

56. Nate Chinen, *Playing Changes: Jazz for the New Century* (New York: Pantheon, 2018), 49–50.

57. Stuart Nicholson, *Is Jazz Dead? (Or Has It Moved to a New Address?)* (Abingdon and New York: Routledge, 2005), 76.

58. Chinen, *Playing Changes*, 51.

59. Bill Maher and Wynton Marsalis (interview), "Season 20, episode 26," *Real Time with Bill Maher*, New York: HBO, September 9, 2022.

60. Teal, *Jazz Places*, 56.

61. Dan Oullette, "JALC's Big Ed Outreach," *DownBeat*, January 25, 2022, https://downbeat.com/news/detail/jalcs-big-jazz-ed-outreach.

62. Scholarship on this phenomenon is relatively rare, though a notable exception can be found in Zachary Wiggins's recent doctoral dissertation on the teaching of historical jazz performance. I was fortunate to serve as a consultant to Wiggins's project and to participate in a recent panel with him along with fellow ASU student Jayson Davis and their mentor Christi Jay Wells at the Rhythm Changes conference in Amsterdam in August 2022. See Zachary Wiggins, "Mediating Tradition as a Traditional Jazz Scholar-Performer" (PhD dissertation, Arizona State University, 2021).

63. Kimberly Hannon Teal, "Posthumously Live: Canon Formation at Jazz at Lincoln Center through the Case of Mary Lou Williams," *American Music* 32, no. 4 (2014): 407–8.

64. Thomas Clavin, "Conductor at Top of the Jazz World," *New York Times*, January 23, 1994, LI 9.

65. David Berger, *Life in D♭: A Jazz Journal* (Such Sweet Thunder Publishing, 2017), Kindle edition, chapter two. In addition to providing transcriptions of Ellington's work, Berger served as the initial conductor of the Jazz at Lincoln Center Orchestra, a post that he held until 1994. He continues to serve as a consultant to JALC and Essentially Ellington.

66. Ben Ratliff, "Critic's Notebook: When High School Bands Get a Chance to Play Real Ellington," *New York Times*, May 4, 1999, https://www.nytimes.com/1999/05/04/arts/critic-s-notebook-when-high-school-bands-get-a-chance-to-play-real-ellington.html.

67. See Wynton Marsalis, "What Jazz Is—and Isn't," *New York Times*, July 31, 1988, https://www.nytimes.com/1988/07/31/arts/music-what-jazz-is-and-isn-t.html. While many have attributed this essay to Marsalis's relative youth at the time, it is worth noting that the text still appears on the trumpeter's official website.

68. Ethan Iverson, "The 'J' Word," Do the Math (website), accessed July 27, 2022, https://ethaniverson.com/the-j-word/.

69. Laura Andrews, "Composer Horace Silver Distraught Over Deficit in Jazz Education," *New York Amsterdam News*, July 5, 1997, 34.

70. For a contemporary discussion of this term, see "Interview in Los Angeles: On Jump for Joy, Opera, and Dissonance as a 'Way of Life,'" (1941). Reprinted in Mark Tucker, *The Duke Ellington Reader* (New York and Oxford: Oxford University Press, 1993), 150.

71. Natalia Navarro, "'These Guys Don't Sound Like High School Students': Denver Jazz Band Takes Act to National Competition," *Colorado Public Radio*, May 7, 2019, https://www.cpr.org/2019/05/07/these-guys-dont-sound-like-high-school-students-denver-jazz-band-takes-act-to-national-competition/. Emphasis added.

72. United States House of Representatives, "Summary: H Res. 958–115th Congress (2017–2018)," *H Res.958*, June 22, 2018, https://www.congress.gov/bill/115th-congress/house-resolution/958/text?r=56&s=1. The passage referring to Adderley "gaining fame" at Dillard is, I would suggest, somewhat questionable.

73. Eric Felton, "Vintage Artists, Vintage Art: Reviving Ellington Jazz for a New Generation," *Philanthropy*, Summer 2018, https://www.philanthropyroundtable.org/philanthropy-magazine/article/young-artists-vintage-art.

74. Nicholson, *Is Jazz Dead?* 76.

75. In a 2001 episode of *The Charlie Rose Show*, Burns describes Marsalis's response to his inquiry as "I'll do whatever you want" with respect to assisting with the *Jazz* project. Marsalis would end up as the project's main creative consultant as well as the most frequent "talking head" in the film. This interview can be found at https://www.youtube.com/watch?v=YeGqvn89YBw (reference point for this discussion is the 15:49 mark).

76. Information in this discussion was gathered from publicly available US Census data as well as from *School Digger*, a website that aggregates school enrollment and performance statistics.

77. A comprehensive list of finalists can be found at https://en.wikipedia.org/wiki/Essentially_Ellington_High_School_Jazz_Band_Competition_and_Festival#Finalists.

78. Jazz at Lincoln Center, "Equity and Inclusion Initiative," *Jazz Academy*, accessed April 17, 2021, https://academy.jazz.org/ee/participate/equity-and-inclusion-initiative/.

79. Ibid.

80. As of 2022, Roosevelt has been an Essentially Ellington finalist twenty-one times, while Garfield has made seventeen finals appearances.

81. Paul de Barros, "Jazz Hits a Pale Note: Despite Roots, It's a Mostly White Activity in Seattle Schools," *Seattle Times*, April 13, 2003, https://archive.seattletimes.com/archive/?date=20030413&slug=hsjazz13. De Barros notes that about 23 percent of Seattle public school students at the time of this article were Black; meanwhile, Black students represented only 6 percent of students in school jazz bands.

82. Ibid.

83. Ibid.

84. Ibid.

CHAPTER 5: JAZZ PEOPLE AND PUBLIC PEDAGOGIES

1. Nielsen, "2014 Nielsen U.S. Music Report," accessed June 3, 2022, https://bird.jazzline.com/tjl/uploads/2015/03/nielsen-2014-year-end-music-report-us.pdf.

2. David La Rosa, "Jazz Has Become the Least-Popular Genre in America." https://news.jazzline.com/news/jazz-least-popular-music-genre/.

3. Patrick Jarenwattananon, "You Aren't Too Dumb to Like Jazz," *A Blog Supreme* (NPR), August 27, 2010, https://www.npr.org/sect.ions/ablogsupreme/2010/08/27/129476048/you-aren-t-too-dumb-to-like-jazz.

4. Ibid.

5. Ibid.

6. Ibid.

7. "Jazz is The Worst" (Twitter account), accessed November 13, 2021, https://twitter.com/jazzistheworst.

8. The scene in question is available at https://www.youtube.com/watch?v=DAjNoNUqsoQ; the segment referenced here begins at approximately 1:30.

9. Django Gold, "Sonny Rollins: In His Own Words," *New Yorker*, July 31, 2014, https://www.newyorker.com/humor/daily-shouts/sonny-rollins-words.

10. Django Gold, "Notes from the Backlash: New Yorker Humorist Django Gold Speaks," *JazzTimes*, August 18, 2014, https://jazztimes.com/features/columns/notes-from-the-backlash/.

11. The program in question was called *Jackass*, which ran on MTV from 2000 to 2002, and was known for featuring its cast of Gen Xers performing dangerous, outlandish, and sometimes repulsive stunts. The popular series also spawned several films, including one that was released in 2022.

12. Marc Myers, "Sonny Rollins + The New Yorker," *jazz.fm91*, CJRT-FM, August 4, 2014, https://jazz.fm/sonny-rollins-the-new-yorker/.

13. Howard Mandel, "Most Scurrilous, Unfunny New Yorker 'Humor' re Jazz," *ArtsJournal*, August 2, 2014, https://www.artsjournal.com/jazzbeyondjazz/2014/08/most-scurrilous-unfunny-new-yorker-humor-re-jazz.html.

14. Sean O'Connell, "Sonny Rollins Fans Go Ballistic About *New Yorker* Article," *Village Voice*, August 6, 2014, https://www.villagevoice.com/2014/08/06/sonny-rollins-fans-go-ballistic-about-new-yorker-article/.

15. Will Layman, "The Sonny Rollins/*New Yorker* Controversy and Jazz's Image Problem," *Popmatters*, August 18, 2014, https://www.popmatters.com/184681-the-sonny-rollins-new-yorker-controversy-and-jazzs-image-problem-2495629647.html.

16. Ibid.

17. Ibid.

18. Ibid.

19. Justin Moyer, "All That Jazz Isn't All That Great," *Washington Post*, August 8, 2014, https://www.washingtonpost.com/news/opinions/wp/2014/08/08/all-that-jazz-isnt-all-that-great/.

20. Mandel, "Most Scurrilous."

21. Quoted in Layman, "Sonny Rollins/*New Yorker*."

22. Ibid.

23. Taylor Wofford, "Jazz Legend Sonny Rollins: *Onion* Writer Was Mean To Me," *Newsweek*, August 6, 2014, https://www.newsweek.com/jazz-legend-sonny-rollins-onion-writer-was-mean-me-263307.

24. Gold, "Notes from the Backlash."

25. Rollins himself made this claim in his interview with Primack, but it is worth noting that some of his comments seemed to be contradictory.

26. Richard Brody, "Getting Jazz Right in the Movies," *New Yorker*, October 13, 2014, https://www.newyorker.com/culture/richard-brody/whiplash-getting-jazz-right-movies.

27. Nate Chinen, "An All-Year Season of Discontent in Jazz," *New York Times*, December 30, 2014, https://www.nytimes.com/2014/12/31/arts/music/jazzs-year-of-complaint-citing-whiplash-and-the-new-yorker.html.

28. Ibid. The reference to Dumont alludes to her performance in a number of Marx Brothers films, generally serving as a foil or victim of the brothers' antics (most notably Groucho). Dumont's voice, couched in a dramatic, quasi-British "high-class" accent was a distinctive feature of these films, often expressing anger or shock in a sharp contrast with Groucho Marx's deadpan comedy.

29. Jazz at Lincoln Center, "The Jazz Congress," accessed November 1, 2018, https://www.jazz.org/events/t-7034/jazz-congress/.

30. Kareem Abdul-Jabbar, "Kareem Abdul-Jabbar: Sharing the Passion for Jazz," *JazzTimes*, March 16, 2018, https://jazztimes.com/features/columns/kareem-abdul-jabbar-sharing-passion-jazz/.

31. Jennifer Sandlin, Brian Schultz, and Jake Burdick, "Understanding, Mapping, and Exploring the Terrain of Public Pedagogy, in *Handbook of Public Pedagogy: Education and Learning Beyond Schooling*, edited by Jennifer A. Sandlin et al. (New York and London: Routledge, 2009), 1.

32. William Pinar, "Foreword," in *Handbook of Public Pedagogy: Education and Learning Beyond Schooling*, edited by Jennifer A. Sandlin et al. (New York and London: Routledge, 2009), xv.

33. Hugh C. Ernst, "An Experiment in Modern Music," Program Notes, February 12, 1924. Reprinted in Robert Walser, ed., *Keeping Time: Readings in Jazz History* (Oxford and New York: Oxford University Press, 1998), 38–39.

34. Kelsey Klotz, "Dave Brubeck in the Living Room: Race, Gender, and Respectability in the Conversion of a "New" Jazz Audience," paper delivered at the Annual Meeting of the American Musicological Society, San Antonio, November 1–4, 2018. Abstract available at https://cdn.ymaws.com/ams-net.site-ym.com/resource/resmgr/files/abstracts/2018-san antonio.pdf, 177. As this book goes to press, Klotz's book *Dave Brubeck and the Performance of Whiteness* (Oxford University Press) is also nearing publication. Klotz engages in a deep and probing examination of Brubeck's life and career "as a starting point to understand the ways in which whiteness, privilege, and white supremacy more fully manifested in mid-century America."

35. Negri was, in fact, the jazz guitar instructor at the University of Pittsburgh during my doctoral studies, a fact that I was delighted to discover—having grown up seeing him on the show—during my first visit to the department in the late 1990s.

36. "International Jazz Day," UNESCO, *International Jazz Day and the Herbie Hancock Institute of Jazz*, accessed November 21, 2021, https://jazzday.com/interview/travis-kemp-united-states/.

37. "About the Calgary Jazz Orchestra," *Calgary Jazz Orchestra*, access November 23, 2021, http://www.calgaryjazzorchestra.com/about.html.

38. Terence Hsieh, "Yiling Lin: Jazz in Beijing has a Bright Future," *Forbes*, July 31, 2016, https://www.forbes.com/sites/terencehsieh/2016/07/31/yiling-lin-jazz-in-beijing-has-a-bright-future/?sh=63c68aa65fc1.

39. "FAQ," *Jazz Appreciation Month*, National Museum of American History, accessed November 23, 2021, https://americanhistory.si.edu/smithsonian-jazz/jazz-appreciation-month/faq.

40. "Jazz Snob, *Urban Dictionary*, accessed November 21, 2021 https://www.urbandictionary.com/define.php?term=Jazz%20Snob.

41. Ken Burns et al., *Jazz*, episode 10, 24:05–24:16, PBS Home Video, 2001, DVD. Ben Ratliff, reviewing the series for the *New York Times*, astutely noted that Cecil Taylor was "the only musician in the film to be disrespected by one of its talking heads." See Ben Ratliff, "Fixing, for Now, the Image of Jazz," *New York Times*, January 7, 2001, Arts and Leisure, section 2, page 1.

42. Ibid., 24:18–24:28.

43. Branford Marsalis with Bill Milkowski, "Like It Is: The Branford Marsalis Interview," *JazzTimes*, November 1, 2012, https://jazztimes.com/features/interviews/like-it-is-the-branford-marsalis-interview/.

44. Ibid. Emphasis added.

45. https://twitter.com/JazzIsTheWorst/status/352805517460127744.

46. In strictly rhetorical terms, many statements about jazz's relationship to other concepts might be more accurately described as similes, which are fundamentally comparative in nature, as opposed to a more direct equivalency between concepts. The statement "life is like jazz" would be an example of a simile, whereas "life is jazz" would be better understood as a metaphor. However, given the ubiquitous use of the term "metaphor" to describe such statements and initiatives, I have opted to follow that convention here in reference to rhetorical structures that could be described in this way.

47. Stephen Crist, "Jazz and Democracy: Dave Brubeck and Cold War Politics," *Journal of Musicology* 26, no. 2 (2009): 137.

48. Penny Von Eschen, *Satchmo Blows Up the World: Jazz Ambassadors Play the Cold War* (Cambridge: Harvard University Press, 2004), 33.

49. VOA News, "Willis Conover Jazz Hour Clip, *YouTube* (Voice of America channel), accessed December 2, 2021, https://www.youtube.com/watch?v=TZVpHOSqJpE&ab_channel=VOANews.

50. Von Eschen, *Satchmo Blows Up the World*, 16–17.

51. Anna von Veh," Let's Improvise! Jazz as a Metaphor for Publishing Progress," *Publishing Perspectives*, May 12, 2012, https://publishingperspectives.com/2012/05/lets-improvise-jazz-as-a-metaphor-for-publishing-progress/.

52. Dwight Zscheile, *The Agile Church: Spirit-Led Innovation in an Uncertain Age* (Harrisburg: Morehouse Publishing, 2014), 108.

53. Ibid., 108.

54. W. David Buschart and Kent Elders, *Theology as Retrieval: Receiving the Past, Renewing the Church* (Westmont, IL: InterVarsity Press, 2015), 268

55. Ibid., 268.

56. Columbia Theological Seminary, "Apply Now to Attend Jazz as a Metaphor for Ministry: The Power of Improvisation" (website), accessed June 3, 2022, https://www.ctsnet.edu/apply-now-attend-jazz-metaphor-ministry-power-improvisation/. An archived version of the page can be found at https://web.archive.org/web/20221212072858/https://www.ctsnet.edu/apply-now-attend-jazz-metaphor-ministry-power-improvisation/.

57. I. A. Richards, *The Philosophy of Rhetoric* (London: Oxford University Press, 1936), 89.

58. Ibid., 89.

59. Ray Malewitz, "What Are Vehicles and Tenors?" *Oregon State Guide to Literary Terms*, Oregon State University, accessed December 2, 2021, https://liberalarts.oregonstate.edu/wlf/what-vehicles-and-tenors.

60. Ken Burns and Lynn Novick, "Q&A with the Filmmakers," *Jazz*, PBS, accessed December 2, 2021, https://www.pbs.org/kenburns/jazz/q-a-with-filmmakers/.

61. Dale Chapman, *The Jazz Bubble: Neoclassical Jazz in Neoliberal Culture* (Berkeley: University of California Press, 2018), 158–59.

62. Mark Laver, "Freedom of Choice: Jazz, Neoliberalism, and the Lincoln Center," *Popular Music and Society* 37, no. 5 (2014): 553.

63. Teal, *Jazz Places*, 59.

64. Ibid., 60.

65. Benjamin Givan, "How Democratic is Jazz?" in *Finding Democracy in Music*, ed. Robert Adlington and Esteban Bruch (Abingdon and New York, 2021), 34–35.

66. Ibid., 35.

67. Theresa Riley, "What Do Democracy and Jazz Have in Common?" Bill Moyers (website), October 12, 2020, https://billmoyers.com/story/democracy-jazz-wynton-marsalis-amazing-grace/.

68. *Organization Science* 9, no. 5 (1998). This is a special issue which emerged from the "Organization Science Jazz Festival" in 1996.

69. Jim Kalbach, "About Me," *Experiencing Information*, accessed July 28, 2022, https://experiencinginformation.com/about/.

70. TEDx Talks, "Jazz Improvisation for Radical Collaboration," *YouTube*, March 15, 2015, https://www.youtube.com/watch?v=j8Gmp194zbI&ab_channel=TEDxTalks.

71. Greg Thomas and Jewel Kinch-Thomas, *Jazz Leadership Project*, accessed December 1, 2021, https://www.jazzleadershipproject.com/.

72. Ibid.

73. Ibid.

74. Ibid.

75. Ibid.

76. "Syncopated Leadership," Jazz at Lincoln Center, accessed December 1, 2021, https://www.jazz.org/business-leadership-workshop/.

77. Ibid.

78. See Mike Ford, "An Agile Musicology: Improvisation in Corporate Management and Lean Startups" (PhD dissertation, Columbia University, 2022).

79. This section is adapted from conference papers given at the Rhythm Changes conference in 2016 (Birmingham, UK) and the Beyond Genre: Jazz as Popular Music conference in 2018 (Cleveland).

80. J. R. Jones, "*Whiplash*: A Jazz Movie That Has Nothing to Do with Jazz," *Chicago Reader*, October 29, 2014, https://chicagoreader.com/film/whiplash-a-jazz-movie-that-has-nothing-to-do-with-jazz/.

81. Quoted in Nick Clark, "*Whiplash* Movie Hit by Backlash from Disgruntled Jazz Fans," *The Independent*, January 23, 2015, https://www.independent.co.uk/arts-entertainment/films/news/jazz-thriller-whiplash-hit-by-backlash-from-disgruntled-jazz-fans-9999858.html.

82. Quoted in Philip Conklin, "It Ain't Got That Swing," *The Periphery*, January 2015, http://www.theperipherymag.com/on-the-arts-whiplash.

83. Richard Brody, "Getting Jazz Right in the Movies," *The New Yorker*, October 1, 2014, https://www.newyorker.com/culture/richard-brody/whiplash-getting-jazz-right-movies.

84. Ibid.

85. Ibid.

86. Ibid.

87. Excerpts of these tapes can easily be found online; one version can be heard at https://www.youtube.com/watch?v=3Ia95oiS5LE. The tapes were made by Rich's then-pianist Lee Musiker on a small portable cassette recorder. See Will Friedwald, "'Just in Time: The Final Recording' by Buddy Rich Review: He Kept Pushing to the End," *Wall Street*

Journal, October 6, 2021, https://www.wsj.com/articles/just-in-time-the-final-recording-by-buddy-rich-review-he-kept-pushing-to-the-end-11576012836.

88. Patrick Berkery, "*Whiplash* Confirms What This Drummer Already Knew: Jazz is Full of Arrogant, Sadistic Jerks," *Salon*, February 21, 2015, https://www.salon.com/2015/02/21/whiplash_confirms_what_this_drummer_already_knew_jazz_is_full_of_arrogant_sadistic_jerks/.

89. Bruce Klauber, "Damien Chazelle's *Whiplash*," *Broad Street Review*, November 1, 2014, https://www.broadstreetreview.com/articles/damien-chazelles-whiplash.

90. Quoted in Conklin, "It Ain't Got That Swing."

91. Ibid.

92. Ibid.

93. Redditsauce57 (username), "Watching the movie *Whiplash* brings back some memories. Jazz education is a crazy world," Reddit (discussion), March 6, 2022, https://www.reddit.com/r/jazzguitar/comments/t802ol/watching_the_movie_whiplash_brings_back_some/.

94. Polarshed (username), comment in response to "Watching the movie *Whiplash*," March 7, 2022.

95. Unnamed user, comment in response to "Watching the movie *Whiplash*," March 6, 2022.

96. Chinen, "An All-Year Season."

97. David Marchese, "*La La Land* Director Damien Chazelle Breaks Down Jazz's Popularity Problem, *Vulture*, December 19, 2016, https://www.vulture.com/2016/12/la-la-land-damien-chazelle-jazz-nostalgia.html.

98. The "KJAZ" call letters are actually assigned to a radio station in Texas that has been "silent" (i.e., not broadcasting) since at least 2008. See "KJAZ," *Wikipedia*, accessed September 2, 2022, https://en.wi*kipedia.org/wiki/KJAZ.

99. Anna Silman, "*La La Land*: A Musical Ode to Men Who Love Loving Jazz," *The Cut*, December 13, 2016, https://www.thecut.com/2016/12/la-la-land-two-hours-of-ryan-gosling-explaining-jazz.html.

100. Bjorn Heile, "Renaissance or Afterlife? Nostalgia in the New Jazz Films," *The Routledge Companion to Jazz Studies*, ed. Nicholas Gebhardt, Nichole, Rustin-Paschal, and Tony Whyton (New York: Routledge), 423–31.

101. Krin Gabbard, "*La La Land* is a Hit, but Is It Good for Jazz?" *Daedalus* 148, no. 2 (2019): 99.

102. Ibid., 99.

103. Kareem Abdul-Jabbar, "How *La La Land* Misleads on Race, Romance, and Jazz," *Hollywood Reporter*, February 15, 2017, https://www.hollywoodreporter.com/news/general-news/la-la-land-disappoints-bigoted-race-portrayal-childish-romance-975786/.

104. Seve Chambers, "*La La Land* is Clueless about What's Actually Happening in Jazz," *The Cut*, January 13, 2017, https://www.vulture.com/2017/01/what-la-la-land-gets-wrong-about-todays-jazz.html.

105. Ethan Iverson, "The Drum Thing, or A Brief History of *Whiplash*, or 'I'm Generalizing Here,'" *Do the M@th*, accessed October 4, 2021, https://ethaniverson.com/rhythm-and-blues/the-drum-thing-or-a-brief-history-of-whiplash-or-im-generalizing-here/.

106. Rebecca Ford, "Making of *Whiplash*: How a 20-Something Shot His Harrowing Script in Just 19 Days," *Hollywood Reporter*, December 9, 2014, https://www.hollywoodreporter.com/news/general-news/making-whiplash-how-a-twentysomething-753283/.

107. Oliver Gettell, "Screening Series: *Whiplash* Director Damien Chazelle on his Real-Life Inspiration," *Los Angeles Times*, November 11, 2014, https://www.latimes.com/entertainment/movies/moviesnow/la-et-mn-whiplash-damien-chazelle-real-life-inspiration-20141111-story.html.

108. Damien Chazelle, "Divide and Conquer: Damien Chazelle on Why You Should Make a Short First," *Moviemaker*, October 9, 2015, https://www.moviemaker.com/damien-chazelle-on-why-you-should-make-a-short-first/. *Guy and Madeline* is a reference to Chazelle's 2009 independent film *Guy and Madeline on a Park Bench*, which involved the relationship between the two titular characters, the former a jazz trumpeter.

109. Gabbard, "*La La Land*," 99.

110. Emma Bezilla and Elliot Wailoo, "PHS Alumnus Releases Nationally Acclaimed Film Recounting High School Band Experiences," *The Tower*, November 26, 2014, https://thetowerphs.com/2014/11/arts-and-entertainment/phs-alumnus-releases-nationally-acclaimed-film-recounting-high-school-band-experiences/.

111. Ibid.

112. Ibid.

113. Nicolas Pillai, *Jazz As Visual Language: Film, Television and the Dissonant Image* (London: I. B. Tauris, 2017), 119.

114. Pillai suggests that *Whiplash* might be better understood as a "horror film" that "unsettles any fixed definition of what the "jazz" in jazz film might be and so sharpens our awareness of how particular films use jazz metaphorically or symbolically. See Pillai, *Jazz As Visual Language*, 10.

CODA: WHAT'S IN A DOMAIN NAME

1. David La Rosa, "Jazz at Lincoln Center Domain Change Sparks Outrage," *Jazzline*, January 15, 2015, https://news.jazzline.com/news/jazz-at-lincoln-center-domain-change-petition-jazz-org/.

2. "Wayback Machine," *Internet Archive*, accessed July 6, 2022, https://web.archive.org/web/20010424073002/http://www.jazz.org/servlet/webmail?MainScenarioId=enter&InterfaceId=EnterForm&refreshAction=true&InitSession=true.

3. Nate Chinen, "The Gig: JALC Takes Over jazz.org," *JazzTimes*, April 2015, https://jazztimes.com/features/columns/the-gig-jalc-takes-over-jazz-org/.

4. Andre Guess, "Remove Jazz.org as Jazz at Lincoln Center's Domain Name and Develop a Separate Inclusive Community-Wide Site with the URL," *Change.org*, accessed July 13, 2022, https://www.change.org/p/wynton-marsalis-remove-jazz-org-as-jazz-at-lincoln-center-s-domain-name-and-develop-a-separate-inclusive-community-wide-site-with-the-url.

5. Ibid.

6. Chinen, "The Gig: JALC."

INDEX

AAJC/HBCU Student All-Star Big Band, 133
Abdul-Jabbar, Kareem, 167–68, 191
adolescents and jazz, 104, 111–12, 118
Aebersold, Jamey, 46, 209n1
Ake, David, 207–8n68
Alapatt, Egon, 135
All-American High School Stage Band Festival, 9, 134–36
Allen, Eddie, 85
Allen, Geri, 6
alternative names for jazz, 29–30
American College Jazz Festival, 130
Anderson, Benedict, 5
Armstrong, Louis, 5, 28, 35, 47–48, 55, 63, 69–71, 76, 78, 91, 163, 172, 204n76, 207n61, 209n87
athletics, jazz and, 111, 113

Baker, David, x, 6, 46, 54, 126, 133, 214n8
Balkan music, 100–101
Barnet, Charlie, 104
Barnhart, Scotty, 87–88
Basie, Count, 63, 73, 88, 95, 105, 141
Batiste, Alvin, 131
Battlestar Galactica. See science fiction
"Beale Street Blues" (Mole), 31, 96
Beatles, The, 73–75, 116
bebop, 53, 76, 92, 104
Berg, Shelton "Shelly," 186
Berger, David, 145–46, 148, 217n65
Berk, Lawrence, 128
Berklee College of Music, 83, 128, 134, 159
Betton, Matt, 129, 214n13

Biancosino, Anthony, 193–95
Biden, Joe, 4–5
Billboard (magazine), 107–8
"Birdland" (Ferguson), 109
Birdland (jazz club), 105
Blackboard Jungle (Brooks), 118
Black Jazz Music Caucus, 132
Black Power movement, 125–26, 131–32, 138
Blake, Ran, 100
Blakey, Art, 3, 130, 192, 209n85
Blanchard, Terrence, 3
blog (web log), 159, 189, 198
Bolden, Buddy, 61, 91
Boston Consolidated Gas Company Band, 23
Bowden, Mwata, 131
brass instruments, 18, 23, 54, 104, 107, 114, 118, 120, 202n33, 213n75
breaks, musical, 30–31, 35–43, 49
Brecker Brothers, 7
Breeden, Leon, 9, 81, 85–87, 94–95, 99–100, 123, 130, 210n15
Bridgewater, Dee Dee, 4
Brockton, Lester. *See* Lake, Mayhew
Brubeck, Dave, 6, 93, 100, 101, 168, 172, 220n34
Brunies, George, 32
Burns, Ken, 69, 97, 141–43, 151, 170, 175, 206n53, 216n52, 218n75
Byrd, Donald, 6

Calgary Jazz Orchestra, 169
Calloway, Cab, 136, 215n39
Canadian Stage Band Festival, 112

Candoli, Conte, 94
Candoli, Pete, 92
canon, 9, 27, 50, 59, 62, 70–72, 75–77, 79–80, 117, 142, 144–45, 148, 198
Carl Fischer (publisher), 22, 44
Carnival (Ferguson), 108–9, 119
Carter, Benny, 80
Carter, Jimmy, 98
Carter, Ronald, 140, 216n51
Cashbox (magazine), 108
Cass Technical High School, 76
Castellaneta, Dan, 160
Catlett, Sid, 80
Center for Black Music Research, x, 9, 62, 205n21, 205n33, 206n35
Chattaway, Jay, 102, 107, 119
Chazelle, Damian, 10, 165–66, 182–95, 198, 224n108
Chevan, David, 91, 203n60
Childers, Buddy, 94
Chinen, Nate, 143–44, 165–66, 184, 188, 197
Clarke, Kenny, 79
Clayton, John, 130
Clinton, George. *See* Parliament (band)
Coker, Jerry, 202n48
Coleman, Ornette, 6
Collier, James Lincoln, 47, 56, 71–72, 207n65
Collins, Arthur, 26
Coltrane, John, 3, 4, 54, 56, 70, 73–74, 76, 80, 90–91, 112, 187, 208n68, 209n85
Coltrane, Ravi, 4
Columbia College. *See* Center for Black Music Research
Columbia Records, 106–8
Commitments, The (Parker), 171
Conquistador (Ferguson), 107–9, 119
"Coon Band Contest, A" (Pryor), 13–14
Corea, Chick, 6
Costa, Johnny, 139, 169
COVID-19 pandemic, 6–7, 153–54
Crispus Attucks High School, 76
Crouch, Stanley, 6, 70, 151, 183, 207n57, 207n68
"Crow Jim" (phrase), 96, 99
Crozier, George, 38–40
Cry of Jazz, The (Bland), 6

Damrosch, Walter, 200n5
David, Keith, 170
Davis, Meyer, 30
Davis, Miles, 4, 70, 71, 79, 90, 103, 112, 160, 166, 178
Davis, Nathan, x, 6
Davis, R. N., 15
"Deed I Do" (Rose and Hirsch), 42
de Koenigswarter, Panonnica, 70
democracy, jazz as, 10, 145, 151, 153, 156, 172, 174–80
DeRosa, Clement, 214n13
"Dinah" (Armstrong), 69, 78
dirt (musical description), 44–45, 49, 203n67
disco, 108, 119
diversity in jazz education, 138, 154
Dolphy, Eric, 54
Dorsey, Tommy, 38, 40, 43–44, 47, 49
Dorsey Brothers, 56
Douglas, Dave, 100
DownBeat (magazine), 6, 9, 59–62, 64–68, 85, 95–96, 98, 108, 122–23, 151, 162
drug use in jazz, 84, 106
Durante, Jimmy, 33

Edwards, Eddie, 33
Eldridge, Roy, 55
Ellington, Duke, 3, 5, 9, 63–66, 70, 71–72, 78, 105, 125, 142, 145–46, 148–49, 151, 154, 163, 172, 173, 207n65, 209n89, 217n65. *See also* Essentially Ellington (program)
Ellis, Don, 101, 182, 185
Elmhurst College, 130
Ericsson, K. Anders, 74–75
Ernst, Hugh, 168
Essentially Ellington (program), 9, 125, 138–56, 217n65, 218n80
Experiment in Modern Music (concert). *See* Whiteman, Paul

Facebook, 198
Feather, Leonard, 54, 85, 92, 95–96, 109, 127–28
Ferguson, Allyn, 92

Ferguson, Flo, 106
Ferguson, Kim, 109
Ferguson, Lisa, 106, 212n53
Ferguson, Maynard, 9, 92, 94, 102–21, 141, 191, 212n60, 212n62, 212–13n63
Fillmore, Henry, 8, 12–13, 17–29, 31–32, 200n7, 200n8
Fischer, Clare, 92
Floyd, George, 138, 198
Fontana, Carl, 92
Foxx, Jamie, 135
Franck, Cesar, 16
Fuller, Curtis, 6

Gabbard, Krin, 72, 118, 191, 194, 206n51, 207n55, 214n84
genius (in jazz), 69–73, 76–77, 207n57, 207n60, 207n61
Gershwin, George, 11, 35, 63, 65, 168
Giddins, Gary, 71
Gillespie, Dizzy, 55, 172, 213n75
Gladwell, Malcolm, 9, 59, 72–75
Glasper, Robert, 157
glissando, 11–24, 26–27, 31–32, 34, 36–37, 41–42, 44–45, 117, 200n7
Gold, Django, 160–61, 165, 190
Goldkette, Jean, 38, 40, 203n52
Goldwater, Barry, 96–98
"Gonna Fly Now" (Chattaway), 102, 107–8, 119
Goodman, Benny, 41, 61, 63, 66, 160
Gorman, Ross, 11, 30, 32, 40, 200n2, 200n4
Gosling, Ryan, 190–92
Gourse, Leslie, 71
Granoff, Isidore, 73
Granz, Norman, 79
Green, Charlie, 32, 203n54
Grofe, Ferde, 11, 65
Guess, Andre, 197
Gushee, Lawrence, 27–28, 30–31, 72, 203n67
Guy and Madeline on a Park Bench (Chazelle), 194, 224n108

Hall, Morris E. "Gene," 95, 214n13
Hampton, Lionel, 96

Hargrove, Roy, 6
Harlan, Byron, 26
Harris, Kamala, 4–5
Harris, Richard, 107
Harrison, Jimmy, 35
Hasse, John Edward, 71
Hayes, Isaac, 107
Heath, Percy, 79
Hefti, Neal, 86
Henderson, Fletcher, 35, 38, 40, 63–64, 203n54, 203n60
Hentoff, Nat, 6
Herbert, Trevor, 14
Herbie Hancock Competition. *See* Thelonious Monk International Jazz Competition
Herman, Woody, 83, 141
Holman, Bill, 83, 92
Howell, Bill, 131
Hurst, Charles, 132

International Association for Jazz Education (NAJE/IAJE), 128–29, 132–33
International Jazz Day, 169
International Tchaikovsky Competition, 147
Iverson, Ethan, 148, 192
"I Wish I Could Shimmy Like My Sister Kate" (Piron), 34

Jacobs, Walter, 201n28
James, Harry, 55
Jarrett, Keith, 97
Jazz (Burns), 69, 97, 141–43, 151, 170, 206n53, 216n52, 218n75, 220n41
Jazz Ambassador program. *See* State Department (US)
Jazz Appreciation Month, 169
Jazz at Lincoln Center (JALC), 3, 7, 9, 57, 71, 125, 139–40, 142–45, 150–51, 166, 176, 179–80, 196–97, 217n65. *See also* Essentially Ellington (program)
jazz community, 5, 79, 144
Jazz Congress, 166–67

jazz history, teaching of, 7, 50–52, 57–58, 71, 134, 196
Jazz is The Worst (JITW) (Twitter profile), 159–60, 171, 195
Jazzmobile, 168
jazz.org (web domain), 196–97
jazz snob, 170
Jen Education Network (JEN), 133, 138–40
Johnson, Bunk, 54–55, 91
Johnson, Charles, 69, 78–79
Johnson, Conrad "Prof," 135–37
Johnson, J. J., 77, 84
Jones, Elvin, 192
Jones, Quincy, 86
Joseph, Donald, 214n13

Kalbach, Jim, 177–78
Kashmere Stage Band, 9, 125, 127, 134–38, 215n39
Kendor Music, 141
Kenton, Stan, 9, 79, 83–85, 92–102, 104–5, 107, 118, 120, 121, 130, 141, 148, 210n4, 211n39, 212n51, 214n13
Kernodle, Tammy, 52
King, Thomas, 16
Kingsley, Walter, 17, 25
"Klaxon, The" (Fillmore), 12
klezmer, 11, 200n4
Konitz, Lee, 6, 79
Koza, Julia Eklund, 89–90
K-Pop, 167
Krampe, Ralf, 74–75

Lake, Mayhew, 8, 21–23, 28–29, 32, 44–46, 49, 201n22
La La Land (Chazelle), 10, 166, 189–91, 195
Landsman, Mark, 137
Lane, Nick, 119
Langey, Otto, 24–25
Lanin, Sam, 42
"Lassus Trombone" (Fillmore), 13, 200n8
Lateef, Yusef, 6
Leary, Timothy, 106
Lebrecht, Norman, 11, 200n4
Lee, Bill, 214n13

"Let Freedom Swing" (program), 144, 177
Levy, Hank, 101, 182, 185
Levy, Morris, 105
Levy, Stan, 84
Lewis, Mel, 92
Lhotak, Frank, 33
Liszt, Franz, 111
"Livery Stable Blues" (ODJB), 27, 29
Lombardo, Guy, 86
LSD (drug). See Leary, Timothy
Lunceford, Jimmie, 136, 148

"MacArthur Park" (Drover), 107
Malcolm X College, 9, 125, 127, 130–32, 138
Malone, Tom, 87
Mandel, Howie, 161–62, 163–64
Manne, Shelly, 105
Marini, Lou, 87
Marsalis, Branford, 170–71
Marsalis, Ellis, 6
Marsalis, Wynton, 3, 54, 69, 125, 139–44, 146–51, 154, 170, 176–77, 197, 207n68, 217n67, 218n75
masculinity, 111, 118, 120
"Maynard Ferguson" (Kenton and Rogers), 104–5, 212n51
McBride, Christian, 4
McMullen, Tracy, 122–23
McNeely, Jim, 131
McPartland, Marian, 6
McShann, Jay, 80
Meadows, Edward, 129
Melrose Bros. (publisher), 35, 40, 47–48
Memphis State University, 130
metaphors in jazz, 10, 166, 172–82
method books, 8, 11–49, 66, 90, 201n27
Miller, Glenn, 40–44, 47
Miller, Paul Eduard, 8–9, 58, 59–69
Miller, Ray, 32, 34–35
Miller High School, 76
"Miss Trombone (A Slippery Rag)" (Fillmore), 13
Mister Rogers' Neighborhood (Rogers), 139, 169
Mobile Jazz Festival, 9, 134

Mole, Milfred "Miff," 30–38, 41–42, 47, 49, 56
Morgan, Lee, 77, 209n85
Morton, Benny, 77
Morton, Ferdinand "Jelly Roll," 40, 63
Moyer, Justin, 163
Muhoberac, Larry, 86
Murphy, John, 186–87
Murray, Albert, 6, 151, 207n68
Music Educators' National Conference (MENC), 128–29, 133

National Association of Jazz Educators. See International Association for Jazz Education (NAJE/IAJE)
National Endowment for the Arts, 3
National Stage Band Camp, 93, 134
Negri, Joe, 169, 220n35
neophonic music, 92, 94
Nestico, Sammy, 86, 141
Nettl, Bruno, 113
New Vintage (Ferguson), 108, 119, 212n62
Nichols, Red, 32–33, 35, 42
Niehaus, Lennie, 92
Nokomis Regional High School, 103
Notre Dame Collegiate Jazz Festival, 9, 85, 93, 103, 130–32, 215n22
novelty (musical concept), 12–13, 17, 19, 21–22, 26–29, 44, 51, 107, 202n38
Nugent, Ted, 120

Obama, Barack, 3
Original Dixieland Jass Band, 26–27, 33, 64
Ory, Edward "Kid," 27–28, 32
"Ory's Creole Trombone" (Ory), 27–28
Outliers (book). See Gladwell, Malcolm
Outliers (statistics), 9, 59, 72–76, 78, 80, 88, 153, 206n50

Paganini, Nicolo, 111
"Pahson Trombone" (Filmore), 13
Parker, Charlie, 4, 70–71, 73–74, 75, 76, 79–80, 90, 162, 171, 184–85, 209n85
Parks and Recreation (Daniels and Schur), 160
Parliament (band), 126

parody, jazz and, 26, 160–61, 163
Pelleas und Melisande (Schoenberg), 14
Peyton, Dave, 90
Poehler, Amy, 160
Pollack, Ben, 40–42
Pomp and Circumstance (Elgar), 168
popular music, jazz and, 12, 17, 21, 25, 28–29, 61, 65, 69, 103, 110
Powell, Bud, 162
Powell, Morgan, 93
Primack, Bret, 164
Primal Scream (Ferguson), 108
"Prince of Wails" (The Cotton Pickers), 34
Princeton High School, 186, 193–94
private instruction, 87, 115, 155
Pryor, Arthur, 13–14, 23, 26
public pedagogy, 10, 166–69, 172, 177–78

Quarantine Big Band Helsinki, 7
Quinichette, Paul, 80

Ramey, Gene, 73, 185
Ramsey, Frederic, Jr., 54–55, 61, 91
Ratliff, Ben, 147–48, 220n41
Redman, Don, 35, 63–64
revisionism, jazz history and, 51–52
Rhapsody in Blue. See Gershwin, George
Rich, Buddy, 83, 141, 183–86, 189, 191–92, 222n87
Ridley, Larry, 132–33
Roach, Max, 57, 70
Robert, John, 214n13
Rocky (Avildsen), 102, 107, 108
Rogers, Fred. See *Mister Rogers' Neighborhood*
Rogers, Shorty, 104–5, 212n51
Rollins, Sonny, 110, 160–64, 212n62, 219n25
Rosolino, Frank, 92
Russell, George, 46
Russo, Bill, 92

"Sally Trombone" (Fillmore), 13
Schildkraut, Dave, 79–80
Schoebel, Elmer, 47–48
Schoenberg, Arnold, 14

Schuller, Gunther, 6, 67
science fiction, adolescents and, 119–20
Scofield, John, 4
Seals, Sonny, 131
Severinsen, Doc, 83
Sharp, Gus, 33
Shore, Dinah, 116
sight reading, 81–91
Silver, Horace, 79, 148–49
Simmons, Gene, 120
Simmons, J. K., 183, 189, 194
Simon and Garfunkel, 107
Simpsons, The (Groening), 160
Slater, Neil, 82
"Slidus Trombonus" (Lake), 21, 44
"Slim Trombone" (Filmore), 13
Smith, Charles Edward, 54–55, 61, 91
Smith, Wadada Leo, 4
Smithsonian Institution, 140, 169, 214n8
Solis, Gabriel, 71, 76–77
"Some of these Days" (Mole), 31
Soph, Ed, 86, 87, 123
Sordillo, Fortunato, 8, 23–25, 28, 32, 201n26, 201n29, 202n33
Sousa, John Philip, 12, 13–14, 23, 26
Southern University. *See* Batiste, Alvin
"So What" (Davis), 112
stage bands, 9, 93, 109, 127–28, 134–37
Star Trek. See science fiction
Star Wars. See science fiction
State Department (US), 172
Stearns, Marshall, 8, 59, 64, 67–69
Stewart, Rex, 55
Stitt, Sonny, 76–77
Stoll, Todd, 138–40, 144, 150
Stone, Emma, 189–92
Suber, Charles "Chuck," 93–94, 127, 133–34
Sudhalter, Richard, 52–53, 55–56
Sullivan, Ed, 92, 104–5
Sundance Film Festival, 165, 182–83
Syburg, Bob, 130
syncopep, 30–31

tailgate trombone, 33
Taylor, Billy, 115, 168

Taylor, Cecil, 143, 170, 182
Taylor, James, 107
Teagarden, Jack, 35
"Teddy Trombone" (Fillmore), 13
Teller, Miles, 182
10,000-hour rule, 73–75
Terry, Clark, 129
Tesch-Römer, Clemens, 74–75
Thelonious Monk International Jazz Competition, 147, 216n50
Thunder Soul (Landsman), 135–37
Towson University. *See* Levy, Hank
Trump, Donald, 3, 4, 167
trumpet, "screech," 102, 107, 109, 116
Tucker, Sherrie, 51–53
Twitter, 159, 165, 166, 195, 197
Tynan, John, 54
Tyner, McCoy, 77, 209n85

Ulanov, Barry, 92

Van Cliburn International Piano Competition, 147
virtual music performance, 6–7, 154
virtuosity, 9, 13, 48, 69, 74, 103, 110–18

Wallace, George, 97–98, 136, 211n36, 211n39
Walton, Charles, 131, 215n24
Weather Report (band), 109
Weber, Carl, 14–15, 24
weightlifting, 112
Wein, George, 6
Wells, Christi Jay, 53
Werner, Kenny, 159
Westinghouse High School, 76, 208n80
Wheaton, Jack, 86, 214n13
"When I First Met Mary" (Pollack and Miller), 42
"Where Is that Old Girl of Mine" (Miller orchestra), 34
Whiplash (Chazelle), 10, 101, 165–66, 182–95, 198, 224n114
"Whiplash" (Levy), 101
White, Anderson, 112

Whiteman, Paul, 11, 34–35, 42, 53, 63, 68, 168, 200n2, 200n5
Whyton, Tony, 207n68
Widor, Charles Marie, 14–15
Wikipedia, 197
Williams, Cootie, 55
Williams, James, 130
Williams, John, 92, 119
Williams, Leona, 33–34
Williams, Mary Lou, 145
Williams, Tony, 192
Wright, Rayburn, 86

Yeo, Douglass, 21, 200n8, 201n27
Young, Lester, 73, 80, 148
Yurochko, Bob, 71

Zawadi, Sabu, 131
Zoom (online platform). *See* virtual music performance
Zuckerberg, Mark, 198

ABOUT THE AUTHOR

Photo by Harley J. Seeley for Michigan State University. Used by permission.

Ken Prouty is associate professor of musicology and jazz studies at Michigan State University, where he teaches courses in jazz history, popular music, and American music. His first book, *Knowing Jazz: Community, Pedagogy, and Canon in the Information Age*, was published by University Press of Mississippi.

www.ingramcontent.com/pod-product-compliance
Lightning Source LLC
Chambersburg PA
CBHW030620230426
43661CB00053B/2078